D0176801

A Good House

Building a Life on the Land

RICHARD MANNING

PENGUIN BOOKS

PENGUIN BOOKS
Published by the Penguin Group
Penguin Books USA Inc., 375 Hudson Street, New York, New York 10014, U.S.A.
Penguin Books Ltd, 27 Wrights Lane, London W8 5TZ, England
Penguin Books Australia Ltd, Ringwood, Victoria, Australia
Penguin Books Canada Ltd, 10 Alcorn Avenue, Toronto, Ontario, Canada M4V 3B2
Penguin Books (N.Z.) Ltd, 182–190 Wairau Road, Auckland 10, New Zealand

Penguin Books Ltd, Registered Offices: Harmondsworth, Middlesex, England

First published in the United States of America by Grove Press 1993
Published in Penguin Books 1994

10 9 8 7 6 5 4 3 2 1

Grateful acknowledgment is made to:
Capra Press for permission to quote from Wendell Berry's Introduction to
The Toilet Papers by Sim Van der Ryn, copyright © 1978 by Sim Van der Ryn.
North Point Press, a division of Farrar, Straus & Giroux, Inc., for permission to quote
from Gary Nabhan's *The Desert Smells Like Rain: A Naturalist in Papago Indian Country*,
copyright © 1987 by Gary Nabhan.
The Taunton Press for permission to quote from *Fine Homebuilding* 67 (April/May
1991), "Composition Panels" by Charles Wardell, copyright © The Taunton Press,
Inc.
Tracy Stone-Manning and Michael Gallacher for photographs.

THE LIBRARY OF CONGRESS HAS CATALOGUED THE HARDCOVER AS FOLLOWS:
Manning, Richard, 1951–
A good house: building a life on the land/Richard Manning.
p. cm.
ISBN 0-8021-1503-9 (hc.)
ISBN 0 14 02.3407 1 (pbk.)
1. House construction.   2. Missoula (Mont.)—Description and travel.
TH4812.M236   1993
690′.837—dc20   92–31685

Printed in the United States of America
Set in Janson with displays set in Birch Woodtype
Designed by Kate L. Thompson

Praise for Richard Manning's *A Good House*

"Behind the whole project, this book, this house that [Manning] builds, is an effort to move from his head to his heart and his hands . . . [and] it is fascinating to watch him handle the materials and tools of home-building. . . . The man built himself a house in Montana. And it was Good."

—Susan Salter Reynolds, *Los Angeles Book Review*

"This is a very American tale: In no other nation do people take so much pleasure in the simple act of building things for themselves . . . . Manning offers advice that anyone can use—even if they don't go the extremes that he did—to help preserve resources."

—Graham Friel, *Audubon*

"Manning has built a book as solid and durable as his subject. . . . Its graceful, unflinching honesty will endure as far into time as the home; a book to be picked up and held over and again as one would a fine tool."   —Paul G. Hawken

"Throughout the book, the reader is treated to Manning's inner musings . . . [raising] this book above the level of most other 'country home' chronicles."

—*Library Journal*

"Manning's joy in the work is infectious. . . . By the end of this fine book, the building of the house has taken on a powerful meaning. If you're thinking of building a home, you owe it to yourself to read *A Good House*. And if you have ever regarded the roof over your head as more than mere shelter, this book will open your eyes."   —Stephen Goodwin, *USA Today*

"It took great wisdom to write this book, and it will take a certain simple kind of courage to read it and listen to it. *A Good House* is delightful, as crafted as a novel. Please read this book."

—Rick Bass

"Anyone who is thinking of building a house should read this first. And even those who aren't will enjoy the read of [Manning's] experiences."   —Helen L. Mershon, *The Oregonian*

"Manning combines the nuts-and-bolts concreteness of a how-to book with a lively sense of history and a genuine dedication to principle and self-reliance: this one has the potential to become a modern American classic."

—*Kirkus Reviews*

PENGUIN BOOKS

A GOOD HOUSE

Richard Manning was born in Flint, Michigan, in 1951. He worked as a reporter for fifteen years, including four years at the *Missoulian*. A three-time winner of the C. B. Blethen Award for Investigative Journalism, given by *The Seattle Times*, he has also won the Audubon Society Journalism Award and the first Richard J. Margolis Award for environmental reporting. His first book was *Last Stand* (Penguin), an exposé of the logging industry, which was a finalist for the Sigurd F. Olson Nature Writing Award. His work has appeared in a variety of magazines and newspapers, including *Outside*, *Sierra*, *E Magazine*, and *Buzzworm*. Richard Manning lives with his wife, Tracy, in the house they built themselves near Lolo, Montana.

For Tracy

Acknowledgments

THIS BOOK owes a great debt to the people who helped build the house. Most of those have been named herein. The house got some added help along the way from C. E. "Abe" Abramson, who lent valuable advice to our attempts to negotiate the treacherous waters of real estate, banking, and the local regulatory bureaucracy. Anna Vandehey at First Federal Savings & Loan Association went beyond the call of duty. Steve Laber at Intermountain Lumber was more than a salesman; he provided considerable counsel on matters of building materials. And the staff at Thurmans Electrical and Plumbing Supply was extraordinarily patient in handling my ignorance on issues of pipes and wires. My friend Jim Ludwick overcame his fear of heights long enough to lend a hand with the roof. Rasim Babamento was an aid and comfort throughout. Andy Kulla, weed expert for the Lolo National Forest, offered his vast store of information on the care of our land.

Henry E. Martinson, economics research assistant for the National Association of Homebuilders, was a great deal of help in researching the book.

Useful comments, advice, and support on the manuscript came from my friend Michael Moore, from my agent Tim Schaffner, and especially from my editor, Bryan Oettel.

Contents

Illustrations follow p. 114

It only gradually occurred to me that our wounds are far less unique than our cures.

—JIM HARRISON

A Good House

A Notion

IT IS A MEASURE OF THE CONFUSION of our times that the simplest words tease out the most complicated questions. Words like "good" and "house." What do we mean by these? A year of my life turned on this question, a year in which I built my own house.

I am only guessing, but I suspect the phrase "good house" once was perfectly clear. People understood what it meant, or if they didn't at least it raised no confusion worth settling. Ours is a different time. Now the phrase "good house" is a riddle. It is a koan. This is how I understand it best. It is an important question because it leads to a larger one: What is the good life? A house is a simulacrum of a life. It is my thought that the idea of "good" can flow from the part to the whole.

In a simple and true sense, I built my own house in Montana because I needed one, as all of us do. Need, as in food, water, sleep, and shelter. A creature need. When pressed, this is the excuse most of us give for owning houses, but of course this isn't what we mean. Through most of the half-million years of human history, most of our species lived in huts, yurts, tipis and piles of sticks, unheated tents the size of a modern bathroom—nothing we would consider acceptable shelter. To our way of thinking, these people needed houses. We consider them deprived, their lives nasty, mean, brutish, and short. Yet by some accounts they were happy as toads. Houseless, maybe, but not home-less. Only in the past few generations and only in a handful of cultures have people claimed to need houses. Now almost all of us have houses, but most of us are still homeless. Over time we have come to reverse the relationship. We inhabit houses, but neither we nor our houses inhabit their places.

I already had a house when I decided to build. Maybe it was a noisy, expensive, and cramped apartment, but it was better than most dwellings throughout human history, better than what many have in our privileged nation. I had shelter. Still, there was no denying I believed I needed to build a house. The phrase "to build" is important here. It wasn't just the house I sought; it was the building of it. In another simple and true sense, all of this had nothing to do with a house, or rather the house was surrogate for the larger issue. When I began this odd and ordinary project I was more concerned with "good life" than "good house," although at the time I could not bring myself to put it just that way. Now I have the blistered, hard hands of a man who has built, and the callouses have taught me what I was seeking.

That was the summer of 1991, and there was much that needed to be rebuilt. I turned forty that year and was at the turning point of a years-long midlife upheaval more severe than most. One could see that reflected in the places where I recently had lived.

Through most of the first half of my adult life I had lived in comfortable houses that are the wages of devotion to career: single-family bungalows in old but sound neighborhoods. There were trees and sidewalks, and new coats of paint when the stucco needed it. Fixer-uppers, but still solid and serene. Flower gardens doted on by my wife, and the bicycle of our only child tipped onto the lawn. I had been married when I was twenty-one. The marriage lasted for seventeen years. When it ended, the comfortable little houses became cheap apartments in student ghettos—all I could afford. Besides, I didn't need much space; my son stayed with her. No need for a lawn to hold a kid's bicycle.

Living in apartments and in a state of confusion, I lost track of my son for a while. His name is Josh. Through all of this he was in high school, about to graduate to apartments of his own. Realizing this also pushed me toward the building of my own house. I thought I might be able to involve him in the process. I no longer could provide a home for him, but I could show him how to build. My father did that for me. I wanted to do it for Josh. I suspect someday he will need to know.

This break in my marriage occurred in Missoula, Montana, still my hometown, still my son's and hers. It was an odd place for such an explosion, largely because my ex-wife and I considered Missoula our place for settling down. During our marriage we had lived in eleven houses in six different towns, first in Michigan, where we grew up and were married, then in Idaho, then in Montana. The superficial reason for all this mobility was my other first marriage, my career. For fifteen years I was a newspaper reporter. I was paid to watch how the world worked, or, increasingly, how it didn't. Newspaper reporters are mobile. Much of this has to do with advancement to better jobs at better papers, but when one is in the business of printing the news and raising hell, sometimes it's just more comfortable to move on to a new town every now and again.

Mostly I wrote about politics, but late in my career, in 1988, in Missoula, I took on a new beat. I became an environmental reporter, which in western Montana means I wrote about logging. Nature plays big in the northern Rockies, and so do the people who see nature as plunder. Accordingly, I became something of a war correspondent, filing dispatches from the latest skirmishes in our culture's conflict with the rest of the living world. My particular free-fire zone was occupied by timber corporations laying siege to forests.

This new work of mine came just as Americans, as if cued, decided they wanted nothing so much as bigger and flashier houses—increasingly, our idea of good houses. The lumber to grant those wishes nationwide came heavily from the Northwest—the logging states of Washington and Oregon, northern California, Idaho's panhandle, and the mountains of western Montana. For timber corporations there was opportunity for profit. It was an era when American business in general was concentrating on short-term gain above all else. Timbered lands suffered especially during this binge. For nearly a century it had been the practice of the logging companies to follow a doctrine called "sustained yield." Trees were cut only as fast as they grew back;

if it took one hundred years to grow a usable tree of a given species, then a company would cut no more than one-hundredth of its trees in any one year. The demand for more and bigger houses, however, sundered the doctrine of sustained yield. The timber corporations clear-cut the Northwest in the matter of a few decades.

I had written all of this for my newspaper, the *Missoulian*. I had been among the first reporters in the Northwest to do so. The timber companies took issue and complained to my editors. The editors, in turn, thought it might be better for all concerned if I transferred to a less controversial beat. I quit the paper in such a huff that it precluded my moving on to the next town. Besides, I had seen some things that made me want to stay. In our country most towns have become one-paper towns, so my staying effectively dissolved my other marriage. The two breaks coincided within a year.

Given this coincidence, I suppose I can be forgiven the thought that all of these events were related, that the destruction of my marriage and my career, the corruption of industry, and our disrespect for nature all spring from the same bad seed. I have spent the years since reading, walking, and roaming the vast wilderness of Montana mostly with these notions in my mind, considering the fabric that weaves it all together. Still I think something is terribly wrong in the way we live our lives.

There came a point nearly two years into this upheaval when I realized that the time for thinking and sadness had ended. A time to build had begun. I needed a house. I had remarried. Like many newly married couples, Tracy and I wanted a place to anchor our life. Not a stand-in for our lives as some houses are, a construct of show and pretense. The fact is, we were and are deeply anchored in each other. Owning or not owning a house will not change that, but the idea of our own place grew out of our marriage. The building of a house seemed a simple, straightforward act of love, and slowly it was occurring to me that such acts are what we need now. I thought it might be possible to conceive a house in love, somehow separate from the violence brought to the once-forested hills around me, the basis of many other houses of our time.

In this wish a bias of mine was surfacing. The upheaval of the past years had sent me into a deepening spiral of thought, but I believe fundamentally that we cannot think our way through our lives. Sooner or later we must live our lives. Somewhere this idea of a good life must bring us into direct touch with the forces that make us. To live a good life one must touch it as one touches a mate. One must touch a house. One must swing a hammer and drive nails.

We must honor this physical aspect of life because life is ultimately physical. We are nature. Our houses are nature, or at least good houses are nature. This idea built my house—this and my hands.

My environmental reporting, my investigations, the thing that had smashed my career, had taught me that there is enormous consequence to the way each of us lives our lives. Distilled to its simple forms this means a house takes forests from mountains. A house takes coal from the hills. A house takes life from the planet. Yet each of us must have a house. For those of us who value nature, this is the primary contradiction of our lives.

It occurred to me that I was uniquely situated to investigate this matter from one end to the other, not by reading or interviewing or thinking but by asking the question in a more basic manner, by asking the questions of each board and wire of my house. Could I build a house in such a way as to ensure my happiness and still do minimum damage to the earth? On a practical and straightforward level, could I build an environmentally sensitive house, one that was wood-efficient, energy-efficient, Spartan, and everywhere shaped by its respect for nature's limits? Deeper still, could I build a house that would help rebuild my life? What should such a house look like? Will its frugality preclude beauty? Will its asceticism preclude its art?

Asking the questions just this way seemed to steer me toward the ultimate shape of the project and especially toward an answer to a particularly problematic aspect of it. All of this—the living, the building—was informed by the idea of context, by which I mean nature. That seemed a necessary beginning. It followed that this could not be a city or suburban house slapped up in a squared, subdivided, and sidewalked lot. It needed to be a rural house attentive to the land. The building would include more than just the four walls and a roof. It would include gardens, fruit trees, deer for the freezer, and woodlots for heat, all cared for as if the house and its environs were an island, the way we need to begin thinking of our place on earth.

My house would have something to say to all houses, rural and urban, but it needed to gather its information by living in the trees.

This idea of rural landscape guided the project onto its most dangerous ground, the problems of people living in the woods. Writing about the joys of rural living is even more dangerous still, in that publicity can amplify a bad trend. Environmentalists of my region are coming to regard subdividers and rural newcomers as an even greater threat than loggers, and in many ways they are.

We now believe, with justification, that we protect nature only where we succeed in excluding people. I have seen what people have done to the countryside, so I understand this rule's origins. Still, if we adopt this exclusion as our ultimate goal then we have lost the fight. We have succeeded only in reinforcing our distance from nature, which is the root cause of the hubris that has caused so much damage. There must be another way to go about this, a way my house would seek. Ultimately, then, this house was about seeking, picking a quiet path among the trees.

There are a couple of stories that frame this house's issues in their largest perspective. The first comes from the work of ethnobotanist Gary Nabhan. In his important book *The Desert Smells Like Rain* Nabhan writes about the traditional lives of the Papago Indians in a region straddling the border between Mexico and Arizona.

Our experience tells us that where humans venture, wildlife instantly becomes troubled. As a species we are notorious for making little room for the rest of nature. We are Shiva the destroyer. We are the engine of extinction. Accordingly, it has become our habit to set aside areas free from human intrusions, areas we consider wildlife sanctuaries. Normally this is considered one of our good acts, but in another sense it is an admission of our greatest failing.

With the goal of protecting nature the federal government in the 1950s set aside a bird sanctuary in Papago country by evicting farmers whose culture had inhabited the place for thousands of years. Decades later Nabhan visited the sanctuary with a group of ornithologists. They found thirty-two species of birds. The next day, visiting an adjacent and traditional Papago village, they found sixty-five species of birds living among those people. Nabhan asked his Papago friend to explain this phenomenon. "I've been thinking over what you say about not so many birds living over there anymore," he said. "That's because those birds, they come where the people are. When the people live and work in a place, and plant their seeds and water their trees, the birds go live with them. They like those places, there's plenty to eat, and that's when we are friends to them."

I've carried that story with me now for years, revisiting it often. Many of us have come to accept the destruction of nature as inherent to the human condition, yet the cases of the Papago and of hundreds of traditional cultures around the world suggest otherwise. The common denominator of these traditional cultures is an awareness of nature, an awareness of the context of their lives. They consider themselves part of the weave, not the weavers.

My other story is also about context.

I was flying back to Montana one clear winter's morning early in 1991. I had been on a magazine assignment of a curious sort, one that had originally been my idea. I had been chasing groups of people who live in motor homes, a new sort of nomad class. Most are retirees, people we call "secure" when what we mean to say is that they have a lot of money. They must have to afford the life they have chosen: cramped "houses" that cost well over $100,000 on average, sometimes going as high as $500,000 or more. These behemoths stalk about the country at the rate of about 5 miles per gallon, seeking nothing so much as the road. We see them mostly queued up at the gates of national parks or, during the winter in the Sunbelt states, stanchioned cheek by cowl in RV parks, aluminum ghettos wrapped around golf courses. We conclude that these people are seeking scenery or sun or something like that, but this turns out to be not at all true. They are not seeking, they are fleeing.

They flee the death of cities or small-town America or community, or, in a darker sense, they flee people different from themselves. They flee change and loss of control. In their refugee status they are not that different from all of us, a lost and wandering people, a people without place. Whenever I visit the suburbs I am amazed at how few people walk. The curtains are all closed, making windows useless. Virtually all houses face not outdoors to their land but indoors to the television, our identical window on our identical world.

I once talked to a motor-home nomad who had been camped for

months in the middle of the California desert. Outside her $100,000 motor home an inverted garbage can lid served as a bird feeder.

"What birds are those," I asked her, because I was new to the region and couldn't identify desert species. "What are those shrubs they use for cover?"

"Those," she said, "are just birds. Just birds you always see. And that is just brush."

There was no use in her learning the names of the birds that had come to live there. She watered no trees and planted no seeds. In a short time she would be gone, down the road. Her culture—ours—is incapable of inhabiting a place for thousands of years.

Her husband pointed out the nearby mountains as the scenic advantage of their place, and I asked him their names.

"Those are the foothills," he said, as if mountain ranges required no more identity than "the mall," or "the strip," or "McDonald's."

In this, the motor nomads are simply a distillation of what all of us have become: a people without a place. We have taken our lives out of the context of the land, above the land. Literally. One can see this most clearly on airliners. Watch the new class of flying itinerant merchants, men in gray suits and laptops. Watch them board and stash carry-ons in the overhead, then throw identical folds into identical jackets and stow them at the top of the rack. Even before takeoff, briefcases are snapped open, calculators are powered up, and numbers are crunched. Watch them land in a new place and never notice the window, as if the view were identical to that of the last place they did not see. To them, whose job it is to distill all places to the ultimate line of a profit and loss statement—the new map of the landscape—this place is indeed identical to the last. They are at ease here above the land, distant and disdainful of Earth.

As I flew around the country chasing motor-home people, I watched such scenes play repeatedly. I saw America, and then I flew home to Montana. I was convinced it was time I built a house. The clear winter morning that I headed home was a Sunday. In a half-full airliner the sun broke hard through the right bank of windows. Few gray suits were present. These were different people. The crowd ran heavy to jeans and nylon jackets. As the airliner neared Missoula, I noticed people moving around the plane, shifting to the right side and watching the sun play across the snowcaps of the Continental Divide. Most of us, it appeared, were going home. We began naming names. People pointed out the Bob Marshall, the Swan Range, the Mission Mountains, the Garnets and the Sapphires, and below, the sedate, winding valley of the Clark Fork River. They said the names.

Then the airliner banked over Mount Sentinel and began its descent to a runway at Missoula. A descent to a landing. Land that I know. As we approached, I could see it all coming into focus on progressively more intimate scales: first the mountain ranges; then individual valleys; then creeks and draws; and finally, tucked behind a softly rounded but hard-cut mountain, a gulch that held the very land that is the context of my house. As the focus shifted from the grand sweep to the minute and individual bits of land, it occurred to me that this is how we find our homes. We find them, then we build them.

Water

ONCE MORE I HOBBLED ACROSS THE FIELD that had come to hold my favorite ideas. I hobbled because I was injured—a chronic bad back. My pacing of an area the size of a football field only aggravated the problem, as a dwindling bottle of ibuprofen demonstrated. I should have been home in bed. How do I relax, though, when two kids who seem to understand only hot rods are going to use a 30-ton machine to dump more money than I have into a 6-inch hole in the ground?

The hot-rodders were drilling a water well. Wells begin houses; wells make land humanly habitable, so more than money was at stake. So I paced, and I worried. I began to comprehend the odd assertion that my body is mostly made of water. My moisture content was slipping. A slight and natural dehydration of my spine, a process I reluctantly identify by its simple name, "aging," was the cause of my pain and cursing. We hold to life only to the extent we hold to water.

I live in the West, in the mountainous West where the Pacific-drained slope of the Rockies rolls out of Montana toward Idaho. Like most of the West this place is coarse and arid. Habitability here is and always has been tenuous enough to make the population agreeably sparse. The Westerners' favorite myth says we are held here solely by a mix of stubbornness and ingenuity, but in truth our presence is only suffered to the degree that we are able to mine water. The water grab is the history of all land west of the Mississippi. For the sake of water, white Westerners have killed Indians with abandon and other whites only slightly more reluctantly. For the sake of water, we have engaged our most vicious attorneys and conducted bold raids on the federal treasury. Aridity is our general predicament made specific and intense at the moment to me and four of the people who matter most in my life.

Of these four, the one I consider first is Tracy, my wife. At forty, a bad back is not my only injury, although I probably have suffered our time's troubles no more than most of my generation. Tracy was twenty-five when we started the house. Now twenty-six, she is beautiful, vigorous, and redheaded. She is honest enough in her affections to more than offset any suffering my half-lifetime has amassed. When we began the house we had been married less than a year. I am hopelessly in love. I am not used to this affection offered without guile or psychological peregrinations. I cannot tire of the thrill of watching her charge straight at the world as if her charging counts. She stands up to life like a flagpole that bears a bright banner. She is intelligent without melancholy, challenging without spite. She's as honest and easy as mountain air.

She comes from a large and close family of brothers, Easterners, and never questions her prime notion that the world is glued together by love. She has lived in Montana just three years but has settled on this place as home. An environmentalist, she believes that the earth is in need of saving and considers it her personal responsibility to do so, probably within a week or so if all goes well. Tracy earnestly believes all will go well.

In this she is very much like Wendy Moore, and if I were at all sober-minded about this whole enterprise I would consider the involvement of two visionaries as serious trouble. In its simplest incarnation this project is really about the building of two houses, not just Tracy's and mine. That's where Wendy comes in. Houses are built of concrete, nails, and boards. All demand correct behavior, precision, tradition, discipline, and work. Above all, work. Concrete, nails, and boards do not respond to optimism and vision, or so I believed at the outset.

Were it not for vision, though, in particular Wendy's vision, I would not be gimping around this field drilling a water well. This whole house project was her idea. Since she hatched it six months ago, since I took an airplane ride and agreed to the idea a few months later, we five principals have planned for little else but this idea's fruition. As conceived it was not an idea cast in concrete and boards. It had mushier foundations: wistful notions about the resurrection of community, especially as community plays out in its most intense form, as family. We—the Moores, Tracy, and I—are not family but would like to behave as one.

Wendy is twenty-nine, stubborn-quiet, gentle, and pretty as a doe. She and her husband, Michael, are my oldest friends in Missoula. Like Tracy, Wendy is a graduate student in environmental studies. This program at the University of Montana in Missoula is something of a haven for idealists, so both fit right in. She and Michael met eight years ago after both came here to work for a Ralph Nader spin-off group formed to defend the public good. Neither remained an activist; instead they settled to responsibilities of family and career. Still, Wendy has dreams.

Michael and I are often mistaken for brothers, even by each other. We wear the bruises and bond of fraternity. We once were newspaper reporters at the same paper. Seven years ago I hired onto the paper as something of a veteran just as he took a job as a rookie. He was always better than a rookie, though, and we grew together out of mutual respect. The newspaper business is one of those odd callings that focus the whole of your life in its intense beam. Then you come to love especially those people who love the craft as you do.

Four years after our professional partnership bloomed I quit the paper in that messy blowup. Michael still works there, is still an unsoiled deacon in the church that I have left. This is a strain on our friendship, but the bond has held. We fish for trout together. We play guitars together. We share friends.

My suspicion, though, is that these friendships and intersecting lines of affection are the secondary push of the project, at least for Michael and Wendy. The primary is the fifth member of the group, who is Kate. She is Michael and Wendy's seven-year-old daughter, a precocious and engaging blonde. The Moores are typical of our generation, people who have moved from long-standing roots. Wendy is from a big family of girls in New Jersey. Michael's move here stretched ties to a brother and doting parents in Mississippi. It is difficult to understand why Americans believe they are better off away from home. Telephones and jetliners cannot adequately maintain our bonds to the places and people who made us. I believe we are coming to realize this mistake, but it's too late to cancel it. We've already moved. We're here and so we might as well make the best of it.

We do what we can. In our cases, Wendy decided we should buy a piece of land, build a couple of houses, and share some work like real extended families do. The wistful pull of family may not be reason enough to get the nails driven and the bank paid, but it got us onto the land. Just a week before the drilling of the well we had signed the papers on 38 acres of mostly wooded land near the burg of Lolo, Montana, 8 miles out of Missoula. Up Lolo Creek, to the west and out of Lolo, run two paths emblematic of our region's history. In 1805 Lewis and Clark traveled within sight of my house, heading west. In his journal William Clark described the tight valley that holds Lolo Creek:

> One Deer & Some Pheasants killed this morning, I shot 4 Pheasants
> of the Common Kind except the tale was black. The road over the last
> mountain was thick Steep & Stoney as usual.

Still is.

The Lewis and Clark expeditions opened the way for the gradual but inexorable catastrophe that has befallen the indigenous people. As the white explorers crossed into Idaho in 1805 their hides were more or less saved by the friendly Nez Percé living in what is now northern Idaho. The encounter began a generally amicable partnership with white people that lasted until late in the century. But after a series of provocations by land-hungry settlers and troops, a group of braves responded by killing eleven whites, the first such killing in the tribe's history. To avoid a reprisal the Nez Percé people took flight. In 1877, under the leadership of young Chief Joseph, they reversed the route of Lewis and Clark and followed their buffalo-hunting route back into Montana. A few miles from my house they met up with about two hundred hostile soldiers protected behind a quickly assembled log breastworks. There was no fight. While several of the braves engaged the enemy in negotiations, Chief Joseph and the seven hundred Nez Percé in his charge used a little side gulch to slip by the soldiers in the main canyon. A few days later there was a fight. The Nez Percé scored a convincing victory near the Big Hole River, then traveled several hundred miles southeast, much to the alarm of the tourists in what was already Yellowstone National Park. At a nearby mining camp they stole silver bullion and melted it to bullets. They fought on, escaping capture and heading north a few hundred miles en route to freedom in Canada. Reinforced troops eventually caught and subdued the Nez Percé just shy of the border. Unlike most of the tribe, Chief Joseph survived to be sent to prison at Leavenworth, Kansas. He never was allowed to return to his home in northern Idaho and died in 1904 of a broken heart.

Joseph's path around the troops at Lolo Creek probably was a small canyon called Sleeman Gulch. This is where we will make our stand.

In April 1991, $42,500 bought a piece of land that slides up a barely walkable slope to a ridge top. Most of the land we bought is not humanly habitable, which suits us. That's why we bought it. We had looked for about two months at many other pieces of land, but none of them ever hit us just this way. Mostly we liked it for its seclusion. Although close to Missoula, the narrow canyon cuts off the rest of the world. In it we feel alone.

It is covered by second- or third-growth ponderosa pine and an ample population of elk and deer. From a grassy park just at the zenith of our ridge we can see the guarding rows of snowcapped peaks that surround us on all sides. The day the five of us first huffed our way to this spot was the day we decided to buy. Standing there I imagined being buried under the grassy park some day, and I still do. We will build well below this ridge top. If I have anything to say about it (that's the real value of owning land—I do have something to say about it) this bit of our land will remain uncut, unplowed, unscraped, and unroaded until it is my grave. If my life has any effect on the people closest to it, my grave will remain unmolested long after I am gone.

From atop my ridge I can see Montana's most recent history played out on the hills. Up Lolo Creek, up the Bitterroot Valley to the south, for most of the thirty or so miles I can see from my backyard there are clear-cuts, vast splotches of land that loggers have stripped of trees. In the nation's rush to build its suburban sprawl Montana was logged hard over the course of the last decade. That's why this spot on my land will be logged no more.

The ridge top rolls back to a shallow, grassy mountaintop valley we call a "bowl," guarded on all sides by towering ponderosa pine. This is our land too. Steep slopes protect it from pickup trucks, bulldozers, chainsaws, and even house builders. Because of its isolation and relatively low elevation, it is an important winter range for elk and mule deer. Montana is still rich with wilderness, high peaks, and protected alpine valleys where elk spend summers. That's because humans consider high ground unusable. The valley floors, however, have been logged, roaded, and roofed. The elk need low-elevation winter ranges, places like my land. It is the scarcity of such land that limits the number of elk, so this little draw of ours is an important place. It will stay as it is.

Yet in preserving it I understand it offers me only a slight hedge against the problems of our world. It is not the moral high ground. Just down the hill from this elk's ridge I plan to build a house—a house that will use lumber. Land will be logged in my name. This house will be heated with wood, so some of these very trees will be cut to preserve a human winter range. I wish to sustain the lives of these elk, but primarily I wish to sustain my own. This is the paradox that defines this project. The wild land and I need to cut a deal. As much as the pull of family, the need to explore this paradox brings me here.

The trees on the ridge, though, are merely the obvious manifestation of the contradiction that will run straight through my house. The building of a house is an environmentally destructive act. Its multiplication by the millions across the country is responsible for the degradation of some of our best land, for deforestation and urban sprawl, for highways and the wanton use of energy. Still, we must have houses, so I see no ground to be gained in my not playing the game. I see ground to be gained by building with attention to the dangers. In this endeavor the land will be the first teacher.

From the ridge top gravity propels us straight down the face of the hill to the floor of Sleeman Gulch. The ridge top stands 4,230 feet above sea level. The valley floor is 650 feet below. This little valley holds the other part of our land. The skipping, sliding route down weaves among a few limestone outcrops, a healthy young stand of ponderosa, and the full complement of dryland flowers, shrubs, and grasses. The aspect is south-southwest. The slope of the hill plays out suddenly, and in a 100-foot belt of transition, life switches radically from hillside forest to flat valley meadow. A road runs up through the center of this valley floor, the human place. Four or so acres of our land lie in this flat. On it a good 2 feet of undisturbed grassland topsoil lie over the glacial till. This is where I shall face the consequences of my life. This is the land that balances the wild lands above. This, too, is a place to take a stand.

I have not yet forgotten that recent American history was dominated by a war in the Mideast. We were told this derived from some sort of notion of defense, but I can make no sense of this. Like most Americans I am not uninterested in the idea of defense. However, my own notion of such matters steers me toward the study of tomatoes, not tanks.

As the well was drilled there was no physical evidence of the house. It existed only as pixels on a computer screen. There was, however, evidence that building—the broader notion of construction that concerns me—had begun. There were six dozen stripling tomato plants pulling at the light in my rented apartment in Missoula. They were not just any plants. Their several varieties were chosen with careful regard to Tracy's and my tastes. We matched their habits to the fragility of our soil and fickleness of our climate. They were tomatoes committed to place. They were my closest approximation of hope.

Eventually I took them outside to our land and planted them in rows, my first lines of defense. I understand this is not what is meant by most Americans, but I wish to differ. It's not that I am completely at odds with our people. I agree that we face a clear and present danger. I am frightened. I agree there is a threat to our lives, and that in our lives there are at least some things worth defending. I am with them in my willingness to go to extraordinary lengths in this defense.

It's just that I can make no sense from what we have chosen to defend and of how we have chosen to do so. The threat to our communities is not external. The threat is the way we live our lives. We feed, house, and clothe ourselves in ways that are not sustainable. We do not farm the soil—we mine it.

To me, defense makes sense only if it rings through that antique phrase: "defense of the soil." It is the soil that supports us. We can begin to justify our making a stand only if it includes defending that on which we stand. It seems that true defense must proceed from the ground up, a specific piece of ground, my ground. Here I will plant tomatoes, cut wood, build a house. I do not regard these things merely as products, accessories to my life. They are my life, my teachers. They attach my senses to the earth. These are not merely philosophical issues, nor is my attack on them intellectual. We have spent decades now thinking about the problems that plague us, screaming, posturing, and theorizing until we no longer speak to each other. I am tired of thinking as if thinking alone would save us.

I know of people who believe the solution to our troubles is in preservation. We have used so much that we can use no more and so all of unspoiled nature ought to be left alone. I have great sympathy for this view and try to pursue it to the extent it is possible, but in truth it is not possible. Like the rest of creation we humans re-create our own lives at the expense of others.

I know of people who believe that our salvation lies in development, in use, in the conquering and taming of a piece of land. They are wrong.

I plan to build my house at the toe of the hill, on the line between steep and flat. Here a thin line of 60-foot-tall Douglas fir gives way to a few pine that rim the bottom of the hill, the edge of the meadow. Behind my house will be wild land, largely preserved. Before it will be flat land, not tamed but farmed organically, with attention to nature's pattern for life. The house itself will stand in the trees between. Resting as it will in this crease, this house will inform the rest of my life. Because of this I wish to touch every square inch of it with my work.

In *Walden*, Thoreau said:

There is some of the same fitness in a man's building his own house that there is in a bird's building its own nest. Who knows but if men con- structed their dwellings with their own hands and provided food for themselves and families simply and honestly enough, the poetic faculty would be universally developed, as birds universally sing when they are so engaged? But alas! we do like cowbirds and cuckoos, which lay their eggs in nests which other birds have built, and cheer no traveller with their chattering and unmusical notes. Shall we forever resign the pleasure of construction to the carpenter? What does architecture amount to in the experience of the mass of men? I never in all my walks came across a man engaged in so simple and natural an occupation as building his house. We belong to the community. It is not the tailor alone who is the ninth part of a man: it is as much the preacher, and the merchant, and the farmer. Where is the division of labor to end? And what object does it finally serve? No doubt another may also think for me; but it is not therefore desirable that he should do so to the exclusion of my thinking for myself.

The day the well drillers came in April was a typical Montana spring day. It was snowing. While I waited for them I hobbled down to the south end of the property as a bitter-toothed canyon wind quartered off my right shoulder. In a line down the south edge of the property were seven short spars of apple trees, our first flags planted on the land. I stopped to feel a wispy purple pasqueflower (a wild crocus) blooming in the grass. It was hunched into a cup against the weather, but if the sun came out later it would stretch open like the rest of us. Down near the trees five mule deer raised their heads to confront me. Mule deer are a brazen lot, especially when they have the advantage of a steep hill at their backs. They can pogo straight up a hill that would rip the lungs out of anything else living, especially middle-aged humans. I once watched a doe thrash the conspiracy out of two coyotes that were eyeing her fawn.

Deer are pests down here on the flat where the fruit trees grow. This time of year especially, when the grass is not yet green, they enjoy nipping buds off freshly planted apple trees. Michael, Tracy, and I had spudded in these trees just a day before, and we were worried about the deer. While we were planting the Hendersons had stopped by to talk. It's the first time we had met them, new neighbors, nice people with a couple of young daughters Kate's age. We could tell he was a logger by the brace of chainsaws stabbed into a rack in the back of his pickup truck. Mrs. Henderson allowed as how the deer already had punished fruit trees on her land just up the gulch. Accordingly she had raised hell with the Forest Service. Following a political logic I do not quite understand, rugged individualistic Montana now lays its problems on the desks of the federal government, which is constituted here as the Forest Service. Even odder, the federal government has to a degree accepted this role. Mrs. Henderson told us the local ranger gave her some blood meal to fend off the deer.

I, too, was in a defending mood and so bought some blood meal of my own. Tracy, generally a vegetarian, liked the idea that deer were such strict herbivores as to be greatly offended by even the slightest whiff of blood. The woman at the nursery said it's true, they are, but only for a while, and then even deer adapt. I took quiet comfort in the fact that some neighbors only days before had seen a mountain lion, a more effective and natural form of pest control, stalking the valley. By the morning of the drilling either the deer hadn't yet found the trees or the lion had found the deer. The fresh apple buds were beginning to unwrap unmolested to test the bitter breeze. Soon these new bits of life would need water.

In the West one does not simply plant and pray for rain. One irrigates everything: gardens, fruit trees, and golf courses. I was especially reminded of this as I stood on the 38 acres where the surface contained not a drop of water.

A crude picture of western Montana's subsurface geology can be assembled through a collection of horror stories. Virtually anyone associated with rural living has such a story. I heard my first from an official of the local power company when I went to ask about his rates.

"Got your well in yet?" he asked. Then when he found I didn't he grinned the smug smile people here reserve for the obvious tenderfoot. Who would be fool enough to spend good money on a piece of land without knowing a thing about the water table? Failure to find water can render property "useless."

"Wells can get expensive," the man said. "Seventeen dollars a foot." Rural Montanans can quote this number as readily as city people quote subway fares.

This man learned the figure first hand, having recently built a house and having recently installed a 600-foot shaft of dry light into the earth. "I spent the price of a new car on a long posthole," he said.

A friend of mine had just spent $5,000 squeezing but a trickle of water from the earth. In one area nearby, which just happens to be adjacent to the biggest freshwater lake in the West, wells are routinely drilled to 800 feet. Other holes, however, yield geysers of fresh, clean water at 40 feet. The explanation for all of this capriciousness is as obvious as the mountains all around us.

The area's subsurface is every bit as rilled and rifted as the surface. The inclines and anticlines continue well below this temporary and shifting line we call the surface to form underground canyons and fissures filled between with pockets of glacial gravel hundreds of feet thick. Most of the water that sustains this place is in pockets formed at least 10,000 years ago as the glaciers waxed and waned. The ice chewed channels, bulldozed up banks of gravel, and filled these pockets in the earth with water.

My land stands just on the edge of the Missoula Valley, which once was covered by a pool the size of Lake Michigan. The retreat of the glaciers destroyed and rebuilt the lake several times, sometimes draining it in a matter of days. Evidence of it remains today, however, as a monster aquifer sometimes only 40 feet beneath the city of Missoula.

A property owner becomes more of a gambler as he moves away from the aquifer. As one walks up the canyons that finger the mountains, there are corresponding canyons weaving secret paths below. Some are above the aquifer; some are not. Some are dry. Here, well drillers use stone-cutting, diamond-tipped bits to drill not in gravel but in bedrock, seeking out pockets of water folded therein. Some of the water from these wells is older than the hills.

There is no precise map of this substrata, and so the mountain well driller and his unwilling partner, the home owner, are like wildcatters. They confront mystery. Science can offer no hard information on this. It has no predictive powers here. Yet information is just exactly what the singularly focused mind of the check-writing home owner seeks. The custom hereabouts among modern people is to react as people always have when confronted with mystery. We hire seers, sorcerers, water shamans, dowsers, or, as they are most commonly known around here, well witches.

Bruce Zemliska's aging Dodge had pulled onto my land a couple of days before the well drillers arrived. I felt greatly comforted by his presence. He was a big, old guy in bib overalls and had that grandfatherly sureness to his walk that told me everything was going to be all right. He unloaded from the car the tools of his trade: two 3-foot brass wires, each with a 90-degree bend toward one end and a gnarled old willow stick, the sort of stick one would expect a witch to carry. Bruce called me "young feller" a couple of times just to stake out the folklorish high ground, and then he strode off across my land to confront mystery.

Tracy had come with me for this event, being seriously interested in the intuitive arts. She strode off after Bruce, rapt. I followed. Bruce didn't say much, and Tracy and I had too much riding on the quality of his trance to disturb him. We simply watched his face for hopeful signs, even though we weren't sure what a hopeful sign might be.

Bruce cut straight across the flat part of the land several hundred feet toward the toe of the mountain. Drawing him along were the two brass rods, one in each hand held at the bend so that the long parts of the rods floated parallel and horizontally out across the dry earth. I was reminded of cartoon versions of somnambulists. Most people think of forked willow sticks when they think of dowsers, but the metal rod method is about as popular. It probably developed in England at least a century ago, although the art of dowsing itself is at least 7,000 years old. The Chinese, Egyptians, and Babylonians did it. In a statue dating to 2200 B.C., an early emperor of China carries a forked stick. In the first textbook on the matter, issued in 1556, Georgius Agricola outlined techniques for locating underground mineral deposits.

Martin Luther denounced it as ungodly in 1516, although his damnation seems to have had no effect. The practice flourished, especially in England, and spread to those countries blessed by England's taste for empire. Over the centuries forked sticks, wires, needles, pendulums, human bodies, phials, Bibles, keys, fiberglass fishing rods, whalebones, pliers, barbed wire, dowels, grass, and railroad spikes all have been employed with some success. Dowsers have located, besides water, water pipes, buried cable, precious metals, bodies in graves, gold teeth in bodies in graves, and buried treasure. One dowser in the Southwest uses his stick to forecast the outcome of elections. In Montana this year authorities commissioned a witcher to wave his wands over a map of the mountains in an attempt to locate a crashed airplane. Usually, though, the target is water, and the forked stick and parallel wires remain the methods of choice.

The latter technique spread to the United States from England just after World War I. Although not much is said about it, virtually any road construction crew operating any place in America has at least one member skilled with a set of wires. Any rural community in the country probably has a dowser, although you won't find him listed in the Yellow Pages. One simply asks around. That's how I found Bruce.

As my dowser and his rods approached the toe of the hill, the rods crossed over each other like a salute of swords, rested a second together, then, as Bruce took a few more steps, they uncrossed to their former parallel position. Bruce's deadpan face changed not a bit. He only tipped his head skyward for a second, as if seeking divining inspiration, then backed up a step and carved a line in the dirt with the heel of his boot.

In earlier centuries, when it was politically correct to burn witches, Bruce's predecessors opted to rename the craft. They became known as "water philosophers." The title seemed apt as evidence of his contemplation of the subterranean verities spread across Bruce's face.

Tracy and I exchanged hopeful glances but didn't speak, out of respect for the trance. Then Bruce executed a crisp 90-degree turn and charted a course perpendicular to the last. Presently the two rods snapped across each other again. Another glance to the sky, another line with a boot. Bruce stopped and thought for a moment to establish a couple of imaginary lines, then extrapolated them to their intersection. He walked to the point and approached it first from one direction, then another, rods crossing and uncrossing over what Tracy and I imagined to be a Niagara just beneath the soil. For a second I thought I could hear it.

Once Bruce had established this point of maximum convergence he put away his rods and drew his gnarled willow stick, which had a bit of a curve toward its fat end. This, too, is a very old device, the customary method of ascertaining the depth of the alleged water. With the thin end of his stick in his hand he held it at an angle so that the fat end extended to about 6 inches above the surface. It rested a second and then began to bounce in a vertical arc like a baton. Bruce counted the bounces until it stopped, shifted from side to side once, then stopped again. "Forty-two," he announced, and then the stick started bouncing again. It stopped, shifted side to side, then stopped for good. "Forty-four more." I had no precedent for reacting to this information, so I simply wrote it down. Bruce then grinned as if to invite conversation, and I took the hint.

"Bruce, what does this mean?"

He informed me that he had detected not one but two streams of water, one at 42 feet and a second 44 feet below that. He was sure of it. Said he never missed by more than 4 feet. This was good news, but Bruce had bad news. They were small streams. "Make a well, but not a good well. Can't leave you with a trickle like that, especially young people and two houses and all." And so Bruce grabbed the brass rods again and sallied forth. He walked about 60 feet. The rods crossed. Bruce pivoted and walked. The rods crossed again. Another point in the dirt. He said all the recrossing business was to allow him to find two underground streams and then the point where they crossed, giving his customers a doubled chance for a producing well. This thoroughness came at no extra charge.

The willow came out again. Bouncing and counting. "Thirty-seven." More bouncing. "Sixty-three more." It occurred to me then that Bruce was particularly fortunate to have obtained a witching stick that had its bounces calibrated in feet. It would have been difficult to convert from a bounce measured in, say, meters. Considerate the way nature adapts to Western human convention. I didn't mention this observation to Bruce. He grinned again. Much better streams this time, he could feel it. This was the place to drill.

About this time Michael drove up to the property. He had sneaked away from his office, not wanting to miss the spectacle. Michael watched until the proceedings finally provoked his instincts. Being from Mississippi he is possessed of a Southerner's love of conversation. His regional drawl still pokes through his Montana cover like underwear through well-worn jeans. He is a reporter, and so the conversation often comes as questions. Michael shifted his drawl up two notches, something he does more or less automatically when dealing with just folks. He wanted to know how Bruce had learned his business. Bruce was pleased by the question.

"That's all I get out of life anymore is to visit a little," he said, and then he drew back to indulge us in a full explanation. Said it wasn't often he found young people these days interested in a dying art. He had learned to witch wells in 1957 while working on a construction job. I had last seen witching done on construction, typically underground construction, such as the installation of sewer lines. People who dig in the ground with huge machines are keenly interested in what has been buried before. When a backhoe ruptures an unexpected water line it can cost days of down time. I had seen this apparently magical and verifiable feat of location performed many times using Bruce's method.

After learning to witch water lines correctly, it became apparent that Bruce had the "gift," and so he went on to a career of witching. He said he had no idea how it worked, but it worked, he was sure of it. Michael was impressed not so much with this explanation as with Bruce's general idea of where our water lay, just at the toe of our hill and below the end of a dry gulch that sliced the face of it. Michael's father is a geologist. When Michael had described the lay of the land to him his father had predicted the water would lie where Bruce had found it.

Imagine that the hill is only the very top of the hill and that the slant of the bedrock that makes it continues beneath the surface. The flat land is only a pool of glacial gravel banked against the slope of the rock. The belief is that the porous gravel drains groundwater through it until the water comes to rest against the bedrock or in channels below its surface. At least that is the hypothesis, according to an actual geologist who had made a solid living finding oil beneath the earth. Still, Michael's father had advised that navigating the subsurface mysteries is a risky business. He had advised us to hire a witch.

So had the surveyor who had helped me find my property lines that day. A man of straight lines and hard answers, he believed in witches, particularly in Bruce. This surveyor said Bruce had never missed a well.

Tracy took over Michael's line of questioning. She is inherently suspicious of science and so is drawn to anything that smacks of an intuitive understanding of the earth. This witching business appealed to her, and yes, Bruce said he'd be glad to show her the tricks, especially since it wasn't often he found young people interested in witching these days, especially pretty female young people.

Bruce showed her how to thread the rods through her fingers so that they swing free of the power of the opposable thumb. The theory behind this grip is that the holder can't turn the rods even if she wants to. This overcomes any bias. Tracy began the somnambulistic shuffle and soon had rods swinging like barroom doors on a Saturday night. She tried the willow shillelagh and established some general agreement with Bruce's assessment of depth. Reproducible results. Science. A sorting of the subterranean mystery. We paid Bruce $60, and I recorded it as one of my soundest investments. Bruce left.

Tracy became fascinated with witchery and began making plans for a serious study of the matter. She vowed to call Bruce and offer her services as an apprentice and later turn 60 bucks an hour divining the mysteries of the earth. It made sense. Michael was similarly smitten. That evening he built a set of dowsing rods out of coat hangers. He and Kate then successfully located a sewer line, his toilet, a glass of beer, and the Clark Fork River as it wended through downtown Missoula.

A well driller's rig is not science, it is industry. I felt its presence as my first compromise. On a snowy morning, the rigs arrived like tanks rolling into a sacred city. The drilling rig itself was first, a 30-ton truck bearing the steel cage of a 30-foot boom, hydraulic lines, air hoses, a welder, a winch, a compressor, and a second diesel engine to power the works. Trudging behind the drill truck came a flatbed truck of similar size full of 6-inch steel pipe in 20-foot lengths, another welder, and a rack of rods that served as the drill's shaft. Certain attending pickup trucks and small vans followed.

The drill rig left the road first, striking out across the grass and pasqueflowers. It left a wake of 6-inch-deep tire tracks pressed in the virgin loam. Randy jumped from the rig as it stopped. He was the crew's boss, the master driller, about thirty years old, a Corvette fancier, cigarette-ad blond, and polite. I showed him the spot Bruce had witched, placing special emphasis on the fact that I knew where the water lay so there would be no shenanigans directed toward the amassing of an enormous bill. Randy caught my meaning but made no response. His understudy, Kevin, alighted from the cab of the flatbed, and they set to drilling.

Outriggers on the drilling truck suspended it off the ground like a cork on a wave, then set it level. Hydraulics swung the boom to a perfect vertical, 30 feet in the air.

A well sinks 20 feet at a time in a series of short, two-step shuffles. One step is the progress of the casing, the 6-inch pipe that holds back the dirt and gravel from the hole. An air hammer beats the casing down as the hole progresses. Inside the casing turns a thick steel shaft with a drill bit at its head. A rotary air motor on the rig spins the drill, which chews a few feet down, then the air hammer forces the casing to follow. After the shuffle presses on for 20 feet the drillers unscrew the shaft, raise the hammer and motor, and insert another 20 feet of casing and shaft into the breach.

As Randy and Kevin set to this task I settle into the rhythm and the security of watching hands turned to their work. Pipe drops, shafts turn, wrenches as long as softball bats stroke a series of error-free singles. I stand maybe 40 feet away from the rig in a trancelike state induced by the earplugs Randy gave me and by the unreality of the amount of money being consumed. The casing has quarter-inch-thick steel walls. I try to imagine what it would take to drive it with a hammer. Sometimes, when the air hammer whacks it, the casing drops 2 feet into the earth all at once. Then I feel the *whompf* of its progress as vibrations course through the soles of my feet. Where the casing penetrates the surface the soft earth rises in a vulval swell. I ignore the lurid symbolism, though, more concerned with the rape of my wallet. I count casings: one, then two; 20 feet, 40 feet; $340, then $680.

Now the rig pauses again and the operators add another length of casing and shaft. This takes about twenty minutes, mostly spent as Kevin and Randy weld the steel collar that couples the lengths of casing. Since the tip of the casing rests about 3 feet out of the ground, I figure the time has come. It's at 37 feet. The bottom of the casing must be resting directly atop the vein of water Bruce found. The welding ends and the drilling begins. Randy stops the drill and sends a blast of compressed air down the center of the shaft to the base of the hole. This is how the rig ejects the gravel, busted-up rock, and, when all goes well, water from the base of the hole. I stand next to the exhaust pipe awaiting the geyser. I catch instead a handful of dusty gravel. It appears Bruce is off by a few feet. The drill presses on, more air sends up more dust. Interesting dust, mind you. Musty smelling dust that has not seen daylight for ten thousand years, but dust all the same.

The drill presses on, and I am somewhat relieved old Bruce allows for error, that he always finds the intersection of two veins of water. Then $1,020, then $1,360, then $1,700 and in the matter of about four hours, the drill bit rests on the dank but otherwise dry gravel 100 feet beneath the surface. Air hisses, winch drums turn, a welder arcs, and another 20 feet of casing and shaft are loaded into the breach. We press on, long past Bruce's predicted moisture.

It occurs to me now that there can be no stopping this process, pushing toward bedrock at $17 a foot. In this area 500 feet is not an unusual depth for a well. (My brain hears that number now as $8,500.) When do I chicken out? Do I stop this madness at, say, 300 feet, when the water I need might be resting only a few more feet down? Do we then move the rig only to drill another long, dark, dry posthole? Well drilling is a cruel art.

Randy sees all this begin to play across my face and so now takes pains to explain exactly what is happening, shows me how to read the gravel flying from the exhaust. Look for black-edged rock, which is freshly fractured rock. This means the drill is beginning to chew into bedrock. Water rests on top of bedrock.

One hundred twenty feet. One hundred forty feet. Now I am half pacing, half hobbling my chosen bit of land in full circles. Any illusion of comfort the well witch's "information" provided has vanished against the reality of a steel bit and rock. I feel like I am on my own. The well drillers tell me later that they never dispute a customer's belief in witches, because witches are right as often as they are wrong. Drilling is a crapshoot, so everyone gets lucky once in a while.

"Besides," Kevin says, "it gives us a place to start."

I worked for fifteen years as a newspaper reporter, exchanging information with people. It is true that people believe what they want to believe. But sooner or later you've got to drill a well, an enterprise that forbids the luxury of selective belief. No matter what one chooses to call them, water is water and dust is dust. I watch as more of the latter pours from the drilling rig's exhaust.

At 150 feet I scoop a handful of something new, first a gob of clay, then black gravel, freshly fractured edges. The drill, for the first time, is breaking rock, bedrock. And then at 157 feet, there is a plop on the ground, the noise of a handful of mud falling from the exhaust tube. No more than a soft plop, and yet the sound seems loud, even through earplugs and above the industrial roar. Water. Still it is not a well. We've hit only the top of a water-laden vein of fractured bedrock. There is no telling if the vein is an inch or a mile thick. Still, it is water.

The drilling goes on. Just past 180 feet the hole comes up dry again, and so decisions must be made. We've hit a small, workable vein of water. Randy believes it will produce about 7 gallons a minute, a modest but adequate flow.

Or at least considered modest. The average family of four people uses about 260 gallons of water a day. Pumped at 7 gallons per minute, my modest well could produce more than 10,000 gallons a day. Yes, says Randy, but when you want lots of water, you want it now, and not as a trickle. What about the dishwasher and the clothes washer and the shower and all those things, and then there's two families and sometimes you will want to run all those things at once. That would be the most convenient way. "The more the merrier," he says. The more the better. Ought to have 10 gallons per minute for each house so you can face a morning shower that feels like a fire hose. Randy is for drilling on into the bedrock in search of ancient pockets.

These pockets of water are a gift laid down by nature through sheer accident, happenstance that occurs on the order of once every few thousand years. Thirty five states, including all those in the West, now are pumping this gift of water faster than it can be replenished, mostly in the interest of a bracing shower, golf courses, and the landscaping of exotic species of plants, particularly grass that nature designed for the sodden Midwest. I have made my compromises for the day. A 30-ton hunk of industry has pressed a trail of deep grooves into an unworked bit of nature. Diesel fumes, dust, and noise have pounded a larcenous bit of steel pipe 180 feet into the earth. I've had enough. This house will be built on compromise. All houses are. But this house will make its stand on the lean side of the line. More is not better.

I have resolved that as I build this house I will assert as often as necessary that less is better. I know that this is a profoundly un-

American notion, yet the measure of our task is to reverse a culture's ethic, to hatch a world that values frugality. Conservation can no longer be a notion bandied about as an anthem at conferences of environmentalists. Frugality needs to be built into houses, gardens, cars, and the minds of the people who make them work, even people who run drill rigs.

I mention the 260-gallon figure to Randy and tell him that 30 percent of that goes through a house's toilet. I speak of water-saving toilets and the recycling of household wastewater for garden irrigation. I suspect I will sound self-righteous, impractical, and preachy, but I don't care. It's my house.

Now Randy looks at me and smiles. He acknowledges that what I have said makes sense. He agrees. He says he's drilled a lot of holes in the earth and somewhere along the line it has to stop. He shows me a trick called perforation that can make my well more efficient but not deeper. It costs $25 a foot, and he needs to do about 20 feet worth to make it work. He does it, and I count the feet. His boss will never find out, so he throws in 10 extra feet for free. Then he asks me about the apple trees I have planted. He needs trees for his lot in town. What grows best around here?

Then he and the drill rig rumble off, returning my land to the deer, the flowers, and its new range of possibilities.

Money

EVEN AT AGE THREE, KATE MOORE SHOWED a gift for language. It could be unsettling to hear whole and proper sentences issue from a toddler's body, as if she were a movie's special effect or a gadget with a recorder inside. At about six years old she turned that talent to the telling of jokes, which fascinate her. She doesn't get them; she doesn't even seem to understand what there is to get. She understands, however, that jokes entertain adults, so she treats them like magic.

As Tracy and I began seriously scheming a house, Kate told me a joke. It involved a frog who had outgrown his lily pad. He required a home-improvement loan. The frog had nothing to offer as collateral except his large collection of knicknacks. Most bankers were unimpressed with this offering, and the frog foundered financially. Eventually he heard of a woman named Patty Black, who was a soft touch for kitsch. She was reputed to frequently accept knicknacks as collateral. The frog went to see the woman and won her approval. When Patty Black presented the completed loan package to her superiors they not only concurred but, according to Kate, did so by breaking into song: "Knicknack Patty Black give the frog a loan."

Kate went around giggling and singing her punch line for weeks, and, I admit, so did I. I am a sucker for irony, and the frog stood a better chance at loan approval than I did. The Moores, Tracy, and I had hatched a subversive scheme. We planned steps such as cooperative land ownership, simple, even austere houses, rural settings, composting toilets, shared wells, and owner-built structures. All are red flags in the conservative world of banking, rendered even more conservative by the savings and loan scandals. Further, I am a free-lance writer, a thin euphemism for "unemployed." When I quit my newspaper job my income collapsed. My financial pedigree showed a gross income of ten thousand dollars in the previous tax year. I had no savings and was obscenely in debt. Tracy was a graduate student in environmental studies, a field that qualifies one only for large student loans but provides no marketable craft with which to settle the notes. We felt as financially adept as frogs.

Nonetheless, our house would need a bank loan. We had spent all available money (the remainder of a loan from Michael's father to lever the land) putting in the well, but with that gamble over and with water flowing we had at least proved the land was habitable. A few weeks after the drilling was done we began the next inevitable but shaky step. Clearly the moment required a cleverly conceived scam.

I looked at the situation thusly: My financial straits were a reality, and the banking world has nothing to do with reality. If nothing else, the savings and loan scandals taught us exactly this. The banking world rests on paper and abstractions. These are concepts I am trained to understand. Who should know better how to manipulate a paper world than a writer? Bankers and writers share common roots.

Toward the earliest morning of Western consciousness there arose a story of the Greek king Gyges. Who cares whether its true. We have told it all these centuries so we must need for it to be true.

In Greek legend, Gyges was the archetypical tyrant, a status he attained with a magic ring. By manipulating the ring on his finger he could become invisible. Then he would slip about unnoticed in the real world, spying on enemies, friends, and lovers and obtaining the information he needed to manipulate people as well as rings. His power of slipping back and forth from visible to invisible, literally his sleight of hand, allowed him to both seize and hold the throne.

The power of this story is only slightly encoded. We need to understand the significance of the ring. It was the Greeks who first began breaking rings in half to seal contracts, a giving of one's word that survives in our use of wedding rings. This use predated the invention of money, and so the ring evolved. Early Greek coins had holes in the center, copies of rings. Rings became money. Goods and services were rendered invisible by a twist of the ring or, as it was known in a more revealing word, "symbola."

Records of commercial transactions were simply drawings of pieces of these rings, these symbola, that eventually became the alphabet that became written language. Gyges the tyrant founded the world of paper—both money and writing—that we inhabit today.

The manipulators of the savings and loan scandal, a scam so huge we are still unable even to calculate or comprehend its scale, were the heirs of Gyges. The thrift industry arose in this nation in the last century simply to amass and lend the money to build houses. Building is about as real and necessary an enterprise as one could imagine. Through most of its history, which began in 1831, it varied not at all from its original mission of bricks and mortar. The spirit of the 1980s, however, sent it awry.

A series of "reforms," capped with a new law signed by President Reagan in 1982, allowed the thrifts to stray from the path of reality. Specifically, savings and loan institutions were allowed much wider latitude in commercial real estate and began playing in the speculative world of money markets. That is, they began transforming money to money, not money to houses. They twisted a ring and entered the invisible world. Most of the manipulation rested on wildly inflating the value of property, trading bad loans for bad loans, and deliberately inflating loans and rolling loans to collect imaginary service charges.

The people running these institutions were not aberrations. They were a species evolved and suited to our times. We consider them criminals today but forget that the rest of us were living off credit cards, stocks bought on margin, and leveraged buyouts. The federal government itself lived and lives off a budget deficit. These are the symptoms that suggest the American dream is collapsing.

The epicenter of that dream was once the American house, the dream house. This we sacrificed to a dream world of illusory wealth, the smoke and the mirrors. The forces that controlled our lives became invisible and we lost control. I had concluded that the antidote to all of this lay in the simple act of reclaiming reality. Reality I chose to define as the tangible, something my hands could hold, something as simple and as sensible as a well-built house.

That left me in an interesting position. My first step toward escaping the power of the tyrant was to approach a savings and loan bank to borrow money, a dose of the hair of the dog. In April 1991 the four principals in this scheme issued the following letter to nine savings and loan or commercial banks doing business around Missoula:

Dear Bankers,

We have begun an interesting housing project near Lolo and are writing this letter to local banks to find financing. Because the project is a bit unusual we thought it best to outline the oddities up front. We need to find a financial institution interested in the project's creative aspects.

As housing projects go, this is a small one: two houses. They will be the houses of the undersigned partners. Therefore, all we really need are two construction loans and two end loans to build the houses on 38 acres we have bought near Lolo. There are, however, some additional opportunities or difficulties here, depending on your point of view. We are trying to build a project that meets the environmental concerns of our time and so will require bankers that will give us the flexibility to do that.

Our environmental goals are many, but let us state a few here:

- A 30 percent reduction in water consumption compared to national averages
- Energy efficiency to meet or exceed Super Good Cents standards
- Installation of superefficient lights and appliances to further reduce energy load
- Recycling of gray water for garden irrigation
- Joint ownership of facilities such as workshops, greenhouses, well, and a guest house to avoid duplication of little-used amenities
- Granting of open-space easements for wildlife habitat on about 33 acres of the property

We understand the project presents some problems, but none seem beyond the reach of creative solutions. Further, they are the sorts of problems builders and bankers must address to meet the needs of customers and the earth in the coming decades.

If you would be interested in working on this project, please contact any one of the partners.

Of the nine letters sent we got one response, but it turned out to be all we needed. A few weeks later we met with Mike McKee, a president at the Missoula-based First Federal Savings and Loan. McKee is old-school savings and loan in that he understands bricks and mortar better than treasury bills. In 1982 federal regulators urged him to diversify his small-town S&L by participating in loans in Texas, the same sorts of loans that torpedoed many similar institutions.

"I told them 'no thanks,' " he says. "I'm not a very smart person. If I don't understand it, I don't do it."

He liked our ideas and seemed to trust us. He heard our plans and foresaw no problems. He told us to proceed and then allowed that a certain amount of paperwork would ensue. Four months later, when we closed the loan, I had to agree he was right about the pile of paper.

I still do not know how to imagine a house. I have only planned and assembled the parts of one. The origins of the whole are a mystery. Let us say, though, that the idea of a house springs most confidently from the driving of a stake into the heart of one's own land. Even before we had bought the land Trace and I had begun the hopeful pacing of the place, searching for the spot that most looked like where we ought to live. We had naturally gravitated toward the transition zone between hill and valley, between grassland meadow and forested slope: a pine park straight at the toe of the hill. It was no accident this spot sloped south.

In Montana the aspect of a slope makes all the difference in its character. Twist the face of a hill around toward the north and there the snow lingers into spring, meting moisture as it goes. In such places the vegetation springs lush, dank, and green under a smothering coat of Douglas fir. But twist the same slope's face south, and the soil bakes. A few stately ponderosa spar such places. The subplot includes a cast of pungent sage and juniper. The latter's crushed blue berries smell like gin. On south slopes the grasses grow low, brown, and wispy. The wildflowers tend to be light and airy reds, purples, and sky blues—paintbrush, larkspur, horsemint, and lupine.

I had it in my mind that such a place would be home, and so to find it I always dreamed house dreams with a compass in hand. Native people would not enter even the smallest of enterprises without orienting to and honoring the four directions. Native architecture is marked by its scrupulous attention to orientation. Here in Montana tipis always had their entry holes faced to the east to catch each day's rising sun. It seemed to me that my house, too, would be better for being tuned to the world that raised it. I wanted a life attentive to its sources.

On a more tangible level, the south slope is a practical matter in that it is the ideal site for an earth-sheltered, passive-solar home. Slope gives shelter; south gives sun. I favor simple solutions and so wanted a passive-solar home. Tracy did too, so we drove a stake just where we thought such a home would be. Then we sat on that sunny hillside all one late winter's afternoon making plans. The stake we drove that day still stands about 30 feet out of this house's back door. We didn't miss our spot by much.

The driving of a stake led us back to paper. More than its being earth-sheltered, the key decision had been to make the house small and simple. House designers use the term "footprint" to describe the area consumed by contact between house and earth. I like that word. It gets to the deeper notion of the need for each of us to leave a smaller footprint on the earth.

As a practical matter small size would keep the house stingy in its use of materials, both in its construction and, more important, in its year-to-year sustenance. Keeping it small and simple would also keep the house affordable. Its owners, now becoming builders, relative idiots in their new avocation, could do most of the work themselves. This included the work of designing it.

Banker McKee had told us that if he trusted someone detailed plans of a house were unnecessary for loan approval. Sketches of houses, literally on the backs of envelopes, have been sufficient to pry loans from McKee. We planned a more polished approach, but the banker's informality gave us an important boost. We did not have to hire an architect. We could design the house ourselves.

After a preliminary discussion established some shared ideas between Tracy and me, we each independently sketched floor plans. They were close. We finagled some rooms around a bit, made a couple of minor compromises, and in a matter of hours there was agreement on the broad outlines. I set to work drawing the plans with simple graphics software on my Macintosh computer.

The guiding hand of my work was anger provoked by the logging of the area. In the past decade loggers shaved this area and the rest of the Pacific Northwest like a dog. As a newspaper reporter I had investigated these timber predations. I had followed the logs down the logging roads through the mills and onto the trains that shipped the trees to the sprawl that has become America. In this country we build big. Environmentalists consider the timber barons the villains of our world, but they are simply willing conduits. At times leaky, greedy, and inefficient conduits, but in the end only accomplices.

Some of that funny money during the years of the savings and loan scandals did worm its way back to reality, for reasons other than practical ones: simply for layering loans on loans, the money built or partially built unneeded houses, offices, and malls. I remember one vivid image from the period, a television report on the savings and loan scandal underscored by a videotape of bulldozers razing acres of partially built houses. This was physical evidence of the collapsing house of cards. Yet those cats buried real lumber, real studs, stripped from the hills of Montana. This waste was the cost of our losing touch with reality.

During the mid-1980s the nation built about twelve million new structures a year when only nine million were needed. But more to the point, the houses were huge, suburban sprawlers. Three and four and five thousand square feet for two to four people. According to the National Association of Home Builders the median size of a single-family home in 1980 was 1,595 square feet. That figure actually dropped slightly but steadily to 1,520 square feet by 1982, when the Reagan years began in earnest. By 1990 the median home was 1,905 square feet, an increase of nearly 20 percent over the decade, 25 percent over 1982.

There was no physical push to this excess. During the same period the price of a new home nearly doubled from $65,000 to $123,000. If anything, this should have been a disincentive to larger houses. We didn't need the space; families got smaller, but our appetites got larger. I don't remember the nation as being terribly cramped in 1980. Are we that much more comfortable in our bigger houses today?

At the outset Tracy and I established a rule. We decided our apartment was close but adequate space for our lives, so we had measured it room by room. It was about 1,000 square feet, so that's roughly what our house would be. By American standards this is cramped quarters for two people, particularly when both work at home. Our living space also is our office space. By world standards, though, I suspect such space is considered palatial. The average Japanese house, for instance, was about 850 square feet in 1990. Small became our standard for a notion that was important to us, that of living within limits.

The size teamed with the passive-solar aspect of the house to make design a relatively simple process. The inside had to be free of interior walls. The open design lets heat and light circulate freely and makes a small house seem larger.

These details seemed to almost dictate a design. I suppose it would have been automatic for someone in the trades, someone familiar with the conventions of the craft. I was, however, building my skills as well as a house, so I remember this time best as one of sleepless nights. Daily I would draw and scheme, adding new tidbits from research I was doing and whims that would arise. For instance, I designed an entire electrical system based on solar generation and photovoltaics all because the notion seemed forward-looking, right-thinking, and politically correct. At the outset I did not bother to calculate two factors—photovoltaic generation is wickedly expensive and electricity on my site is stupidly cheap.

Using photovoltaics would have driven the cost of the house out of my reach or would have meant I had no money left to spend on other less glamorous but equally effective environmental considerations. I scrapped the solar cells and went on with other details.

I am by nature a tinkerer and am fascinated with the workings of pipes, wires, braces, and beams. Even in my simple house these details created a seductively complex pattern. In a sense a house is nothing more than a giant puzzle to be solved, an addictive Rubik's cube. I became obsessed.

Still the obsession matured from an infatuation to a plan, a drawing.

In May I shoved this drawing into a manila folder to shield it from my sweaty, nervous hands. This and a few sheets of depressing financial statements were what I presented to Mike McKee in arguing that he advance a destitute writer and an even more destitute graduate student what we regarded as the princely sum of fifty thousand dollars. We were in luck in that real estate loans have very little to do with the borrower and everything to do with real estate.

McKee was interested in the design but not so much in the aspects that drew my attention. It was not, after all, my house, at least not in his mind. As far as the banker is concerned he is not building the house for the borrowers; he is building the house for the people who will buy it after the borrower defaults.

Accordingly, McKee cast a quick look at certain aspects, searching for obvious red flags for the market. There were faults with the design that may well have sunk it in a more rigidly standardized market, details like its size, wood heat, and single bedroom. McKee, however, knew local real estate well enough to understand there was a niche for my odd little house. He could sell it if we defaulted.

McKee is maybe fifty, tall and thin with a mustached face that looks like it still gets outdoors. Before he became a banker he was a captain in the army. He appears as if he still could be. He left Saigon in 1970, not wanting to serve in what was then becoming a peacetime army. He smiles a lot, jokes in the Western vernacular. He once came to a late-Friday meeting in motorcycle garb, carrying his helmet and ready to leave town on a road trip.

In this May meeting Tracy and I sat across from him in his office in a wonderfully restored Victorian building in downtown Missoula. He shuffled the papers, raised an eyebrow here and there. He asked informed questions for which we had informed answers. On impulse I had brought to the meeting all my gleanings of the sleepless nights: computer printouts, brochures, clips of magazine stories—about 20 pounds of paper in file folders in a blue canvas bag. As McKee would question some eccentric method or material we had planned—for example, a mortarless brick floor—we'd produce a magazine clip on the topic. This went on not long at all until the conversation began undermining all my expectations.

I was raised a poor kid and so I still have a poor kid's phobias about money, that I have no right to it and am simply begging when I apply for a loan. Because of this I despise money and anything to do with it. The only time I am tempted toward sympathies with Christianity is when I am reminded of Christ driving the money changers from the temple. Often I have wished for a thumping big scourge and a batch of Philistines to beat senseless.

Now I am a writer and hate money even more, mostly because I have none but more, I guess, because the manipulation of money is too close to what I do. I suspect writers are a neurotic bunch because they are frightened by their magic. They are unwilling tyrants. When we twist our rings of words to make the visible invisible and then visible again, we haven't the foggiest notion of how we do it, just as we haven't the foggiest notion of how money renders the invisible visible. Money is a bedeviling bit of sorcery and I want no part of it. When I write I feel not at all separate from the savings and loan swindlers, that I am one of them. I don't wish to be reminded of this.

Borrowing money scares me. But there is no way around it if one is to build a house, and so I faced McKee. But I was not at all prepared for what was to happen, which was not mysterious or ugly in the least. I had conducted enough interviews as a reporter to realize quickly that McKee's questions in that meeting were following a preconceived line. The line had less to do with the mechanics of money and more to do with Tracy and me. McKee was attempting to establish trust.

He was trying to find out whether he could trust us to make our dreams work. We had met some objective criteria, true enough. On paper we had enough equity in the land to swing the deal, but every day loans, especially construction loans that stand on sounder ground, are denied. I suspect this is not universally true, but in Montana a loan still can be cut as a matter of trust. Ours was.

Tracy and I convinced McKee we could do what we said we would do, that our word could be translated into reality. This was not a manipulation of the ring in the modern way, not a scam or deceit. It was a giving of the ring, a giving of our word.

We left that meeting in May with an invitation to formally apply for a loan, which in bankerese translates to an opinion that the deal would fly. McKee estimated we would have a formal loan commitment in two weeks. He'd be ready to cut checks two weeks after that, then we could start building. McKee was wrong about this. To close the loan certain matters of public record would need to be verified and certain regulatory matters would need to be settled.

Toward the beginning of World War II the British became alarmed about certain inefficiencies in their military. About the same time, the Americans were pioneering the field of improving efficiency, so the Brits hired some American time-and-motion men, the guys with clipboards and stopwatches, to come have a look. One such efficiency expert drew the task of monitoring a gunnery crew. He was disturbed by what he saw. The crew appeared to be all business, a veritable extension of the machine, as the men scrambled about to reload, aim, and prepare to fire the massive gun. There came a point in the proceedings, however, when two of the Brits would simply stand to one side, snap smartly to attention, and stand idle while their colleagues labored on.

Naturally this matter puzzled the time-and-motion man, and so he questioned the slackers. They said they had no idea why they did what they did. They simply were performing as they had been trained. No one else knew what the two were doing either, only that the training manual specified their behavior. The efficiency expert dug deeper and finally located a wizened coot who had trained gunnery crews in World War I, in the days before lorries towed guns. He well knew what the two men were doing; they were holding the horses so that they would not bolt at the shock of the gun's report.

Those phantom horses survived not only to World War II but well beyond. I suspect they graze invisibly today in a remote but pleasant little gulch in Montana. We were to learn that the government still pays people to hold them, people such as filers of plats and inspectors of septic systems.

To close the loan the Moores, Tracy, and I needed to create a bit of a legal fiction, a phantom minisubdivision. Because mortgages are issued to individuals and because mortgages must be attached to real property, we needed to split off two 2-acre pieces of land from the total parcel. One would secure the Moores' mortgage, one Tracy's and mine. The remaining 34 acres we would hold jointly. Luckily there was a method in Montana for doing this, a sort of minisubdivision procedure. It is meant to allow such splits as dividing a rancher's land among heirs, but it is mostly used by unscrupulous developers to evade subdivision regulations. It suited our purposes fine.

There was, at least by appearance, almost no red tape involved in the split. The only hurdles of substance we would need to clear were obtaining clear title to our land by paying off a series of land contracts tied to it. McKee had agreed to loan us the money to do that, so that step was the real estate world's equivalent of paying a bill and getting a receipt. Also, to effect the split, we would need to have our soil tested and approved for septic tanks by the county.

One June day a county official arrived on the property to lower himself into a 10-foot-deep hole we had dug in the middle of a previously undisturbed piece of meadow. His task was to scoop a hunk of soil from the bottom of the hole, roll it into a glob the size of a golf ball, and pour water on it. He was testing the ability of the soil to absorb wastewater—no small matter in our country's rural areas. Although not much is said about it, septic tanks are the leading threat to water quality in most rural states. The systems often are designed poorly; they become overloaded or fail. Raw sewage then seeps into rivers and streams or aquifers, and then we drink it. As a reporter I had written about such problems in our county, and I considered them serious. In fact, on these stories I had often dealt with the very official crawling around in the hole. I considered his job a valuable and necessary service in protection of the community.

The fellow we had hired to dig the hole thought otherwise. By then we had come to refer to our digger of holes as "Trusty Dave," largely because his name is Dave Trusty. Although not always so aptly named, every small town has such a character, a factotum of subterranean ventures. They are entrepreneurs by virtue of having invested in a creaking and crawling dump truck, a backhoe, and maybe a bulldozer. Dave had all three, rendering him something of a master of the hole world.

Dave and his counterparts are the keepers of the unseen devices, the buried and the forgotten. On short notice—on a holiday or in the middle of the night, if necessary—they will attend to busted pumps and water lines, clogged septic tanks, frozen drains, and broken culverts. The toolboxes in the back of their pickup trucks contain all the parts, one of everything, and if it's not on the truck then it's out behind the double-wide mobile home up a gravel road in a pile that looks like junk to the rest of the world. Finding and cementing a relationship with a Trusty Dave is as important as finding a banker. Like well witches, they are not found in the Yellow Pages, nor would anyone in his right mind select someone so vital as his hole digger through such a random process. A doctor, maybe, but not a hole digger. Instead, one simply asks around.

Before the fellow from the county had come to crawl in Dave's freshly dug hole, Dave had been specific in his counsel to me.

"You just let me do all the talkin'," Dave said. I was to say "yes sir" and "no sir" to the bureaucrat. I was to shuffle, mumble, and avert eyes, but under no circumstances was I to question the inspector's judgment or even discuss salient points. A sewer permit was at stake.

Nonsense, I thought. Bureaucrats are just people; in this case, a person I know. Besides, I am not an unscrupulous developer hell-bent on the pollution of the aquifer. I am an environmentally sensitive person here to do right by water, flora, and fauna. Surely the bureaucrat would recognize this and grant our dispensation.

The county guy climbed into the hole and rolled the dirt into a ball, then squirted it with his holy water. I told him that his work, while apparently interesting and vital, was, in my case, unnecessary. He asked how I came to suffer such a delusion. Dave winced. I said it was unnecessary because I was not nearly so crude as to dump sewage into the ground. I would install a composting toilet approved and sanctified by the National Association of Sanitarians, the poobahs of the inspector's trade. I would recycle my own waste.

The bureaucrat looked at me as if I had just recycled some of that waste into the hole he occupied. I was informed that the county does not encourage the use of composting toilets. Knowing that raw sewage from septic tanks pollutes both the river that bisects the county and the aquifer that underlies it, I found this preference curious. I asked the bureaucrat about its origins.

He said that the regulators view the toilets as a means to circumvent regulation. The county feared evil builders such as I would install the $1,500 composters only to obtain the necessary sewage permit and then yank out the composting toilet and replace it with a $3,000 uninspected septic system. For that reason the county would allow me the composting toilet but would make me install the septic system as well. I prepared to debate this point. Dave noticed my intentions and made menacing gestures in my direction with a shovel. I took these gestures as a suggestion that I should shut my mouth before I caused damage even Dave's diplomacy could not repair. Thus counseled, I inquired of the bureaucrat whether the county would offer some sort of financial inducement toward the virtue of my composting toilet, which, I assured him, I did intend to use.

Reluctantly he regurgitated the policy. Yes, a composting toilet would allow me to scale back the size of my drain field by 40 percent. The drain field is a network of buried pipes that leach to the soil semitreated sewage that passes through the septic tank. Drain fields are a huge part of the costs of a septic system, so this concession was important. Drain fields are priced by length, usually about ten dollars a foot.

Now the bureaucrat returned to the study of his mud balls. I watched with renewed interest. The behavior of this mud would determine the length of the drain field. The bureaucrat squinted at his product and pronounced his judgment: 65 feet of drain field per bedroom. Odd, I thought, because I had never known a bedroom to produce sewage. I didn't state this objection. The bureaucrat had just quoted the lowest possible number, corresponding to soil that yields the optimum leaching conditions. At that rate I calculated a drain field of 39 feet, 65 less 40 percent, $390. No big deal. I shared the results of my calculations with the bureaucrat. He clucked at my stupidity.

He said my number would be correct only in the event that my house had one bedroom. I said, right, that's how many it will have. He informed me one bedroom was impossible, no doubt a subterfuge on my part. He said I lied to obtain the county's sanction. Once I had my permit I would no doubt set immediately to work converting my house to multiple bedrooms spewing all manners of foul effluvia to a short septic system. I said, no, that wouldn't be the case in that only my wife and I would live in the house, and we like each other, and we hate company, and so extra bedrooms would be redundant. Doesn't matter, said the bureaucrat. The county will only allow a system designed to serve a minimum of two bedrooms.

Dave read counterarguments forming on my face and checked my impulse with more menacing gestures of his shovel. More calculations. Okay, 78 feet of drain field. Seven hundred eighty dollars. Not perfect, but I could live with that. Tentatively I disclosed my revised calculations. "Wrong," said the bureaucrat. The county would require a minimum of 100 feet of drain field to accept the nonexisting sewage from my nonexisting bedrooms. A cool grand. I considered borrowing Dave's shovel to kill the bureaucrat but understood the county had more like him to send. Besides, we were still only at the banking stage. I needed this approval only to get the loan. I could fight this drain field battle later. Failing that, perhaps I could use the drain field to fertilize the grass to graze the retired British horses.

The sewer permit was but a preperatory step toward what is in the banking world an accomplishment of substance: the drawing of an imaginary line on a piece of paper. Although all of the would-be residents intended to use the acreage as a commons, the bank insisted we divide it to secure loans. There would be no evidence of the lines on the property, the real part of the real estate. Nonetheless, McKee would not proceed with our loan application until the county assured him the split had occurred, an assurance conveyed in the assignment of a four-digit number. To obtain this number we needed to hire a registered surveyor to draw the lines on our plat, then have the plat recorded with the county.

The drawing of the lines took four weeks. The surveyor was swamped and could not see to it sooner. Unable to hurry the surveyor, I began to work connections in the county to expedite the process. My research showed that the county surveyor's office assigned the number, so I called there to make arrangements to deliver the plat. Couldn't do that, the surveyor's office said. The plat needs to go to the health department first. What does the health department do with it? Nothing. They just send it to us. Why don't I bring it directly to you? Because we don't do it that way. I sent it to the health department early in the week.

"Can this go to the surveyor's office now?"

"No, not until Friday."

"Why Friday?

" 'Cause that's the day we send them."

"What happens to the plat before you send it?

"Nothing."

"Then why can't you send it now?"

"It's not Friday."

The plat, at the appointed hour, wends its way to the surveyor. The surveyor surveys it and pronounces it wanting but nonetheless acceptable.

Does this mean it is now accepted, and I can have my four-digit number?

No, this is only a copy of the plat. We need the original to file it.

That doesn't sound too hard. I'll go get the original from my surveyor and bring it in.

Can't do that. Your surveyor has to send it in.

To you?

No, to the health department. All plats start in the health department.

What will they do with it?

Nothing. They just send it to us.

On Friday?

Right.

A week passes, a week in the prime of construction season. By now it is late June. Later than late here in Montana, where winter comes early and leans hard on people with unfinished houses. Finally the original of the plat makes it to the surveyor's office, where I go to learn my four-digit number.

Do you have the plat?

Yes.

Is it acceptable?

Yes.

What's my number?

We don't do the numbers. The clerk and recorder assigns the number.

I rush upstairs to the clerk and recorder. A clerk (a competent and helpful one—they do exist) checks the plat. Yes, it has been filed and all is well, with one exception. It needs one more signature.

"From whom?"

From the health department.

But they had it first and didn't do anything.

I know. They sign it last.

This woman, though, knows nothing of Friday and simply gives me the plat to take two blocks to the health department. There an official I have long dealt with, an acquaintance of mine, is standing watch.

Jim, old pal, how about a signature on this plat, just a formality, mind you. How's the wife and kids?

Jim surveys the plat and readies his pen to sign the paper that will open the floodgates, and the money that will anoint my long-sought house will come pouring in. He checks his swing.

Wait a minute. The state hasn't lifted the sanitary restrictions. I can't sign this.

There I have him. Sanitary means septic tank and right behind him stands a file cabinet in which, I happen to know, lurks a septic permit for this same property. Someone from this very office, no doubt a buddy of Jim's, had come to my place and rolled mud into balls, not for nothing.

I tell Jim this.

That doesn't have anything to do with the plat. The mud rolling was for your septic permit. This is for sanitary restrictions.

What do state sanitary restrictions have to do with my house?

Nothing.

Nothing?

They don't apply. But under an old law the state has to lift them before we can approve a plat. If we don't send it to them, they give us hell.

How long does this take.

Generally a couple of months.

I consider forgery. I consider killing Jim. What jury would convict me? I consider appealing to a higher authority. I call in reinforcements: a surveyor, my guy, not the county guy. He contends that Jim is wrong about the state, that the law doesn't apply in this case, so the state can enforce its nonexisting restrictions on my nonexisting sewage in what is seeming more and more like my never-to-exist house. Jim buys this argument and signs. I file the plat and a four-digit number is mine. I stop in the street, pull out the plat, and read the number aloud. Several times, as if it is a winning lottery number. I share it with the bank. June ends.

In recent decades, as some ranches of Montana traded their cattle for subdivisions full of summer folks, the ranchers, in effect, became bankers. That is, the land that was diced up and sold was not really sold but was conveyed through an instrument known as a land contract. The sellers, not banks, finance the sale. The buyer pays principal and interest to the seller. In turn the seller agrees to convey title of the land, but only after the land is paid off.

There are a couple of advantages for the seller who doesn't need the cash up front and can, in the argot of real estate, "carry the paper." First, he doesn't receive a big lump of cash and so spreads his taxes on the income over several years. More importantly, he collects the interest. In Montana, ranchers have generally used this income to buy Winnebagos and go to Arizona.

Land contracts are, however, notoriously messy instruments. (In the real estate world one writes on an "instrument," not paper.) Because title does not technically change hands, land contracts create layers of ownership, not clean breaks. They are easy to execute, so they tend to be informal, particularly in rural Montana, where business is considered nobody else's concern, especially nobody in the courthouse downtown where land contracts ought to be filed as part of the public record.

Mike McKee called me in July. He had approved the loan, but we couldn't close on it, that is, he couldn't cut checks, until title to the land was assured. This was a problem. We had bought the land from some people who didn't own it. They had a land contract and we assumed it. The ultimate seller in this case was a well-off woman who held what was left of some substantial business holdings around the town of Lolo. She was, in fact, generally well-off enough that she was nowhere to be found. She was somewhere in Arizona. Our problem was that we needed to give her the large sum of money McKee had loaned us so that she could convey title and all would be well. McKee had been unable to find her to give her the money.

I decided to take an active role in this, largely because I was by now damned mad at the delays in the county's machinery. I was in a mood to start building my house. July was ticking away. By using real estate contacts I was able to track down the woman's stockbroker in Arizona. Then I found her lawyer. I told them I needed to give their client money. This seemed to get their attention. The trouble was, neither the stockbroker nor the lawyer knew where to find their client. She had flitted off to Minnesota, they thought, leaving them only to mind her money. They suggested I check back in a couple of weeks. Maybe then their client would be in a position to receive checks.

I found this unacceptable. More research ensued. It turned out we shouldn't have needed to find the woman, largely because in the real world the deed we needed was supposed to be signed and held in escrow. It wasn't. It also turned out that the woman couldn't execute such a deed because she technically did not own the property. She and her ex-husband had bought it from an old ranching family on a land contract. Resting beneath the layer of ownership tangled up somewhere on the highway between Arizona and Minnesota was yet another layer of ownership settled in generations of an old-guard ranching family.

I called the rich woman's Arizona stockbroker with this new information.

What about the underlying land contract? I asked.

Oh, yeah, we just found out about that a couple of months ago. We paid it off.

Then where in the hell is the deed?

We don't know. They never sent us one.

Who is "they?"

The bank.

What bank?

The one in Alberta.

Meanwhile, the Arizona stockbroker's client remains incommunicado in Minnesota and cannot explain why this blizzard of paper has blown international to come screaming out of the Canadian tundra. I call more sources. It develops that this old-guard ranching family had a curious idiosyncrasy. It was wary of the perils of small-town life. The scions of the family reasoned that putting one's money in the local bank would only lead to one's wealth being bruited about town. Therefore the cash and all attending business was shipped off to financial institutions of proper discretion in LaComb, Alberta. I learn this during the first week in August and call the Canadian banker.

I ask about the deed and he hasn't the vaguest notion what I am talking about. He will, however, have a peek around the vault and see what he can find. Hours later he calls me back. Yes indeed, he does have something that looks awful much like the thing I was talking about. Fine. Be so kind as to fax it off to my pal McKee? No, he couldn't possibly do such a thing without the permission of Minnesota's most unnoticed visitor. I dial Arizona. Negative. Haven't heard from her. Could Arizona extend the needed permission in the absence of his client?

Arizona: "Oh, I don't know."

I explain that I will fly to Arizona and do violence if his fax machine is not revved up and beeping proper permission in a matter of seconds. He complies. Alberta complies. McKee has the paper.

The following day McKee calls. Seems Alberta has misfaxed. Seems he sent a copy of the land contract. We already have that. We still need the deed. I call Alberta, but it's a bank holiday there. I wait not altogether patiently through a long weekend, then call Alberta again. The banker didn't know if he had that other document, but he would have another peek in the vault. Sorry about the mixup. Ring you back when I get a chance. Hours pass. He calls me back. Yes he does have the deed, as it turns out.

Would he be so kind as to fax it on down? I ask.

Don't know about that. Need Arizona's permission. Not sure previously faxed permission extended to new document. Another call to Arizona. Arizona beams Alberta. Alberta beams McKee.

McKee calls again. Good news. Alberta got it right this time. Bad news. Can't proceed with just a fax. Need the original. Would Alberta be so kind as to FedEx same. Alberta doesn't know about this. No permission from Arizona. Arizona is reluctant about releasing the original. Minnesota remains silent. There is further talk of homicide. Further fax transactions and then a FedEx van speeds across the prairie.

McKee calls. There is good news: FedEx arrived. Right document. Bad news: The deed mentions the wrong piece of land. Mind you, most of the information lines up perfectly—mete, bound, and section. The only discrepancy is in the tract number. This raises two possibilities. One: There is an error in the deed. Two: Minnesota, who likely never has seen the land, did not buy what she thought she bought, which means the folks in Baltimore (the people I bought it from) were similarly deluded. Which means I could be strangled by the end of this chain.

This latter possibility gained a further sense of immediacy by a recent development. This land I had come to love despite its checkered legal past now held more than my dreams. It held my concrete. On the strength of McKee's loan commitment six weeks before, I had proceeded with construction, which at the time seemed like not that big of a risk. A thousand-dollar hole had been dug and filled with three thousand dollars worth of concrete, neither of which I could pay for unless the loan closed. Up until then the possibility that the loan might not close had been my worst nightmare, but now a more frightening proposition entered. Perhaps the deed was correct. Perhaps this hole and concrete, not to mention a four thousand dollar freshly dug water well rested on land I did not own. The little valley was full of absentee owners. I could have built a whole house on someone else's land by the time it was noticed.

Then I remembered something. We had found this land in an unusual fashion. No realtor took us there and said this is it. We tracked its owners through tax records, wrote them a letter, and made our offer. Had I misread the plat? Only my own reading of unfamiliar, dog-eared county plat books tied us to this land.

McKee called a huddle of property wizards. They considered the matter and ruled the deed in error. My reading of the plat was right, but still title could not pass. The error would have to be corrected, meaning someone would have to track down the most senior heir to the ranching fortune and obtain an initialed consent to the correction on the deed. I located a junior heir. It turns out he's the manager of the fortune and a lawyer. He had prepared the deed. Could he fix it?

Yes, if I'd bring it on out to his office, he'd run it out to the house. Grandmother was home, and she could initial it. I did and in a half hour the deed was done. The loan closed on August 9. It had taken more than three months to work my way to the bottom line of a pile of papers, none of which made my house real. Paperwork drove no nails. The actual construction of the house would take about as long as the paper chase had.

I felt a curious betrayal in all of this, largely because these paper shufflers were my people. The overclass. The white-collar world. The professionals. The world of bankers, politicians, bureaucrats, and people who write and read books. Unlike carpenters, paper shuffling is what most of us do. I once heard a joke about a town where the economy was based on everybody doing everybody else's laundry. Substitute "paper" for "laundry" and you begin to describe our economy. This paper world was my world, where my allegiance had been. There is another world where people still touch things, where they do real work. I am not arguing that everything in the paper world is unnecessary or waste, but it occurred to me that those of us who do those abstract jobs have lost some wisdom that a touch of the physical world might give us. My allegiance now shifted to the realm of nails and boards.

The notion of real work is mostly lost to us now. I suspect this has much to do with why we ourselves are having so much trouble finding our way.

In August, toward the end of the money time but before the real building had begun, there was a party on the land, a summer's evening gathering of fifty or so people. A few kegs of beer. Barbecue fare and tents, pickup trucks and sleeping bags spread through the meadow and trees. Most of the people were old friends of ours. Then there were a few new people, neighbors and others who had just showed up. By coincidence Tracy's brother and his wife had pulled into town that week, on their way back to their home in Virginia after a drive to the opposite coast. With them was Jeff, an old friend of Tracy's. She hadn't seen him for years. All of them joined us that evening on the land.

I walked the house site many times, pacing off the foundation lines and explaining to people how this thing would work. Thermal mass and solar orientation, earth sheltering, drawing it all with broad swings of my arms, as if gestures could conjure it into being. Some people looked at the lines I had staked on the ground, the lines of what had once been an idea now forming tangibly on the land. Some pronounced these lines beautiful. Their saying it seemed to make it so.

Later we gathered around a campfire, and guitars came from cases to be tuned. Michael and I had often played together. Our guitars paired easily, even in other hands, as they were passed around the fire to play some songs people knew. We sang along with a few anthems or listened quietly to some antique wailing blues that occasionally arose from deep in the Mississippi delta to waft on Rocky Mountain air.

In Montana a summer sky at high latitude glows well into the night, bleeding its pure blue to orange and then pastels that settle on the hills behind the pine. On this night the dark barely settled before it was softened by the glow of a full moon.

Then Jeff began to play, tugging toward the sadder reaches of the songs with a simple blues harp. Jeff has an intense and deep-running mind. In recent years he has become engaged in playing harmonica. I knew this, but I was not prepared for the way he and his notes flowed through those primitive instruments like a sad river. A river we have forgotten runs through us all.

Jeff played along with the guitars, gently filling in the holes. Then he took some leads, some soft Southern songs working their way down to "Shenandoah" and finally to a piece he almost never plays. Like a river, it cannot be visited at will because it is never twice the same. Like a river, it flows only in the context of proper banks. When Jeff played "Amazing Grace," I believed this land was the context of grace, even for this wretch. We had fought long for a banker's sanction, but this song was the real blessing on our land.

Tools

IT HAD BEEN MAYBE THREE YEARS SINCE I had seen that half-inch drill. Normally I do not loose track of such tools. I value and protect tools. If things break, you fix them. If you don't fix them, you do without. Fixing takes tools, simple as that.

In the early days of my first marriage my wife and I were perpetually broke. She was a teacher and I was a newspaper writer, careers that matter little to the market. We bought old houses, euphemistically said to "have potential," and renovated them as best we could. We made a few dollars on the houses, but mostly they gave us better places to live and something to tinker with when the talk wore thin or hot. Sometimes I needed a diversion. Because of this, I collected tools.

In this hoarding there were certain parallels to the caches of the rich. Tools are like leather-bound books in that they hold an aesthetic appeal separate from their use. Finely machined steel meshed to power through crisply ground gears is beauty that transcends our idea of the aesthetic.

Most Native Americans had in their language and therefore in their thinking no separate concepts for utility and beauty. They were the same thing. Accordingly, simple, everyday tools often bore the most elaborate ornamentation. This is a natural outcropping of a life lived close to its sources. Some people still find beauty in utility. I whiffed a hint of this connection in that earlier life of mine.

The years, however, sent me off chasing more wispy, papery notions of the aesthetic. I wrote. The writing jobs got better, and so there was more money. We moved into some better houses and the tools fell from the primary equation of our marriage to a corollary role, to a box in the garage. Then the marriage broke—hell, I broke it—if one can be that conclusively mechanistic about a marriage. Many of the tools went off to garage sales and the few that I still could carry went to boxes in the closets of the cheap apartments I could afford. I ignored them; the rebuilding I was doing still hadn't built anything a tool could fix. Then came Tracy and notions of a new marriage and a house. A life that was drifting for some years came to an understanding of its needs. As that understanding flowed to a house's design, land, and a loan that summer, I began thinking again of tools.

"Thinking" perhaps understates the case. That work of designing the house rendered a curious effect: it claimed my brain in total, wigged-out, and thunderstruck obsession. Obsession not in the form of the big burden, not the great, daunting financial nut of paying for a house. What had infected nearly every available, undamaged, and conscious cerebral cell was an imaginary living of the building. From the design had finally come an understanding of the layers of work that would follow; each job in its turn, literally thousands of tasks.

Because I had no experience in building a whole house, I became terrified and convinced that I would perform some task out of sequence to either preclude or render damned difficult some subsequent task. To avoid this I was building the house, nail by imagined nail, in my head, which became a strange head indeed. Nights I would lie awake using my mental crane to mesh and move adjoining walls. Sometimes I launched out of bed to fire up the computer and record the changes. Even when I finally drifted off to sleep, my brain carpenters refused to punch off the clock. Hammering, sawing, and plotting wound through my dreams.

On one such night electricians were wandering around my synapses to route wires through floors and into the forms of a concrete wall. Mentally I reached for the drill I would need for such a task, but then I remembered I hadn't seen that ½-inch drill for more than two years. I still had a ⅜-inch drill, the smaller cousin that almost every home owner has, the whirring little pistol of a motor that holds various small drill bits and performs small drilling chores. But for the heavy work of a house I would need the larger drill. Somehow I had lost track of that one. I could still see it, a simple, foot-long drill motor with a handle at one end and a chuck (the device that holds drill bits) at the other. A second handle stuck straight out of the side of its cylindrical case to give the operator leverage against the jerking and twisting of drilling a stout hole in stouter wood. I thought about this drill and then saw it clearly sitting on a shelf at the old place, in my ex-wife's garage, right where I had left it.

I called her the next day. By then we had learned to treat each other civilly, so she was not being uncooperative when she said she hadn't seen my drill. I said I was sure it was there in the garage. Would she mind if I stopped by to look? It was there, but it was split in half with three screws missing. Useless. I measured the screw holes and, for 25 cents, found three at a hardware store. That night I spread the drill's vitals on a kitchen table in Tracy's and my apartment, cleaned, oiled its gears, reassembled it, and returned it to life. The rusted gears groaned and whined a bit, but it would drill holes. Then I spent probably more time than necessary wiping and shining its case.

Busy as I was with being obsessed with the house, this was not a good time for Jack Daniels to show up. That's not his real name but should have been, so that's the one I'll use. He's one of my oldest and most exasperating friends. When I went to school in Ann Arbor, he and his wife (his second of what was at last count three) lived next door. We both worked at the beer store downstairs. We hung out with the same group of folksingers, rebels, malcontents, and motorcycle mechanics that was sort of a gritty subculture to Ann Arbor's dominant culture of antiwar radicals. We didn't smoke dope—we drank beer. We tended more toward denim than tie-dye and paisley.

Jack, a potter, carpenter, and folksinger, was the only person I had ever met from Montana. I was a Midwesterner. He spoke of a place of mountains that seemed impossibly distant and mythical. I swallowed what Jack offered on the topic, lies and all.

In the twenty years since then Jack has never held a regular job, not unless you count his marriages. From time to time he has picked up a few bucks as a finish carpenter, but his real avocations have been the often twinned pursuits of alcohol and writing. He has published two novels. He has the biggest brain I have ever encountered. He is the worst alcoholic I have ever known. He has never had a house of his own. He is a sort of nomad, drifting from woman to woman. The drifting took him from Ann Arbor back to Montana and then to Idaho for a while, to California somewhere along the way, and then back to Montana again. Somehow he landed in Missoula shortly after I moved here in 1985.

Just as my planning for the house was swinging into high gear late in May, Jack showed up at my apartment. He had been staying with a friend for a couple of weeks until he exhausted his welcome, and then the friend booted him out. Could he stay a couple of days at my place? Tracy and I were headed out of town for a week, and he had been sober for months, so I didn't see what harm it could do. When we returned he stayed a couple of days longer, then disappeared.

A friend found him a few days later downtown, first passed out and then in convulsions on the floor of a bar. My friend knew Jack. He sought help for him. No, the emergency room at a nearby hospital wouldn't take him. The doctors there already had exhausted their cures on Jack's behalf. A local hospital's alcohol treatment program likewise declined another run at his case.

My friend arranged for a local AA member to drive Jack the hundred miles to the state mental institution, which maintains an accepting but notoriously incompetent alcohol treatment program. Jack stayed a day then released himself. He showed up at our apartment in the middle of one night, snuck in the front door, and crashed on the couch. My first sight of him came the next morning. He could barely stand to his full six-three. Once cowboy-thin, his distended liver now pushed his gut well ahead of him. His wispy, long strawberry blond hair bolted at all angles. As he stumbled toward the bathroom muttering a need for a shower he wore only underwear. He displayed a sallow, nearly transparent hide blotched with the various bruises gathered during the latest binge. He couldn't work the taps in the shower, so I had to turn the water on for him. I let him finish his toilette, then asked him to leave.

The sleep and shower had sobered him enough that he could talk. Sort of. He made a few weepy apologies about his condition and a few testimonials as to my strength of character as his only remaining friend. I repeated my demand that he go. He grew panicky, wild-eyed, and scared and said something about his tools. I told him I knew nothing about his tools and that he'd have to go. He said, of course he did, but would I please drive him across town for his tools? Please? Stupidly I did, delivering a heartfelt temperance lecture the whole way.

We drove to the poor side of town to a run-down house owned by this woman he knew. She wasn't home, so he worked his way in through a back door. In the living room stood two handmade wooden boxes, the kind carpenters carry, about 4 feet long, a foot wide and deep, rope handles threaded through the gabled ends. Each was stuffed with a great array of very good tools. Jack had never had much money, but what he did earn or manage to twist out of friends he spent lavishly. It appeared he had done much of that on these tools. Most were of first quality: intricate and antique hand tools, the stuff of a craftsman; high-tech power tools, state of the art. We lugged the boxes and piles to my car.

I drove him back to my apartment, ready to resume the battle to evict him, but there was none. He said simply that I should keep the tools. Use them. I was building a house and would need them. And then he walked downtown for the first shot of the day, off to die for all I knew. I was glad to see him go.

By late May the garden had begun to come on strong, raising nothing so much as the attention of the deer. Bright young peas and cabbages were nipped off before they much more than cleared the top of the soil. Patches of close-cropped carrots were dotted with the split hoofprints of deer. This was no occasional raid that could be borne as our tithe to the wild. This was pestilence. Only a good fence would make these deer good neighbors.

The Moores, Tracy, and I regarded the garden as our commons, but the commons was under attack. We measured the perimeter, calculated, then counted cash. A fence of substance was necessary, but we had little money, a gap normally bridged with work. We put together enough cash—$185—for woven galvanized wire that would make a fence 7 feet high around the 320 feet of perimeter on the garden. We convened on a fine Saturday in May and began to spud postholes in the soil.

There are motor-driven contrivances for this job of setting fence posts, but we had none. Our tools were round-pointed shovels of the common variety and a 6-foot steel pry bar that weighs about 20 pounds. Hand-operated posthole diggers won't work in the hard-packed glacial gravels of our gulch. To dig a posthole, one must break rock. Posthole diggers won't cut it. The job wants the focused violence of hard, heavy steel.

One swings the steel bar (my Dad taught me to call it a "headache bar") on a vertical stroke like a pile driver. The point finds rocks, smashes them, then pries them loose so that they can be lifted free of the hole with a shovel or a hand. Thus, the hole works its way to 3 feet in depth, an inch or so at a time.

We dug thirty such holes over two days. Then we went to the woods a few hundred feet away and felled some of our land's trees with a chainsaw. We bucked and limbed the trees into 10-foot-long posts that we planted in the holes. We set the poles, eyeballing them straight with a plumb bob as we tamped dirt and crushed rock back into the holes. We braced the corners, then rolled the wire out. I used a makeshift clamp of wood two-by-fours to attach a tow rope to the wire. We hooked the tow rope to Michael's beat-up old miniature pickup truck. Michael got in the truck, revved the engine to a near meltdown, then popped the clutch. The truck lurched its best lurch, not much but enough, and stretched the wire tight until it sang. Then we stapled the wire to the posts and we had a fence. Barely had we finished nailing the wire to posts when a mountain bluebird came to perch atop it, the better to hunt insects in our garden.

I nailed a bracing rail horizontally to span the top of the gap between the two gate posts. The intent was structural, but the brace also made a sort of rustic arched portal into the garden. It occurred to me that this was the very place for an old set of deer antlers I had. Actually, Michael had. During the previous fall's hunting season Michael and I had been driving a highway that winds along the Big

Blackfoot River near Missoula. We spotted a deer down in the river, a nice young whitetail buck, apparently shot and left by a careless hunter. We drove to town, got Michael's canoe, then drove back up the river and retrieved the deer. The meat was still good. The deer had been dead less than a day and had fallen in the near-frozen river, cooling it as if it were in a meat locker. That young deer fed the Moores all that winter, so we took a perverse pride in having a deer we had gathered, not hunted. Its antlers seemed the proper talisman for the garden, so I nailed them there.

Then the principals gathered beneath the arch for a team photo. After two days swinging the headache bar, all the skin was stripped from the insides of both my thumbs. The palms of my hands were bleeding. I couldn't make a fist, nor did I have reason to do so. The camera caught pained but honest smiles from all of us. As the shutter clicked, Wendy said, "We need a preacher now to pronounce us family."

We took trowels and with them planted about three dozen tomato plants, the special hardy varieties Tracy and I had started from seed in February, now grown to strapping plants. We committed them to the soil. A couple of weeks later a late frost came and killed them all, or so we thought. They were hardy plants, though, and a few came back from the roots. They really were Montana tomatoes. Then on June 15, Venus and Mars aligned with the crescent moon of an ice-cold sky that brought a freak late frost. The tomatoes all collapsed again. From a total of three dozen plants maybe five survived this second assault to crawl back from the roots and finally fruit a few marble-sized tomatoes.

Through ensuing days the fence barred the deer as planned, but our plants kept disappearing, depredation we finally traced to a horde of Columbia ground squirrels that had perforated the meadow. Behaving like prairie dogs or gophers, they burrow extensively, ignoring the best of fences. We found burrows in the middle of now-naked lettuce beds. The squirrels sawed off the peas, broccoli, and cabbage, all of the plants, sometimes in a single night. Occasionally a ground squirrel or two would poke out of its burrow in the afternoon to whistle at the day. Although I kept a .22-caliber rifle at the garden, I failed to capitalize on these rare sightings. I was reduced to cheering on the red-tailed hawk that had taken to hunting the meadow each day. It perched in a lone, tall Douglas fir near the edge of the road. Once I watched the raptor scream from the sky in a power dive. Every member of the squirrel colony froze in panic at the sight of the hawk's passing shadow.

The hawk wouldn't save me, though; he was a predator making a living: farming, not decimating the squirrel colony. I was interested in total devastation. I heard about a trick with automobile antifreeze and cracked corn: mix them and stick the results down the squirrel holes. I hate poisons, and besides, the ground squirrels belong here. Who am I to assert my rights to hold garden and property against their long-held niche in the natural scheme of things? What right do I have to silence their afternoon's whistlings as they stand on hind legs to peer across the meadow's grass?

Still, my back was bent and sore from the fence, and the tomatoes were dead from frost. In a matter of a few days the rest of the garden would go to the squirrels. Could I claim this land if I were not willing to kill a few squirrels to hold it? I used the poison. I was careful that the corn was all hidden down squirrel holes and away from birds and other unintended victims. I counted on the squirrels' dying quickly in the holes, away from the hawks and the rest of the food chain. As nearly as I can tell, that's the way it worked. The predations stopped and the garden grew. The meadow's afternoons went silent. In victory, I felt a bit more lonely on the land.

My growing collection of tools began to heighten my awareness of a barrier I faced in building a house. I was entering partly alien territory, the world of craft. This world is conscious and protective of its uniqueness to the point of having developed its own manners and language. It is a self-contained subculture that is comfortable in rejecting interlopers, which I clearly was.

About this time, during those summer months of planning and banking, I also began entering some of the passageways to this world, places like lumberyards and hardware stores. Here I looked at tools, just looked at first, palming familiar ones and trying to figure out the workings of the more novel devices. I talked to no one in the stores, afraid that the manifest ignorance of my questions would expose me. I was as shy as a country teenager in a dirty-book store. I bought magazines and at night would read the tool advertisements, learning a new lexicon: chop saws, planers, compound miters, slides, Delta, Makita, and Porter Cable. Then tentatively I began buying tools.

Tentatively, because I had to speak. I had to try out my new language. I was terrified I would say something stupid, use the wrong acronym or phrase and identify myself as an alien, a wearer of ties and pusher of paper. I figured the second the lumberyard guys spotted me as an imposter they would throw me onto the street, tool-less, or worse, they would laugh at me.

The worst aspect of this came in the early months of the project, the result of my chronic lack of money. I had assembled a weighty collection of tools but was forced to ferry them the 13 miles from my apartment to the land in a 1978 beat-near-to-death Volvo station wagon. The effect of the tools' weight on the car didn't help the impression I presented to the rest of the world. The load tipped the car's tail down, further heightening the illusion that its death was imminent. It looked as if the car already had tipped its nose skyward to begin its ascent to heaven. I was terribly ashamed to be seen like this. It is generally known that any person who does anything useful owns, always drives, and more or less lives in a pickup truck. They are the crowning achievement of utility, a sort of overarching tool that holds all other tools, the bearer of the armory with which one confronts the world.

There was no money for a truck. Appearances be damned, I would build this house without one. Wasn't really looking for one, not really. I'd make do. Then I heard a rumor. A hand-lettered sign soon confirmed the rumor: Cass Chinske was selling his truck. In some circles the sale of one's pickup is a development akin to divorce. I broached the subject with Cass with all the delicacy and tact I could muster.

Cass's truck was a thing of beauty. I always had admired it, a 1978 Ford half-ton, granny-geared four-on-the-floor, 6-cylinder workhorse. Still, it was a baby with only 60,000 miles, the slightest of burdens on its near-pristine soul. It was immaculate but Spartan, an ugly mint green, bench seat, tinny AM radio. No frills. It was, in short, the perfect pickup truck. There was no debating the issue in my brain as if it were some ordinary purchase. This was karmic. Even before talking with Cass I knew I would need the pickup. There was no money, but

I'd scrape some up from nowhere. Besides, Cass, a long-time acquaintance of mine, would be in the mood to sell right. He had to sell. He was going to prison.

He is a former Missoula City councilman, a short, wiry, bald fellow with lively eyes. I knew him mostly as a crusader, especially for environmental causes. He was the sort of motor-mouthed true believer who can talk a listener to exhaustion and tears, with sincerity. People often wondered how Cass was financed in his crusades in that he had no visible means of support. People figured there was a trust fund somewhere and let it go at that.

He had support, but it was not visible for a reason. He was a farmer of sorts. Beneath a secret trap door in his garage there was a room-sized farm sprouting healthy and potent marijuana plants. Apparently business was fine, until federal investigators began cutting deals with some of Cass's business associates. Cass found himself in a bit of a fix. The resolution was a furlough from farming to a federal penitentiary.

Cass barely talks about the prison sentence. Mostly he talks about his house. Because federal law allows seizure of any property used in committing drug "crimes," Cass's house was fair game. Its title passed to the U.S. government.

Cass sold me his pickup from what he called a "messy" house. It wasn't. It's a neat and tasteful split level in a quiet, treed neighborhood of Missoula. The "mess" accrued from boxes of his possessions he had left in disarray on purpose, so that realtors coming to appraise the place for the feds would underestimate. He had disconnected his sprinkler system to let the lawn bake to brown in the dry Missoula summer.

"How am I supposed to start over? This house is everything I have. I own it outright. I live here. I dug the foundation of the room you are in by hand. I planted the trees and bushes in the yard. If I killed you here, right now, they couldn't take my house, but for growing fifteen plants they can. Can you imagine that happening to you? They're going to sell this place for probably seventy thousand. That's ridiculous. How can I afford that? I couldn't even afford to buy my own home. When the federal marshalls came to assess the house one woman stood here and told me: 'Nice house.' 'Don't say that,' I told her. 'How can you stand here and tell me my house is nice when you're taking it away?' I asked them if they knew their history. I told them this country was founded in part because the British would search and seize houses."

When Cass found out I was interested in the truck he immediately took it off the market, even though I gave him no commitment or deposit. He said he wanted me to have it because of my project and because it would be used on the land. He had expected to keep the truck another ten years himself, his work truck. He had treated it accordingly.

I kicked its tires, shifted its gears, tasted its oil, and listened to its engine run like a sewing machine—all the senseless but necessary rituals of truck buying. I didn't want to take advantage of a guy headed to prison, so the ensuing dance was short.

"How much you askin'?"

"Twenty five."

"Will you take twenty-two?"

"How about twenty-three?"

"Deal."

This sounds like haggling, but actually is the shortest number of moves in which a person can, in good conscience, buy a truck. Had I wanted to take advantage of him, I would have gone home "to think on it" overnight and then bought it for twenty-two-fifty the next day.

As Jack Daniel's latest submersion in booze grew near total, I began to consider him dead. I thought this realistic because doctors had told him repeatedly that the next such binge would kill him. He smokes filterless cigarettes incessantly, adding insult to the injury of alcohol. Not yet fifty, he looks seventy sometimes.

Still, he was not dead, apparently not even successfully evicted from my apartment. He began showing up in the backyard of the building in the late afternoon already quite drunk. There he passed out in a sleeping bag he kept hidden nearby. One day I caught him at this and threw him out. He took to sneaking into the yard after dark, figuring I wouldn't see him. I caught on and kicked him out again. Then he called me one afternoon, barely coherent, asking me if I'd drive him to the state mental institution one more time. He said he needed help.

I was fed up with help. I'd concluded that in his case there is no such thing. If a cure was to be effected he would have to handle it himself. If it wasn't, then I only hoped his death would not be terribly messy and too great an imposition on my life. I refused his request, saying I next expected to see him dead or sober. Then he stopped showing up in the backyard at night. He simply disappeared.

A week or so later he was back, this time sober. He had found his way to the state's drunk tank for a proper drying out. The binge had scared him, and he wanted to get back on his feet. Could I help by letting him stay a couple of days? I did, and he stayed sober. I guess by way of amends he asked me if he could help me with some work on the land, and it sounded a fine idea to me. I believe in the healing power of work. He donned his Carhartts, tough brown canvas workman's overalls, then sharpened and oiled his tools and prepared to lay his hands on my house.

But Jack couldn't work. He could no longer focus his brain tightly on the numbers and details. His body couldn't bear the weight of the hammering, the lifting, and the sun. So he tried to work for a few hours but soon grew dizzy, sat in the shade of the pine trees, and smoked cigarettes. He said the antidepressants made him woozy. Then he made a few excuses about getting back to town for an urgent appointment.

Still he wanted to help, so he mentioned to me one day that he knew of a stash of lumber I should have. There had been a sort of father figure in Jack's life, a gruff, gray-bearded old man who taught at a nearby university. The old man's specialty was architecture and work, so he kept a summer home in a nearby rural burg; actually it was more a compound than a home, in that over the years the old man had moved, resurrected, rebuilt, or otherwise restored a series of seven buildings on the property. The center of this tinkerer's universe was a comfortable old farmhouse flanked by log cabins, a studio, a log barn, and even an old saloon refurbished as the town's museum.

It turns out, though, that the old man was not so much working toward a goal as working away from something deep and dark. Depression, I guess. That's what the doctors call it. When it reaches for me, I call it the black hand. Whatever, it eventually got the best of him. In the grip of one unusually deep fit of gloom, the old man, alone, drove his car just outside of his town and killed himself with a gun.

It happened that Jack's nomadic life camped in the old man's compound of buildings for about a year. He had lived there free and alone just after the old man died. Jack found the old man's stash of whiskey bottles hidden in odd cubbyholes around the house. He also found his stash of lumber, in particular a pile of mahogany clapboard siding. Such a thing is unheard of in this part of the country, because mahogany is a rare and valuable exotic hardwood. One does not use it for siding. In fact, as we become aware of the effects of deforestation on tropical rain forests, using mahogany for *anything* has become politically incorrect in the extreme. In Mexico, though, where mahogany grows, such uses are common.

Once, on a trip through Mexico, the old man had found and bought the siding. He had no particular use in mind, but it seemed a good thing to have. He brought it north and stacked it in neat, straight bundles in a dry shed. There it lay when he died.

Jack called the old man's widow. Did she want it? Could we have it? Not sure what it's worth. Figure out something later. Handed to me now was a moral dilemma of the first order. I would never have considered buying an exotic hardwood for my house. I had no interest in deforesting Mexico, preferring to account for the damage from my own life here where it is lived. I had a notion that my house would better slip into its surroundings if it aped them, if its wood came from the same species of trees that grew just outside the door.

On the other hand, by using this mahogany I would be creating no demand for exotic hardwoods. It already had run through the market. Its economic life was over. If I had left it in that shed it would be forgotten, likely to rot with the shed or be whacked into kindling by someone who didn't know what it was. My use of it would be sort of a recycling, I reasoned, a saving of the wood for its highest and best use. I said this aloud. Silently, I imagined how it would look as paneling on my study wall. It is a beautiful rich-rose and full-grained wood. Jack and I made a quick trip in a pickup truck to the compound, where I behaved incorrectly in the political sense.

I piled the mahogany under a tarp on the land, next to a shed full of tools I had gathered. These piles came to feel less like the house's beginning's and more like a collection of other lives' burdens. I regarded this house building as my own reconstruction, but it now seemed as if I had hung out a shingle announcing that service to others. A house is a weave of lives. Now the lives lined up in piles, a dead man's mahogany, a drunken man's tools, and a jailed man's pickup truck. Let them come. They were not a burden; in fact, I needed them. I planned a house of stout timbers. It would support a considerable load.

This time of collecting—both money and tools, they were superimposed on each other—was a time of frustration. I considered these preliminary steps as annoyances. Yet as the end of this time came I began to draw a hint of the importance of the preliminaries. I began to build an actual reverence for the tools, as if I could derive some wisdom from where they had been or the precision that went into their making. Through them and through me would flow a house. Tools are a way to an end, but the way, the process, the path has value of its own.

One day toward the end of all this time of collecting, even before the loan was approved, even before I had any justification for believing the loan would be approved, when Tracy and I faced nothing but the bleak financial prospects of a failing free-lance writer, I committed a series of odd acts. The house had grown so deeply in my brain as to carve a reality of its own. It was this reality that began to drive me.

I went to the local Sears store because it is generally known that Sears sells good tools. I walked the aisles looking at tools, but finally, no longer just looking. I needed to commit irreversible acts. First I bought a circular saw, the hand-held power tool commonly known as a skill saw, a name derived from their original manufacturer. They are a power saw in its simplest form, a disc of a blade driven by a small, hand-held motor. Portable as a kitchen mixer, they handle virtually all of the rough cuts on a house frame.

I didn't want to buy just any saw, but the best one they had, the professional model that cost a hundred dollars more than all the rest. I felt the sublime beauty of hefty horsepower ratings, machined gear drives, and locking spindles. I tested the crisp snap of the blade guard and the heft of the hard plastic handle. I told the man I wanted the best. I was building a house, you understand, a damned important house. It will hold my new life. It is of critical importance that I own a good circular saw.

Then I spotted the table saws and I bought one of those, four hundred dollars worth of power, speed, and precision with a machined, cast-iron table, a ten-inch carbide-tipped blade, and a clean-locking rip fence. A table saw is about the size and shape of a kitchen butcher block but has a fixed and menacing-looking saw blade protruding up through the table. The electric motor that drives the blade is hidden beneath the tabletop. Using a series of guides that ride in grooves in the tabletop and on rails along the tabletop, one pushes the wood to be cut through the stationary blade, achieving far more accurate cuts than can be had with a portable, hand-held saw.

I had always dreamed of owning a table saw but could never justify the expense. They are not tools for the weekend putterer. Table saws are tools for house builders, cabinetmakers, and craftsmen.

I also bought a long-handled, double-bitted ax with a new hickory handle and a black cast-iron head. Two saws and an ax, all on credit. I had not consulted Tracy. I knew she was worried about money and would think I was nuts. Still I knew she would back me on this. She would understand. Not that she understands tools. Her background is solidly in the middle class. Her people hired help for their building. Nonetheless, she has faith in me, and if I say these saws are necessary for the building of a house she'll believe me and at the same time know what I really mean to say. Her faith gives my life its first responsibility.

I took my tools to the apartment and showed them to Trace. It turned out I was right about her reaction. I spent an evening mounting the circular saw's blade, testing its switch, and truing its guides to square. It was ready for duty. Preparing the table saw was more complicated. It was delivered in hundreds of pieces packed in a cardboard box. It took most of a Saturday to assemble, slowly. Each adjustment of the table, fence, and blade was checked and rechecked. A mistake here would have been perfectly replicated in subsequent mistakes in wood. A good saw must be treated with respect, responsible as it is for so much of the house. Its character would determine the integrity of most of the cuts that matter.

Passers must have thought me mad that day, with wrenches, nuts, bolts, casters, squares spread on a sidewalk in front of an apartment house on a busy city street, assembling a table saw. By day's end I fired it up, and it cut square and true. I stored it in the Moores' garage.

Then I gathered the ax and went to work. Tracy and I spent those summer evenings at the land. Her concern there had nothing to do with the ax. She was attacking an infestation of leafy spurge, a particularly noxious weed in the meadow. Technically the spurge is a natural plant, but I choose to think of it otherwise. I consider it a contrivance, a mistake, the result of failed human artifice. I defend this prejudice by arguing that spurge springs from our hands.

The mark of human hands is everywhere on the land. One day our thumb turned around and our brains became fascinated with this business of tools, mostly because we could hold them. The root of all this is encoded in our language: from the Latin word for hand we derive "*man*ipulation." We are hu*man*, and that is what we do. Spurge is an introduced species imported to this country from Eurasia. Speculation is that the seed found its way to this country as a stowaway in soil used as ship ballast. The importation was the intervention of our hand. Spurge is coming to rule the land in several western states and Canadian provinces. A milky stemmed broadleaf weed, it works its way into grassy areas, eventually growing into a carpet of knee-high weeds. Its roots sometimes run to a depth of 20 feet. It has no native enemies.

It is more than an annoyance. Left to its own devices it would supplant all other plant life in this meadow, the native grasses, the fescues, and the wheat grasses. All else would go too: the gromwell, death camas, cinquefoil, snowberry, wild roses, wild currants, sage, shooting stars, serviceberry and the flurry of birds, burrowing rodents, and bugs that live on these. It would level all of this to a biological desert, a monoculture. So we fight the spurge. To do so, we manipulate again. Several enemies have been introduced, including, in our area, the spurge hawk moth. In late summer the clown-colored larvae of this moth, each about 3 inches long, cover the spurge and munch off all leaves. I wonder what these voracious fat worms will do if or when they run out of spurge. How will my garden or some native species look to them then? Will the cure of the spurge become the next disease? I follow this thought not too far, though, thankful now only for the damage the garish moths do to leafy spurge.

Still, my comfort is short-lived. Now we are learning that the moths' damage to the spurge is not much more than cosmetic, a brief defoliation that may check the spurge's advance but will not liberate the territory already occupied. Creatures that destroy their only food source are weeded out by evolution. The weed survives. We manipula-tors are clever, but the spurge is tenacious in its grip on the land. It may be better than we are. The spurge has taken about half of our meadow, so I suppose this will be a battle we will fight for years.

The introduction of the weed was man's meddling with nature's design for grasslands, complex and balanced ecosystems. Now a field full of lemon-flowered spurge is evidence that we are condemned to years of more meddling, the introduction of hawk moths and fungus, flea beetles, and, in extreme and painful cases, herbicides. Paradox-ically, if my field has the slightest chance of recapturing a natural state, the first step will be aided by Dow Chemical Company. We are damned to this because we are tinkerers and cannot leave the world alone. Before we came along this grassland would have been fine without us. Now that we are here we must stay, or its diversity will smother and die under the weight of our sin.

On a summer's evening, though, none of this seems so bad, as the slanting light begins to play across the meadow. The sun has fired Tracy's copper-red hair as she kneels in the midst of the golden spurge, now in full flower. She is pulling weeds by hand, one by one, an act of futility but at least an act. Later we learned that pulling spurge only causes it to secrete a substance that stimulates its renewed growth.

I putter in the garden, help her pull spurge for a while, and then retrieve from the Volvo the new ax. With it I cut a tree, an adolescent ponderosa pine growing near the house site. Usually forest fires would perform nature's work of thinning the pine to the sparse levels that make a few big trees thrive. Ponderosa stands are supposed to be sparse. Physical evidence on these hills shows that these pine usually stood in thinner concentrations than what we would call a forest. They grew as a tree here and a tree there, looming over grassy savannahs. This has been the rule since the last ice age, and that is all we need to know about what is right for this place. If they and all other species here have grown that way for so long, then by now nature has evolved all of the species of this place to consider this normal. Any change in this routine is damaging.

The pine and fir on my own land are in good condition but still stunted a bit from the crowding. Here and there I tinker with my ax. I need the firewood. A few whacks of the ax take out a small tree. A few more blows and the tree is limbed to a straight long pole. In the center of the house site stands a larger tree and I cut it. It's healthy enough but in my way. It crashes hard to the meadow, snapping its butt clear of the stump. I rest for a bit, then perform the customary inquisition of the tree. I count its growth rings. It is forty. Exactly my age.

I buck the tree's trunk to firewood-sized blocks. These I add to a growing pile on each side of the house site. The piles look presumptuous standing alone. No house. At this point the structure is nothing more than four stakes joined by string, an airy web surrounding a bursting crop of spurge. Beside this are neatly stacked rows of firewood, as if there already ought to be smoke curling out of the chimney. Houses begin as acts of faith.

Dirt

IT IS JULY 9. WE HAVE PRELIMINARY approval for the loan, but we are still uncertain we will clear the remaining legal hurdles. I am tired of the paper chase. I am tired of planning. I am tired of tool buying, weed pulling, fence building, wood piling, and navel gazing. In three months the cold will come, and I am ready to build a house. It's time for a gamble that is at this moment growing tangible in the form of diesel smoke besmirching the summer sky.

A few days earlier I had left a message on Trusty Dave's machine: "I am ready to dig a hole."

Dave did not reply. The cussed inhabitants of the building trades consider answering machines one-way devices for monitoring the rest of the world. Dave only receives messages. Responses come in the form of action. Later. Not that Dave didn't plan to dig my hole. He just didn't plan to tell me about it.

I had not yet learned the proper response to his silence was silence, so I took matters in hand. Dave's girlfriend, Judy, works as a waitress at a nearby roadside cafe, the Piney Woods. Its hold on the tourist trade is a box out front advertised as containing live rattlesnakes. It doesn't, but then there's no tourist trade either. The cafe's hold on the locals is a plate of Sunday-morning blueberry pancakes, each bigger than your head, for $2.50. You shoulder up to the counter with the local ranchers, guys in belt buckles big as a full moon and Stetsons big as the sky. If you want wine with dinner it comes from a box, and the waitress will tell you it's "sha-ball-is."

Judy was on duty. "Where's Dave, and when's he planning to dig my hole?"

Judy, apparently part of the conspiracy of silence, said she didn't know about the "when" part, but she did know Dave planned a few days off for some fishin' up at the lake.

I threw back my glass of sha-ball-is and sulked. I calculated how long it would take to dig a 24-foot by 42-foot hole 8 feet into hard-packed glacial gravel with a pick and a shovel. The results of my equations dissuaded me. Dave had the upper hand. I needed his mechanical menagerie, so I stalked off to suffer his silence.

A couple of days later I ran him to ground. I found Dave killing the afternoon lounging around the double-wide. Judy served me a Coke. We talked about the weather for a bit. Finally:

"What about that hole, Dave?"

"I was figuring to start on Tuesday."

And he did.

I sat in the middle of the meadow all morning, fidgeting. Dave had promised to be there "before noon," a phrase I later learned always means 2 P.M. I had plenty of time to consider the gravity of what we were about to do here in a quiet meadow of many grasses. It is a place in recovery now. The land probably had been grazed for a long time—the pestilence of cattle. We celebrate cattle with our most pastoral affections, bucolic prints and images of peaceful Holsteins chewing cud in green pastures. Environmentally these images are far from the truth of the matter.

Montana's biggest water pollution problem is not mining or logging but cattle. They do not belong on these native grasslands. Cows graze in such a way as to wipe out key species of grasses that are vital to the continued health of the land. They deplete the topsoil and kill the trees. They trample stream-bank vegetation, wiping out all the habitat for native trout. Their depredations so unbalance the soil as to open it for invasions by weeds, like leafy spurge.

The cattle have passed from my bit of grassland, though, and now it recovers. The several species of grasses are coming back, dotted with wildflowers. I watch those lives rebuild, and it gives me new reverence for the delicacy of this soil. Once Michael drove his compact pickup truck across the meadow and the tracks were visible for a year.

Up the road comes a dump truck bearing a backhoe mounted on a tractor. Later comes a little bulldozer with its screeching metal-cleated tracks. To build a house I will turn these monsters loose on the soil, decimating a 24-foot by 42-foot web of life.

Dave unloads the machines and clomps them through the woods to the site staked on the side of the hill. Right off he starts moaning that this will be a Herculean task, digging a basement on the side of a hill. Sane people build houses on the flat. Working a hill, a tractor can tip over with only a single careless move. Heads get crushed. Hills belabor engines and overheat clutches.

Then I tell Dave about the concept of earth sheltering, and that I intend to use this south slope to heat my house. I tell him I'm sorry it's a pain in the ass. After hearing the plan, Dave is challenged by the idea. As a hole digger he understands earth sheltering right away. Suddenly this particular hole is not just one more basement but a venture into uncharted territory. He rises to the challenge.

There is nothing new, revolutionary, or complicated about earth sheltering. It is simply an updating of an idea as old as living in a cave. It is simply a matter of burying one's house, or in my case, part of one's house.

Earth sheltering works because the earth is not cold; in fact, it gets progressively warmer at increasing depths. Even in the subzero cold of deepest winter the temperature just below the surface is barely below 32 degrees. It is always above freezing at a depth of about 3 or 4 feet, depending on location. At a depth of about 6 feet the temperature varies only a couple of degrees each year from a constant, which is the temperature of local well water, generally in the range of 60 degrees. A locality's well water temperature is generally 2 degrees warmer than the locality's average annual temperature. In a cold climate, burying one's house simply surrounds it with a warmer medium, or more accurately, insulates it from temperature extremes.

In winter the house is easier to heat. In summer, when outside temperatures scream into the 90s, the temperature in the subterranean zones is still near the well-water constant. In summer, earth sheltering cools. It is not a more common construction method because people associate underground living with caves. That disadvantage can be overcome, however, on a sloped site, a compromise that buries three sides of a house by backing it into a slope. When the remaining side is the south side, the winter sun side, natural light chases out the atmosphere of the dungeon.

To do all of this, someone needs to make a hole happen. Dave sets the backhoe's outriggers down hard to prevent the weight of the swinging shovel from tipping the tractor. Then he sits backward on the tractor, the normal position for operating a hoe, and his fingers instinctively work the four levers that control the great arm of the hoe. It is a giant replication of a human arm, able to reach the length of a car. Hydraulic cylinders control the articulations at elbow and wrist. A wheelbarrow-sized bucket serves as the hand of the beast, a hand fingered by hard steel teeth. The arm reaches toward the center of what has been until this moment an imaginary house and takes that first long bite of earth. In a permanent and irrevocable assault on the planet, the house is becoming real. At once I wince and cheer.

This is no time for contemplation, though; there is work to be done. Now committed to the building of a house, we are committed to do it right, a process that begins with instruments of precision. The first enforcer of precision on any house site is a transit level. It seemed something of a stretch to connect Dave's particular level with the word "precision." It was a cheap, beat-up old Sears model. The grade stake, a separate pole upon which the transit sights and upon which it depends for its accuracy, was homemade, a weathered old piece of wood lathe held together by duct tape. Still it worked well enough for a hole.

Dave told me to fetch the thing from the cab of his dump truck, and I did. I hadn't set up a transit in many years. The operative principle, however, is easy enough, so I took the integrity of the foundation of my house into my own hands.

A transit level looks like a small telescope resting on a tripod that raises it to about eye height of a standing man. They are generally seen in their more complicated use and form, as the primary tool of survey crews along highways. The operative principle here is level. Not flat, but level. An object is flat when it is free of dips and humps. It is level when it is parallel to the surface of the earth (or, for geometry buffs, a plane tangent to the earth's sphere at a single point).

The transit level is set on a tripod and then adjusted so that the telescopelike sight tube is level. When the operator looks through the transit, his line of sight is a perfect parallel to the surface of the earth. The transit is used to set grade, the surface of dirt upon which the bottom of the house will rest so that it is both flat and level. This process begins with picking an elevation, a sort of arbitrary point that will serve as the bottom of the hole. This point determines the elevation of the house, its perspective on the world. When you set that first point of the grade you calculate upward the thickness of the concrete floor above the surface of the hole and then try to imagine your feet resting there, holding up your eyes to just the height where they will see the world. You try to imagine the tie of the house to the surrounding finished landscape: How will it fit? Will it drain right when water comes down the hill?

All else that is to come follows from the setting of this single point. That is, the transit's job is to see that all other points on the house's floor are on the same level as the first point chosen. It is simply a way of making a floor level, the level that will determine the elevation of everything else in the house. It is the foundation of accuracy.

I pick that first point and then set the base of the grade stake on it. Dave sights through the transit and we find the spot where its cross hairs center on the grade stake. I mark the spot with the pencil. Now in other places the task is to dig the hole so that when the stake is placed on the surface the pencil mark will sit in the cross hairs. If the hole is too deep, the pencil mark will rest below the transit's line of site; if it's too shallow, above it. Adjusting the level of the grade at a given point to place the mark in the cross hairs ensures that the bottom of the hole is level at that point, that the elevation of that point matches that of our first point. The process is repeated at coordinates every foot or so until the collection of points describe a plane that is the base of the hole. Dave mounts the tractor and sets to digging. I check grade—really, the depth of the hole.

Periodically I jump into the hole and position the grade stake at a new point of the bottom. This places me right next to the swinging giant arm of the hoe, and I remember how great an act of trust this is. A good operator has control of the swing of his hoe to the fraction of an inch. He can stop it in just that space, even though it can swing nearly as fast as a baseball bat. I've tried to operate backhoes before and always found this control impossible, to connect the push and pull of one of four little levers to the arc and swing of a ton or so of steel. It is awkward and counterintuitive, yet Dave runs the hoe instinctively, with the grace and flow of a dancer. This is the mark of an operator I can trust not to swat me with the swing, a blow that would crush my skull. I do trust him, so we begin to work together.

Dave's strategy is to start digging at the back and deep part of the hole and then shove the dirt forward and to the south, where the house's hole breaks out of the face of the steep slope. The hoe dances on, laying up a huge pile of loose dirt. Once that pile is so big as to block further progress, Dave uses the bulldozer to push it out of the way. Dave notices the job is taking longer than he'd like, so he asks me if I know how to run a Cat. He wants to double-team the hole. I could use the bulldozer to shove dirt while he continues to operate the backhoe.

I do know how to run a Cat, but I haven't done so since I was a teenager. My Dad always had a Cat or two around, and I learned to run them, to guide them not with a steering wheel but by using brakes and clutches to stop one track or the other.

Although these machines are woven into my upbringing, I hate them. They are the behemoths with which we prosecute our abuse of the earth. They are the engines of our most destructive scraping and digging. As a newspaper reporter I had done a series of stories on the depredations of logging on the landscape around me. It was not the logging so much that pained this land, but the Cats. They made possible the building of the roads. They bit their grinding cleats into the fragile soil of hillsides to drag the logs to market. I hate the Cats, but, yes Dave, I do know how to run one.

I hit the starter of the little diesel engine of Dave's Case crawler. It caught in a hollow, resonant roar. I throttled it up and down again, feeling its power through the many vibrations of its hard steel frame. I tried the lever that operated the hydraulics of the blade, up and down, angle and tilt, the movements necessary to effect excavation. Then I dropped it into gear. I was clumsy at first, rocking it back and forth, putting it into some turns. As I jerked back hard on a clutch, the concise little terror began to pivot and teeter on its nose, a characteristic Cat turn. The feel of that rocking rekindled a memory. It returned a lost bit of knowledge.

More confident but still clumsy, I backed the Cat into the hole and snapped it through a hard turn in reverse in the middle of the spot where our living room would be. I set the blade level to the task at hand, pushed for full throttle, and shoved a load of nature's dirt out of my house. I was grinning a kid's grin, as thrilled as if Dave had let me drive a new Porsche. Again I reversed the Cat into the hole, set the blade, and made it roar, smoke, and bellow. Then on through the afternoon, Dave and I dug a hole.

It seems my son is lost to me. This fear wound its way through the planning of my house, which is a hard, real thing, like nothing Josh and I had ever confronted together. The obstacles we faced before were more ephemeral and abstract. In planning the house I pursued a bad idea, that by working on it together perhaps Josh and I could rub from it some of the connection that ought to flow between father and son.

In darker moments I blame the loss of my son on myself. He is an only child and lived at the edge of an intense eruption that was the break-up of a seventeen-year marriage. I guess I lost sight of him out there on the periphery, focused as I was on the center of the storm.

Or maybe he was the center of the storm, the embodiment of a clash of values. In the world that raised me, children were taught to solve problems with work. His mother came from people who used money to shelter children from work. I still believe in the sanctity and power of manual labor. I believe that no matter how brutal the lesson, a parent ought to teach a child to defend himself with his work. Josh's mother believes in sheltering, and she has won.

He was seventeen the year I built the house, gangly and gawky, articulate for his age and smart-ass enough to warm a father's heart. He fancies himself a writer, and I hope he will be, a hope diluted by my understanding that there is no way I can teach him anything useful about that life. The best I can do is teach him more respect for the power of his hands.

After Dave finished the hole, Josh came around for a day. He had no summer job, so he could spend long blocks of time with me, longer than the alternate weekends that had been our usual contact since the divorce. There is no physical reason for our contact to be that sparse. He lives within a few miles. His mother never objects to his visiting me; in fact, she wishes we would spend more time together. But then he's a teenager. He has his life. The building of the house was a chance to make up for some of that.

The two of us set to work with a pick, shovels, and a rake. It was the sort of day I had envisioned when plans were being laid. The teeth of Dave's backhoe bucket set a rough grade, but it was full of small dips and rises. Josh and I set the finish grade with hand tools. We used the transit level and grade stake. I showed Josh how to sight through the transit and find the pencil mark on the stake, then I'd shovel. The day was clear and 90 degrees with the sun pounding straight on the bare gravel grade. I swept the rake and shovel across the humps, spreading the excess dirt from the high spots into the low spots. The process ensures a uniform thickness to the concrete that will rest on the grade. Josh pitched in with his shovel as I had never seen him work. He seemed to understand that the effort mattered.

He peered through the transit as I'd told him: "Down an inch, up a half. On the money."

Toward the latter part of the task and of the day I began to congratulate myself for retraining my eye. The intuitive sense of level, keen in builders of houses, was returning to me. When I was a kid, I could sense a level grade, but the skill had atrophied. It was coming back. I thought Josh was confirming this. Every time I asked him to shoot the grade I figured was level, he agreed.

Then I walked to the transit to check for myself. The grade wasn't even close, and I would have to repeat two hours' worth of shoveling under a July sun. I gave Josh hell, then bent back to the shovel to repair the roller-coaster grade.

Then a notion occurred to me. There was only that single line drawn on the grade stake. I stopped shoveling, walked to the stake, and tipped it over. I drew two more lines, one a half inch below and one a half inch above the original line. These new lines represented, in concrete terms, my limits of tolerance. A kid needs to know that. Here was a standard of behavior reducible to two simple lines. I explained this notion of tolerance to Josh, that a thing could vary only so far, then it is wrong. He immediately understood, and together we finished the job without a problem. I wish I had known how to draw those two lines seventeen years ago.

While we dug most of the hole, Tracy had to work at her part-time job running the county library's bookmobile. Being forced away from the house was torturing her. She had never seen a house built, let alone the one that would be her own. She wanted to poke and play in the process every step of the way, so I saved some work for her. The house would need a frost wall.

The front edge of the concrete floor would protrude from the slope, making it susceptible to freeze-thaw damage unless proper precautions were taken. Normally concrete floors and footings are at the bottom of basements, well below the level that frost penetrates the earth. In severe climates such as Montana's, the ground typically freezes 3 feet deep.

Placing a concrete slab at ground level allows water to seep beneath it and there rest within reach of winter's cold. When the water freezes it expands with enough force to lift a corner of a house. This is called a frost heave. To prevent this one pours a thin concrete wall below the nose of the slab. The wall is deep enough—the standard here is 36 inches—so that water beneath it will not freeze in winter. A frost wall anchors a house in solid ground.

The wall is most effectively made by digging a skinny trench the length of the front of the slab; in our case, 42 feet. The trench acts like a form and is simply poured full of concrete. The problem is, a backhoe like Dave's can't dig the trench. The bucket is far wider than necessary. Filling the resulting hole would be a waste of expensive concrete. A frost wall is best dug with a device called a footing shovel, a skinny, short shovel especially designed for the task. This tool seems to work best in the hands of the house's owners for a couple of reasons. First, almost no one is willing to hire out for the back-breaking stoop labor that is required. Second, although none of the technical manuals advise it, I am of the prejudice that the very bedrock bottom, the foundation of a house, ought to be put in by the two people who will depend most on its stability.

One weekend Tracy and I dug a frost wall. The technique is contortion. We knelt in gravel, our knees grinding in the rocks, then bowed into the narrow trench to work the footing shovel, down the line, like bailing water. Inch by inch we carved this line in the dirt, busting loose rocks with a pick and headache bar, then pulling the loosened fill from the hole. At the end of four days of digging both of us were bent and bleeding, but we had found the bottom of our house, its basis, resting on ancient gravel in a 3-foot-deep hole. We found it together.

Concrete

IN BUILDING A HOUSE, ONE DIGS A hole only to fill it with concrete. Many familiar words derive from this early going; they filter back into everyday talk, words like "concrete," "foundation," notions like "resting on bedrock." The appropriation of these metaphors is our homage to the critical nature of this work. In a house it is not metaphor. Houses can fall. Against this possibility, we set them in concrete.

Oddly though, the use of concrete can in a sense be held as a matter of tradition, not of necessity. Houses are built on foundations of concrete because that's the way it's always been done. Houses don't have to rest on concrete.

The heretics who raised this notion in my mind are John N. Cole and Charles Wing. They are authors of a series of books designed to spawn an owner-builder revolution. Their books use Wing's background as a physicist to cast a jaundiced and skeptical eye at our methods of shelter. They devise methods appropriate and available to all. They are lovers of wood and haters of paint and carpet, prejudices I thoroughly endorse. Above all, though, they are iconoclasts toward traditions of construction, an attitude the planet needs.

Cole and Wing argue against the use of concrete foundations, considering them a vestige of habit. They have a point. The logic behind a foundation is as simple and as clear as the line between living and dead, or more appropriately, living and never-lived. Wood, the stuff of our houses, is the living and as such may not be permanently separated from its relationship with water. All living things are essentially conduits for water and will not cease this relationship, even when they are dead.

When we make lumber we kill trees, but this does not pull them from the life cycle. Placed proximate to water, which is to say in the soil, which contains water, wood rots. This is the ineffable pull of life. Rotting is a decomposition of the organic material of wood, a breaking of the once-living cells to their components so that they may return to the soil, to humus, new sources of food to be drawn into new living things. This is the nutrient cycle, an irresistible cycle for all that is living and has ever lived.

This is why wood makes notoriously poor foundations. Concrete never lived and will not. It is inorganic, a mixture of aggregate (gravel and sand), calcium compounds, and some incidental compounds of aluminum. When it is mixed with water a chemical reaction occurs that unites the whole business. It will not rot. For at least five thousand years some form of the stuff has been with us. The Egyptians used a primitive concrete in the pyramids. The Romans refined it to make the first hydraulic cement, defined as a cement that will harden even under water. This mixture of lime and volcanic ash from Mount Vesuvius was the basis of buildings such as the Pantheon and the Colosseum.

In our time the use of concrete was greatly expanded with the invention of portland cement in England in 1824. The first manufacture of cement didn't occur in the United States until 1875, when it was first used on roads and large public buildings as a replacement for quarried stone. In conjunction with steel it made skyscrapers possible. In our houses, though, it generally was and is relegated to the business of keeping the wood out of the dirt.

This task before had been performed with rock piers, replaced soon by cement piers. As the idea of comfort gradually crept into our expectations of houses around the turn of the century, the piers grew to walls. These formed a sort of a skirt around the house that kept wind from blasting beneath. The skirt made the crawl space frost-free, so it became a cellar, a place to stash garden produce for the winter. In this use the crawl space evolved to a basement, what we now consider the proper foundation of a house.

Cole and Wing argue that this is silly, largely because the vegetable garden—and the need for such storage space—is gone. Further, modern insulating materials make it far cheaper to again build houses on piers and seal the floor against the wind. Further still, concrete piers are simply unnecessary. Chemically treated wood posts, such as salvaged utility poles, won't rot. They will last as long as concrete, making a cheaper alternative.

I didn't want an alternative to a basement, though, because my basement would not be storage space. An earth-sheltered home is simply another way of saying one lives in a basement. Further, I found concrete an attractive building material, not a necessary evil of foundations; it was more than the link between bedrock and wood.

Concrete is attractive because it never lived, but more than its resistance to rot is at stake here. Using it meant I would not have to intervene in the life cycle. Forests would not have to die for at least that part of my house. The chemistry behind concrete is straightforward and inorganic, so no nasty toxins would be spewed in its making. True, the manufacture of cement is a dusty and dirty process. It comes from quarries that are better labeled strip mines. Cement plants are significant degraders of air quality, but mostly their dust inconveniences or irritates humans. The limestone and clays that go into the manufacture of cement are abundant. Their taking seems insignificant when weighed against the taking of a forest. Admittedly, some of this is rooted in a prejudice for forests, but my attraction to concrete had another, firmer foundation.

I planned a sort of alchemy with the concrete. I planned to cancel the drawbacks of subterranean living by marrying concrete to the light.

Earth sheltering's primary advantage is thermal. The solid earth banked against the exterior of the walls is warmer in winter and cooler in summer. This causes an earth-sheltered home to use less energy. Because my house would be built into a south slope, this sheltering occurs on only three sides. The fourth is glass, open to the winter sun.

The sunlight makes the concrete imperative because of a valuable thermal advantage of concrete over wood. The concept is known as "thermal mass." Concrete acts as a sort of storage battery for heat. A south wall full of windows on a sunny day admits far more heat than a house can use, even in winter. Under normal circumstances the house would overheat. One could open a door or window and vent the heat, wasting it. Concrete, however, absorbs the excess heat, then releases it back to the house later, when the sun goes down and the heat is needed.

In the summer the process reverses, in effect storing the coolness of the night air in the concrete to soften the heat of the day. All of this occurs automatically, without any sort of mechanical assistance. Some form of thermal mass is at the heart of any passive-solar home. Other materials such as water or rock will work, but concrete is a common building material. Using it lets one build a house's technical tricks straight into its skin.

Jim Stammers is at once relaxed and quick, a contradiction mediated by an ever-present aw-shucks grin. He wears yellow-tinted aviator glasses and a beat-up straw cowboy hat. He does not walk; he lopes. His music says he's about forty. On the job his truck doors stay open, the better to emit Janis Joplin from the souped-up stereo within. His craft is concrete. He's good at it, but not so serious as to stop him from naming his company "Stone Mountain Erection." He's taller than 6 feet and speaks in a drawl. A fellow who works for him says, "Jim, you're so skinny you scratch the furniture."

In the caste system of the building trades, concrete work falls low, but not because it is trivial. Concrete is the foundation, the basis. Its integrity matters. It's not stupid work. It is, however, stupidly hard. Heavy, dusty, oily, dirty, and fast, like running a marathon around a desert oil spill every day.

Long ago I acquired first-hand knowledge of these facts. I had worked around concrete construction plenty when I was younger. I could finish flatwork—the process of troweling a smooth finish on a concrete floor—in my early teens. My first summer out of high school was spent doing the grunt work on a crew forming concrete walls. I relearned the brutality of the trade during a brief integration in the crew of Stone Mountain Erection.

There are contractors who view the trades as a priesthood, so they will not work with an owner-builder. The people paying the bills at a construction site are regarded, often rightly, as effete and dumb. They are not permitted to touch tools. Stammers, however, was not such a contractor. He said he would allow me to work with him, as if I were a part of the crew. He would deduct my labor from his bill. I hired him.

"You just want to rent me and my forms. Well, hell yes, that's no problem. The work is mostly just lifting shit, anyhow," he said. "I get a kick outa watchin' people try to do my work. By the end of the day they're always ready to write a check for anything I want. They say, 'We're never going to call you a candy ass.' I tell 'em they can call me anything they want."

Both Stammers and his forms were important. I couldn't begin the house without them. Concrete walls are made by pouring the wet concrete into a sort of long skinny wooden box that is the mould of the walls. Generally all of the walls for an entire basement or foundation are poured at once, in the matter of a few hours. The boxes or moulds of the walls are called forms. They can be made from scratch using plywood and two-by-four braces, but this is a waste. Better to use commercially made forms of plywood panels and steel reinforcing, which are reusable. Such forms are ingeniously engineered to slip together rapidly. When the job is done they knock down even quicker to reveal a complete basement. The forms are cleaned and readied for the next set of walls.

Concrete, implacable and massive, shapes the nature of the work. The tools of the trade are rough, rugged, and heavy, an assortment of bludgeons and cudgels shaped to the persuasion of stone, stakes, and steel. The people of this culture are brutes. Jim's assistant on the job was Jim. To avoid confusion I took to calling the assistant Big Jim, distinguishing him from his six-foot-four boss. Jim solved the same problem by calling his understudy "Jimmy."

Big Jim–Jimmy was an out-of-work logger. Machines and overcutting have left a lot of loggers in the region unemployed, so they move on to other work that requires nothing so much as big strong men. Jimmy didn't plan to be in concrete long. He was headed back to school to eventually try to land a job with the Forest Service, something in the back country. He'd always worked in the woods, and while concrete work was okay for a while it was too down country for his tastes.

Jimmy, like his boss, affable and bright, swung a sledge hammer with conviction. On the upswing his body rose off the ground; then he'd send the hammer down with a blow that registered on the Richter scale.

As I held the stake he was thusly driving, Big Jim told me a hammer story. Once he was breaking rock and an assistant (a guy handling the task I was at that very moment performing; in antique days, a guy called "the shaker") had suddenly discerned a weak spot in the rock. The assistant chose to indicate his discovery by telling Big Jim to hit the rock "right here" at a point he marked by covering it with his bare hand. Unbeknownst to the helper, Jim had only seconds before discerned the same crack and had already taken steps to exploit it with a fully realized blow of the hammer. The helper's hand suffered a number of broken bones.

Skinny Jim, however, had developed sufficient finesse to understand his trade was not all naked force, a concept he explained to me once when I was using a small sledge to dislodge a piece of jammed steel.

"Don't beat the fuck out of the motherfucker or it will really be a motherfucker," he advised. There is a sublime understanding buried in the statement, sort of like a koan, but I had to carry it around for a few days before I got it.

During the previous months of haggling, planning, and fretting, the concrete was forever on my mind. This was a yearning for the first rising of the house, the first real lines drawn, not imagined by the computer. But when the real deal went, it went quick. Stammers and his stereophonic truck pulled a trailer-load of forms onto the job one hot, dry morning in July a week or so after ground breaking. Before us stood a flat, blank hole. Jim said nothing by way of preliminaries. He simply hitched on a tool belt and began throwing lumber.

"Mud's coming at eleven."

(It is improper to call concrete "cement." Cement is the gray dust that mixes with water and aggregate to make concrete. Likewise, on the job concrete is never called "concrete." It is "mud.")

Mud it is. A great, gray sloggy unmanageable mass, but when it pours from a mixer truck on a sweltering day, you manage. You have to.

Manage it fast to exactly the shape you wish it to be for all of time. If you fail, the concrete will assume a shape of its own devising and immortalize it as rock.

The phrase "mud's coming" generally is joined to another time-honored and ubiquitous command of the construction world: "I want to see nothing but elbows and assholes." So we hustled.

Jim's timetable left us with about three hours to form 108 running feet of footing. A footing is a sort of long concrete strip; ours was 16 inches wide and 10 inches deep. It is, as the name implies, a sort of base on which the concrete wall, to be poured later, will rest. It is formed by staking two planks parallel to each other, 16 inches apart, all around the perimeter of the house—jogs, corners, and all. The tops of the planks must be perfectly level and the planks must be braced hard against the oozing mass that will be poured therein.

Planks flew into lines, sledges drove stakes, and a 4-foot level set them true. Three hours passed like this. Then came the roar of a diesel downshifting maybe a mile away, straining for the grade up Sleeman Gulch. This bellow meant the house's first load of concrete was on the way in a mixer-truck bearing 3 cubic yards of mud. Footings were poured out by lunchtime, and then the work began.

Forming 108 feet of concrete wall 8 feet tall requires 108 two-foot by four-foot steel and plywood panels. Each weighs about 70 pounds and is flung into place by hand then pinned to the adjacent panel with a series of steel clips driven into slots at the joint. The assembly of panels eventually builds to form one long, unbroken surface. That's the inside of the wall. But a wall form is a trough; it has two sides. The whole business is repeated in mirror image 8 inches away to form the outside surface of the wall. The final assembly consumes 216 panels.

There are four of us drawn to this task: Skinny Jim, Big Jim, Tim Bechtold (a friend of mine), and me. Tim was my recruit and so he was eyed with some skepticism by Jim at first. I deliberately didn't tell Jim that Tim was a nationally prominent player in the radical environmental group Earth First. Later, when Jim called me to try to hire Tim, I did reveal that Tim was a Harvard graduate. Jim said that was okay, that Tim seemed to be a good worker anyhow.

Later still I told Jim of Tim's politics. Jim then surprised me by admitting he harbored some Earth First sympathies of his own. This is a bit like finding a building contractor who supports the PLO.

"Hell, you shoulda told me. We could have had a really good time," he said.

Jim had scheduled the arrival of the wall's concrete for late afternoon the day following the pouring of the footings. That means we have about twelve working hours to assemble and precisely align this massive and stubborn erector set. Again, the ambient temperature is 90 degrees.

I start tipping panels off the truck. Sometimes I tip them; sometimes they tip me. They are not so much heavy as unwieldy. Jimmy grabs them two at a time and begins flinging them as if they are potato chips. We lay them out face up in the sun, then spray them with a mixture of kerosene and oil so the concrete won't stick, much as a baker oils a bread pan. Now the whole enterprise reeks of oil. My jeans begin to feel as if they could stand alone, fortified by a layer of dust and oil. Jim cranks up Janis's white-woman blues on the radio of the Ford F-350 and the lifting and oiling, the sledges and levers, all pick up the pace. Good, hot, mindless work. The cadence lulls me, and worries ooze away with the sweat.

Overhead, against the sun that reminds me this truly is a solar site, a red-tailed hawk spins, shrieks, and glides toward its larder in the meadow. Jim grins, and we talk about birds we know. He is partial to owls, as am I. We share some stories. Jim tells me he likes concrete work and probably will stick with it for a while, which surprises me. Jim is intelligent. Forming concrete is nothing but work, building basement walls to be buried or ignored, never admired. Concrete work seems artless. Jim said he tried to build log houses for a while, but the work was slow and made him flabby, so now daily he straps on a big leather tool belt full of steel clips and a big hammer, plays Janis, and pushes pins in forms.

Concrete work is a gamble. It's big piles of work and money laid down in short order. When it's done it's either right for all time or it's wrong. There's no middle ground. When it goes wrong it goes dreadfully, terribly wrong. All hell can break loose. I watch Jim work and try to understand why he does this awful, grueling work of his. Watching is the only way to find out. I tried asking, but it did no good. The question "Why?" quickly translates to a tradesman's mind as "How?" You don't get descriptions of the attraction of the job. More likely you get a recounting of a series of events that serendipitously landed one in present circumstances. Tradesmen are creatures of cause and effect.

Jim had been working construction jobs since he was fifteen years old, a part-timer, a "weekend warrior," he calls it. He finished high school and even tried college for a while, but it wouldn't stick. He wasn't much for books. Still isn't. The last book he read was Robert Heinlein's *Stranger in a Strange Land* back in the sixties when he was still a kid and the book was all the rage. He still remembers it, still regards it highly. Back then construction paid for his travels. He was a surfer.

Then kids came along. Eight years before I ran into him, a chance came to buy some forms. Jim knew something about concrete work then, enough to stay well away from it, but the forms were a chance to be his own boss. He sold his house to raise the thirty thousand dollars that would make him an entrepreneur. Eight years later the forms are paid for and he has an extra fifteen thousands dollars on hand to stick into the business. He and the family have a new house a mile from the nearest neighbor, up near the Mission Mountains on an Indian reservation. He is not a member of the tribe, but up there the land is cheaper. On weekends he rides Harleys and horses. From his lost corner of Montana, he and his Ford range as much as a hundred miles in any direction each day to pour concrete.

There has to be a reason other than the kids and the money. He'd almost slip inside of himself when he hitched on his tool belt. His head would almost always point straight at the work, as if he were focusing a beam instead of just looking. He was intent, as in meditation. Everywhere potential disasters waited and everywhere he anticipated them, thinking through his work on multiple levels. He was doing a job that fit him like jeans. Maybe that is all there is to it.

The forms rise. The whaler clamps and planks are driven into place to draw the forms into a straight line. We set up a transit to sight a level along the top of the forms, to be the top of the concrete wall. Eventually wood will meet concrete here, a wood wall to extend the house to its full height. Jim's holding the grade stake. I'm shooting the line through the transit. I want to see the skinny wire nail we are using for a mark, want to set the cross hairs dead on its center, to ensure my walls are level within a sixteenth of an inch. Then the labors of a big diesel engine again split the air, and we scurry, speaking of the arrival of mud.

The first truck hesitates as it jockeys into place. We grumble. Much is at stake here. If a driver is good with his rig he can shoot the concrete just where we need it. He can swing the long discharge chute to place the gray, cold lava flow so that it oozes and slithers down the forms just so. If he can't maneuver to the right position, we'll compensate. We will sit atop the forms and shovel, pulling the tons of concrete down the forms and into place by hand, a sort of long, sweating, shirtless bucket brigade. The first driver is ace. He spots the load where we need it. The mixer drum's motor roars, it reverses, and concrete rolls down the line.

I'm standing atop the forms now, straight up with the instep of my boot rocking on the top rail. It is the first time I have risen this high in my house, my first vantage from this level. I remember the hawk.

The second driver arrives. He is not nearly so clever. After about fifteen minutes of trying he is unable to walk the truck up the steep grade where we need it. Chris, a longtime colleague of Jim's, now has joined the team for the pour. Crew cut, blond and T-shirted, he's all attitude. An enforcer, he counterpoints Jim's good-guru routine. Chris puffs and struts like a Marine. His ringside critique of the truck driver's performance soon escalates to direct action. He rather openly alleges the driver is lacking in skill. A discussion between Chris and the driver follows, men with veins popping in their foreheads standing toe to toe. One calls the other a "cocksucker."

My son Josh is on the job playing gofer. I'm glad he hears this exchange. I'm afraid he is bound for a white-collar world where such passions seethe silently, not vented in appropriately violent language here in the open of the afternoon sun. I'm glad Josh sees that to some people the quality of one's work matters enough to arouse passion.

Finally the driver finds low ground where his chute can reach the top of the wall, and we shovel. And then a form begins to shift and shudder, and there is a brief panic; panic because by now we have built this gelatinous gray giant of amoeba to its full potential of power. This is when things can go so very wrong.

There are 8 cubic yards—about 12 tons—of concrete now resting in the forms. Gravity being what it is, all of this weight is pressing now against the base of the forms. Should a single pin or brace give way, the amoeba would push its nose through the resulting crack. The breach in the forms would widen like a hole in a dam, and the concrete would flow from the forms, seeking its own level like a giant gob of pancake batter. There it would harden.

The panic has everyone pulling mud away from the weak spot, some of us with shovels, some with our hands. The pressure's off, and it turns out to be a minor break. We shore it and press on. We dump a third truckload into the forms, filling them level full. Jim grabs a magnesium float and works the top surface smooth. We set the hooked ends of bolts in the wet concrete, leaving about 3 inches of threads sticking out. Later this will be used to bolt the first layer of wood to concrete. The bolts will hold my house to the world.

It is quitting time, an hour known to Jim as "beer-thirty." He grins, cleans his float, and loads his tools. I am beat. Beaten, battered, and slivered. One finger is swollen to twice its size and purple from being smashed between two pieces of steel. My clothes reek of oil and sweat. My muscles have been sucked of carbohydrates. There is no way I could have eaten enough to fuel me through these last two days. I have felt like this only once before in my life, when I ran the full distance, the 26 miles of a marathon. Why do Jim and his colleagues do this awful job day after life-sucking day?

We crawl into our trucks and leave the concrete to stiffen. I'll go home to collapse; Jim to the reservation, his family, and his Solaflex machine. Most nights, he works out. He lifts weights.

"If I don't keep going, I stiffen up. Besides, it's boring just watchin' the lobotomy box, and I'm not much of a reader," he says. "I'm forty-one. The other day I noticed I was the oldest guy on the crew. If I want to keep going, I've got to stay in shape. When you turn forty, you realize you're only halfway through this, and there's still kids to raise. Every day I figure I'd like to turn around and sell these forms, but I figure what else would I do? But I'll tell you what, maybe I'll just win the lottery. Then it would be party time."

I'll give odds that in that event Jim would indeed throw a hell of a party and be back in his skinny tool belt on Monday. He can't quit now; he'd miss the rush. I remember the sound of the diesel, the tension borne by the news that mud is coming up the road, the blur of work, the rhythm of hammers on steel, the push of the wet concrete. I recall the intensity of my focus when I understood the gravity of it all. I think Jim is solidly hooked on a pure adrenalin rush.

We stripped the forms in a day, piled them on Jim's truck, and he was gone. That left me alone, which was how I felt, and I felt good about it. Good enough to pace the perimeter of the walls, first walking on top of them as if they were balance beams, then along the bottoms, the inside and out, thunking them to feel the heft of the young concrete, the smell of concrete curing to its full strength.

The house was not yet ready for wood. It had only its foundation walls, the first floor, north, east, and west. The south would be wood and glass. Before the work of pushing toward the roof ridge began, the foundation would need a floor. More concrete, but this project I would effect alone. Flatwork I could handle. Working around my father and his brothers, I learned to finish concrete when I was about thirteen— the old way, on hands and knees, rolling a trowel until the mud hardens to ring like rock. Then a young back aches and the palms of young hands bleed, but this is how it is done.

Finishing concrete is not simply an act of making it smooth. It is first a leveling of the mass, then a rebuilding of that surface. The flat steel trowel rolls slightly to form a sort of seal against the face of the wet concrete. This creates suction that pulls to the surface the fine slurry of cement powder, water, and sand. The coarser rocks are left below. This slurry is then polished by the trowel as it hardens, making a glassy and impervious surface.

With the walls up just a day, Tracy and I prepared the bare gravel below the house to hold the concrete slab. We laid a sheet of 6-mil-thick black plastic on the compacted earth to block moisture from creeping in. On top came a 2-inch-thick layer of extruded polystyrene foam, a superinsulator that will tolerate being buried. Like my walls, I wanted the slab to store heat. The insulation would prevent the soil from robbing it. On top of the foam board came 6 inches of gravel, more thermal mass. Tracy and I killed a weekend lugging in the gravel with a wheelbarrow and shovels.

Trace went back to work on the bookmobile, and Josh and a friend of mine helped me pour.

For just a few moments, a few rich moments in the days that followed, Josh and I got a hand on that old cycle of shared work that through time has tied fathers to sons. We talked not at all of the usual nags about school and grades, girls and jobs, and what he would ever make of himself. Mostly I talked about concrete. I showed him trowels and how they should be handled. I told him the quality of this work mattered greatly to me, and to ensure it I would need his help, which was true. Then it occurred to me that all of this was coming so very late in his rearing. Why had I never counted on him before? Why hadn't I told him I needed him?

The mud came. Josh by now understood the gravity of this moment, so he shoveled like a convict, pushing the mud back to my screed. A screed is a long, straight wood two-by-four that rides on top of and perpendicular to two parallel pipes. The tops of the pipes have been set to the same level that one wishes the concrete to be. With the screed riding down the pipes like the blade of a miniature bulldozer, the top surface of the concrete finds its level.

There is no art to concrete, no caprice. It is lifeless and formless. Finishing it is simply a matter of shaping it to exactly what one wishes it to be.

Josh tried the trowel a bit, at my urging. I wanted to form this skill in him as it was formed in me. He told me later, "You know, I think I have concrete in my blood." I guess in a way he does, and if he doesn't it's too late for me to do anything about it. It has taken me forever to learn that sons cannot be formed to what one wishes them to be.

In less than a week we finished the floors. Then Josh left. There would be months left of building, but his summer vacation had ended. Besides, after those few days of concrete he basically lost interest in the house. From then on he did help me for a few hours on the alternate weekends spelled out in the divorce decree, but there were to be no more long days on days of father working with son. My plan for rebuilding my relationship with my son by building a house collapsed, owing to a faulty foundation.

He went back to his senior year at high school to edit the school paper. He went off to live his own life, not to live an extension of mine. In a sense this is simply a definition of his growing up. It was me who was building this house to sort through a series of lifelong struggles, and there was no reason for him to suffer anymore in those battles. His claiming his own life is the ultimate measure of the success of a parent, although, as all parents do, I saw it then as a sadness.

He says he wishes to write. He says he's off to the university here in Missoula next fall. He says he will find his place in the paper world. Still, I can't help but think there are lessons for him in work that comes coated in sweat. He will have to come to these on his own terms. This is not the same as saying, as I once did, that my son is lost to me. More to the point, my son is lost as a conduit, as a tool for prosecuting my own wars.

In his book *Home*, Witold Rybczynski reminds us in the subtitle that the concept of single-family houses has existed only a very short time. The evolution of houses coincided with the decline of the Middle Ages. In part, the structures we now know as houses took shape from a separate but growing idea, a regard for family, especially for children. In medieval times many children were sent off to apprenticeship or court service by the time they were seven years old. Thus, houses were not houses as we understand them, but communal halls shared by an amorphous lump of people mostly unrelated. Intimacy, comfort, and ties to children were not part of the deal.

The rise, though, of a society organized by guilds, independent craftspeople and tradesmen, reorganized family relations. Children became apprentices to their fathers and stayed home. Rybczynski credits the Dutch of the seventeenth century with evolving the idea we call home. They literally spread the word; *ham* in the old Anglo-Saxon, *hejm* in Dutch. Its shape grew to something we would recognize as a home today, a shape largely derived from the needs of their children, tied to them by their crafts.

Josh and I lost the first portion of the floor, a miserable and botched job. It was my fault. I was unable to work it to a smooth finish before the August sun beat it to rock. I had anticipated this disaster, though, so had deliberately poured first a portion of the floor that wouldn't show later. It was a trial run, and I could make adjustments for the more critical sections. The rest of the floor, though, had to be finished right. It was an experiment. Tracy and I had found an idea in our research that we had never seen done but wanted to try. The normal practice with a concrete slab in a finished living space, as ours would be, would be to cover it with some sort of a veneer like tile, wood, or carpet. We rebeled against this for a couple of reasons.

First, covering the concrete insulates it from the sun and so undermines its intended function as solar heat storage. But second, any veneer is a waste of material. In function, concrete does everything a floor ought to do. Only prejudice and custom make us cover it.

The idea we liked came from Europe. Concrete is poured between timbers laid down on a 4-foot by 4-foot grid pattern. The timbers add a touch of finish that can make a primitive concrete floor seem handsome. The rub was that I had to rely on my sorry skills to finish this fancy floor.

After the initial disaster I made some adjustments. I bought some better tools and then ordered a smaller amount of concrete to give me less troweling to do before it set up. We poured it and it worked. Better the one day. Better still the next, when we completed the job. It is not perfect, clearly the work of a determined amateur, but the few trowel marks that remain, the imperfections, have sort of grown on us. They are part of our dining room and kitchen floor now, carefully sealed in varnish Tracy applied on hands and knees. It is a floor honest in its flaws, which are not blemishes but a bit of the house's living record.

The Utopian socialists of England in the nineteenth century founded the arts and crafts movement. Its quaint premise was that our salvation from the ravages of the industrial age could be found in the honest exercise of craft. The movement died. The ravages of the industrial age did not.

A signal aphorism of the movement came from the designer J. D. Sedding: "There is hope in honest error; none in the icy perfections of the mere stylist."

Back when we were pouring footings, a wooden form I had built shifted a bit under the weight of concrete. This made for a permanent and visible bow in a short concrete wall, an imperfection that disturbed me. I cursed it properly. Jim Stammers heard me and attempted to settle my anger with an aphorism of his own: "If anybody says anything about it, tell 'em you weren't building a fuckin' piano."

Wood

WE THINK OF THE WOOD IN A house as veneer, as woodwork, which is a layering of thought that hides its more fundamental beauty. We have lost an understanding of the work wood does. Examine beauty from another vantage: A knot-free 4-inch by 4-inch beam of sound Douglas fir (maybe 50 pounds of wood) placed across a 12-foot span will support more than a ton at its center.

A house begins in concrete, the great gray mass that is the bulkhead against the earth. On this pedestal rises the work, the wood, the muscle and bone of a house. Concrete prepares the way for carpenters and for the power of wood. In my house Jim's concrete prepared the way for Bruce. Thus far this story has been nearly as devious as veneer by hiding Bruce. He was always a sort of frame of the house. He was there before the first nailing, even before the planning.

Bruce is first a carpenter. His enthusiasm for his trade infected me about a year before the house began. I met him in a chance social encounter. He was interested in my work as an environmental reporter, and we talked. He became a friend, and I became interested in his work as a carpenter. We discussed environmental issues and agreed that there was profligacy in our society, especially in the excesses of our nation's houses. His solution was building small and simple places where beauty derived from the craft of their making. Bruce said, however, that bankers and real estate people had consistently prevented him from doing this sort of construction, and so he was stuck building houses that he in some way despised.

There are several routes to understanding Bruce's character. The easiest and most obvious is his surname. He is Bruce Haroldson, Norwegian, and attentive to that tradition. Norwegian of Minnesota. He'll tell you he is Norse, and he means it. Quiet, intense, taciturn, stubborn, and devoted to the ethic of work, he was instantly a familiar character to me. Stern men of farms raised him. These were the men I knew too.

He's about my age, a big guy who looks like the college wrestler that he was. His professional training is in botany, which eventually brought him to Montana, a sort of mecca for those who study nature. He knows all the trees and plants by their names, common and scientific. He has worked professionally as a biologist, but a divorce came and blocked his progress toward a master's degree in botany so he fell back on the carpentry he had learned from his uncle. He has the rigorous skepticism of a scientist but a devotion to traditions, Norse as well as Buddhist and Native American. He designs houses with a Macintosh computer and builds them with hand-forged chisels. He is a man of blunt, almost harsh opinions, yet he has the way of a shy, gentle boy. He has the character of a monk in the body of an offensive lineman.

He is a monk in an order of carpentry called timber framing.

All of us who live in houses face a dilemma, but only a few of us are acutely aware of it. The awareness tends to be concentrated in places like mine, in Montana, where we live among the trees. The forests and the web of nature they shelter are a source of wonder and spirit. Yet we understand that they also must shelter us. As I write this, I stare out my window at an unbroken ridge of trees, serene and dignified, beneath a dusting of January snow. But just over the ridge there is another slope, once identical in all regards but now stripped of trees. Champion International, one of two timber corporations that prey upon Montana, owns that latter ridge. The other timber monster is Plum Creek Timber Company, an offshoot of the Burlington Northern Railroad. Together they own about 1.7 million acres of trees, an area the size of Delaware, in this end of the state. Together, partly to feed the building orgy fueled by the funny money of the savings and loan scandal, they have clear-cut most of the land.

I have seen Champion's advertisements placed in national magazines. They suggest that Champion is a tree-planting organization, that timber is a renewable resource. In Montana these ads play like a very bad joke. We have seen the ravages of industrial forestry, a strip-mining of forests in the grab for short-term profits. We are keenly aware that in America this is how houses are built. This is more than an insult to nature, because the corporate system tries to bully us into joining the game.

In the West we can sit in something as personal and sacred as a house and see a clear-cut up the ridge. Then we know the shelter of our lives began in a wanton taking of life. It need not be so.

In the sixteenth and seventeenth centuries the emergence of an independent class of craftsmen began to erode feudalism; they evolved the idea of houses as we know them and, as we have seen, the family. The simple idea of craft created a new class organized as guilds: the artisans. The need for apprenticeships drew them into families. Both the skills and the emerging social organization combined to build the house. In the nineteenth century, industrialism—standardization and machines—decimated craft and, in the process, the integrity of the house, the forests, and eventually the families that were glued together by all of these. A key development in this occurred in the Midwest. Probably it can be pinpointed as specifically as Chicago in 1833. In a church. Then and there carpenters built what is recorded as the first balloon-framed structure, probably for no more reason than that's where the idea first occurred to someone.

Before, most American houses had been timber-framed, a system of supporting houses with massive posts and beams that were either whole trunks of trees or nearly so, trees flattened on one or more sides. The vertical posts are set at the corners of a house and maybe every 10 or 12 feet along the walls. They support a superstructure of horizontal and pitched beams that become the roof. All the timbers are enormous, on the area of a foot square in cross section.

The technique predated even the development of the house. The ancient Egyptians used the system. The great stone temples of Greece probably were merely copies of earlier timber-framed designs. By the time that the temples were built, though, Greece had become deforested, so stone became necessary. The fluting on Greek columns recalls the vertical lines in bark on trees. Timber-framed buildings built in Japan in the seventh century still stand. Archaeologists have dated similar structures in India to 200 B.C. The native people of the Pacific Northwest built a carpenter culture. Their traditional architecture was dominated by elaborate cedar post-and-beam houses.

For two centuries timber framing was the predominant method of construction in white America, but industrialism killed it. The method was ill-suited to the industrial age for a couple of reasons. First, the massive framing timbers were not easily transported. This became important in the early 1800s, when development pushed into the treeless plains. Here easy transportation of building materials was necessary to allow the westward migrations to continue. But second, timber framing uses frame members too large to be nailed, so intricate joinery is required. The Japanese, for instance, developed more than four hundred types of joints, each held sacred and secret within artisan guilds. In this country the joiners were called housewrights and were revered members of the community.

Balloon framing, on the other hand, is driven not by craft but by machine. The method became possible with development of more sophisticated circular saws able to whack logs not into timbers but into smaller planks such as the now-ubiquitous two-by-four stud. With it came machines to make nails, so housewrights became obsolete. The essence of balloon framing is the simple plate-and-stud wall that is today the nearly universal method of house construction. Like the posts of timber frames, the studs are vertical but are nailed in place every 16 to 24 inches, closer than timbers to compensate for the smaller size of studs. Those light, sawed studs could be transported great distances to accommodate settlement of the treeless plains. Relatively unskilled carpenters could frame a house in a matter of days.

Then about two decades ago a few backward-looking pioneers observed the beginning of our postindustrial era by resurrecting timber-frame construction. The process began initially as recovery. It became fashionable to restore old timber-frame structures still standing in areas along the eastern seaboard. Then it occurred to some of the restorers that if these buildings were still standing after in some cases three hundred years, perhaps there was some architectural wisdom locked in the intricate joints. Carpenters who had already learned some of the joinery by replacing lost frame members began a further study, and soon timber-framed buildings were reemerging, cut from whole cloth.

The technique makes sense for our time, an assertion resting on the origin of the posts. Inside a timber-framed structure, one thinks of mass. One thinks of great trees as if the timbers are a reincarnation of an ancient forest, stout and strong. To a certain extent this is an illusion. In England, timber framing arose just as trees became scarce, as a reaction to deforestation. The intricate joinery was a way to conserve trees. The earlier American timber frames to a certain extent ignored some of these measures; at that time there was no shortage of great trees on this continent. There is now, though, so a resurrection of the more frugal forms of the art makes sense. Timber framing is a way to substitute craft for volume in the framing of a house, a notion satisfyingly subversive in the industrial age.

The two-by-four arose from a need for mass production, but there was a cost. Consider the typical 8-inch by 8-inch post of the corresponding timber frame. Simple calculation would suggest that same post can be sawed into 8 two-by-fours, so the use of either would be structural equivalents. First, though, there is the energy used in the sawing. The larger timber post is completed after four passes of the saw to square it, but the manufacture of the two-by-fours has just begun at that point. Six more passes are necessary. Each of those passes extracts a fee beyond energy, a loss known as the "kerf." That's the path the saw makes into sawdust, at least an eighth of an inch wide. The path is waste, not lumber, so some strength of the original tree dies on a sawdust pile.

Once sawed, however, the resultant two-by-four is not complete. The machine age requires uniformity and smoothness, so the two-by-four is planed, a milling process that smooths all four sides but extracts a cost both in energy and sawdust. That's where the concept of "nominal" lumber arises. That is, what we call a two-by-four really isn't. After planing and repeated sawings, a two-by-four really measures 1.5 by 3.5 inches. This reduces the cross-sectional area by about a third and correspondingly reduces the strength of the two-by-four. Put another way, that antique eight-by-eight post is the structural equivalent of twelve finished two-by-fours, not the eight it would produce. And because the two-by-four is so small, it is greatly susceptible to twisting and warping as it dries. The solution is to force-dry it in a heated kiln, another energy cost.

The whole process, now so complicated, becomes industrial—energy-intensive and, accordingly, centralized. Logs must be transported to large mills and then transported back out to markets. The transportation system has become so integrated into the market that here in western Montana, where lumber is the major industry, it is not at all unusual to find studs at the local lumberyard from the west coast of Oregon 600 miles away. Meanwhile, our mills' studs wind up in Texas.

As with most solutions to environmental problems, timber framing is not universally applicable. It is best suited to single-family homes or slightly larger structures, maybe barns, duplexes, and commercial buildings. One cannot build a timber-framed skyscraper, buildings that require concrete and steel. Timber frames are ideally geographically limited to places that have a supply of suitable timbers and small local sawmills that can process them. Timber frames are specific to place. I was not building a house for all people, places, and time. To try to do so would guarantee failure. In many ways that's the whole lesson taught by a house. But in my place the technique made sense.

Without even asking me Bruce ordered the timbers for my house. This didn't bother me, because by this point in the process I trusted him. After Tracy and I had hatched the floor plan, I took my crude computer drawings to him and he made some minor changes. For instance, we widened a stairway to 36 inches to meet the National Uniform Building Code. The house would never be inspected for compliance with the code, but we thought it a good idea to meet the commonsense safety aspects of the rules. In the early going Bruce's hand was light in the process, I suspect because his brain was consumed by other houses in his life. At some point, though, he began waking up in the wee hours with my house on his mind, his normal method for dealing with a new project.

Then one day late in the design process I ran into him at a tavern we both prefer. He announced bluntly and without preface, "Your house is going to have a clerestory."

This was not a minor modification; in fact it would radically change the whole look of the place. My design's sole concession to the south light had been a timber-framed south wall. Each of the 4-foot gaps between the timber posts was to be glass. Bruce wanted to complement this with a clerestory, which is a row of windows set vertically between separated edges of the two roof pitches.

The clerestory windows would shoot light and solar heat to the stepped-back second story of the house, a reprise of the function of the south wall on the first floor. Also, because the clerestory windows stood at the house's highest point, we could leave them open on summer nights to vent off the day's accumulation of warm air, cool the thermal mass of the concrete walls, and prepare a cool house to weather the next day's sun. The whole idea made perfect sense. Tracy and I agreed to add the clerestory without question. More than changing the design, though, it helped build the necessary trust. Later there would be a disagreement between Bruce and me on a minor point of quality, an issue I wanted to settle by compromising quality where I thought it would do no damage.

"No," said Bruce.

"It's my house," I insisted.

"Not yet it isn't." And he was right.

About two weeks passed between the finishing of the concrete walls and the beginning of framing. Bruce had ordered the timbers without telling me of their specifics, and that was fine, but he was finishing another job that was running beyond schedule, as all construction jobs do. This delayed my house. I steamed, fumed, and paced and then finally killed time by building two pine-paneled doors that now close the main entrances of my house. They are 3 inches thick and filled with foam. Bruce calls them "farmer" doors, which tickles me. When he really wishes to be insulting he uses the term as a verb, accusing someone of "farmering" a structure together. His criticism was more a teasing than an objection, though. Had he really objected to the doors he would not have permitted them.

With the doors nearly finished, I happened to learn by accident that the timbers were done, so I decided to speed matters by picking them up from the Finlays, the brothers Myles, Mark, and Mel. It was their sawmill that filled the order.

The brothers are part of the timber industry, although it doesn't seem right to say it that way. In Montana the industry is huge and voracious, descending like a barbarian horde. It is smokestacks, unions, and lunch buckets; company towns; log piles that would cover airport runways; trucks and city-sized aluminum compounds of mills. It is industry. The Finlays' corner of it, however, could be more accurately described as craft.

Their sawmill is hard to find unless you know what you're looking for, although it's just off a main highway that splits the Bitterroot Valley. There's no sign out front and a few trees obscure it from the highway. It's small, an enterprise that covers an area not much bigger than a city lot. An ancient basic saw of the open-air variety sits in the center. Most of the time its tall-as-a-person blade is singing through logs, pushed by an oily diesel engine. The only building is a rough-sawed plank shed, small like an outhouse. It is the office, but there are no chairs. Most of the space is taken by various cans and tubes of lubricants, chains, saws, files, teeth, and a spare blade. The Finlays' bookkeeping occurs within, at a podium-sized desk next to the wall calendar and greasy phone. Sheets of scratch pad are pinned to the wall with orders and accounts penciled thereon. A grimy calculator looks as if it has processed as many board feet as the mill.

Outside, raw logs are stacked around in the mud toward one end of the yard. Planks, boards, and timbers are stickered and stacked toward the other end—green, rough lumber drying in the air. There is no kiln or plane. All three brothers preside over this mill five days a week and half a day on Saturday. They are big men in overalls and flannel shirts. Snuff cans protrude from pockets, the snoose from lower lips. They call ponderosa pine "bull pine," as all old-time loggers do. Mel appears the oldest, maybe fifty, and he is the magician of the saw. He mostly stands at the controls of the mill, peering straight down the kerf. Mark is stern and probably the middle brother. In my mind I see him tossing around six-by-six timbers as if they were kindling. Myles appears to be the youngest, smiles a lot, and asks questions. He was the one who found out in the early going what I do for a living.

"Your card says you're a writer. What do you write about?"

I considered telling a lie. The truth is that I had written frequently about the timber industry, mostly critically. And here in the Bitterroot Valley arguments about the timber industry can become unpleasant, even violent. The representative of that industry inviting me into such a discussion at that moment stood about six-foot-two, a small fellow in comparison to his nearby brothers.

"I write about the timber industry. Just did a book about Champion and Plum Creek."

I stretched the terminal syllable of the sentence, pronouncing it in the local way: "crick." This I hoped would win me some needed points.

"And what did you find out about Champion," the timber man pressed on.

Before I could reply Mark interrupted with his own answer: "You found out they're a bunch of goddamned crooks, didn't you?"

Mark launched into a diatribe against the timber business and what it had become. He said that the valley once supported a half dozen mills just like the Finlays' operation. Everybody made a decent living. Nobody got rich.

"But then they got greedy," he said. "So damned greedy."

The Finlays own a half section of land, 320 acres logged selectively, logged in perpetuity. They don't do clear-cuts, always leaving more trees than they take, always leaving a forest. It provides most of the logs to feed their mill, and yet people who have seen it say you can't tell it's been logged. The Finlays can rattle off the names of the handful of loggers up and down the valley who are the exceptions to the rule, people with regard for the forests and their craft and for the long-term future of both. When the Finlays buy logs, they deal with these people. Such people log gently and selectively. In their hands forests truly can be "renewable resources," but most forests are not in the hands of people who accept nature's limits.

Mark points to a pile of timbers close to the mill, my timbers. That morning they had been green logs. Still full of moisture, they were more than twice as heavy as dried lumber. They pushed my pickup's nose upward as Mark, Myles, and I stacked them in the bed. It took three trips to the Finlays' yard to cart off the skeleton of my house. Cruder, fatter, and heavier than anything I could buy at an industrial lumberyard. Still, I know where these timbers came from.

On the last trip, we loaded the biggest timber, a 10-inch by 10-inch beam 20 feet long, the sort of timber most people believe you cannot buy at any price anymore. It cost sixty-five dollars. It has become the main beam of my house, spanning the space in the ceiling between the living room and dining room. Often I tell its story to visitors. It was not green but was cut from a standing dead western larch killed by a winter storm on Plum Creek land. To the giant timber corporation's computerized, standardized peelers and mills, the log was not usable. It was trash, waste. The corporation sold it as salvage to the Finlays, where Mel's fine eye can pull a beam from most anything. Now it is the single most important piece of wood in my house.

Bruce had forbidden my disturbing so much as a single fiber of the beams, so I simply stacked them in front of the concrete shell of the house and waited for him to finish his other job. Finally, on August 26, maybe eight weeks before the onset of winter, we began framing. It was just Bruce and me working that first day, a day spent pacing and snapping chalk lines, talking through the design details like clearance for walkways, rise and run of steps. Atop the concrete walls we bolted the two-by-six sill plates, special pressure-treated lumber pads on which the frame would rest. They would not rot from the moisture absorbed from concrete and so are a buffer. We checked the tops of the walls for square, an operation performed by comparing diagonal, corner-to-corner measurements. They matched to within a sixteenth of an inch—so far so good. This slavish devotion to the perpendicular seems a cultural bias, a heritage of our Western rationalism that is based in geometry. It's not. Pre-Columbian cultures in the Pacific Northwest performed this very operation using braided cedar-bark ropes instead of 50-foot steel tapes to check square.

Now satisfied that the foundation had been properly laid, Bruce unloaded the sawhorses and placed them on the concrete slab, our work space. We were about to begin framing in earnest. The task of framing is divided into subsets, the construction of a number of subassemblies of the house: decks, individual walls, and, eventually, the roof. Our first task was to frame the deck that would be at once the ceiling of the first floor and the floor of the second. Working on the sawhorses we would prepare each member of the deck frame, then later lift them into place for final assembly. Together we hoisted a raw ten-by-ten beam to span the horses (a sort of operating table) and began to shape it to the task. T-shirted, sweaty, tanned surgeons, we bent over that beam and its mates for two days doing joinery.

That main beam would support the ends of seven 6-inch by 10-inch beams that would be the joists between the first and second floors, a timber-framed deck. In framing, most horizontal members are called joists and support either floors or ceilings or both. The frame, a sort of skeleton, contains no nails. If you have seen the beams in an open-beamed ceiling, you have seen what we were building. What is known as a bedded dovetail joint holds the joists to the beams. From the top, the ends of the six-by-tens joined to the ten-by-ten beam looks like this:

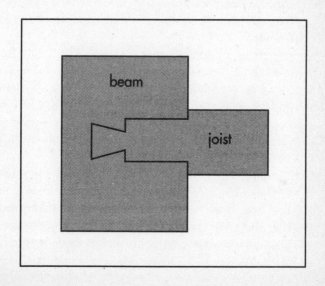

Seven notches, or sockets, that are the exact negatives of the dove-tails on the beams would be cut into the side of the main beam. The joists and the beam slip together like the interlocking pieces of a jigsaw puzzle. All of this precision had to be wrought by hand tools carving into rough, green, and uneven lumber.

Bruce began the layout using a normal number two pencil, instead of a fat carpenter's pencil, to lay down a razor-sharp line. I set to laying out the opposite sides of the joints, and Bruce came quickly to check my work. One cut I had made was found lacking, a sixteenth of an inch off in a spot that would in no way affect the appearance or fit of the joint.

"Do it over," he said, sentencing me to another half hour's work. I complained, pointing out that the error was without consequence.

"Do it over. There are certain standards to be met."

Bruce never did tell me the origins and specifics of these standards, but I eventually learned not to argue with them.

Once the layouts were done we used power saws to square the ends of the beams. I have always thought of the hand-held circular saw, the skill saw, as a sort of crude instrument of butchery, but in Bruce's hands it behaved. With concentration and patience, I soon learned to exactly halve one of these pinpoint pencil lines. When a saw bites a green beam it releases a rush of piney scent like the gush of steam when a fork pierces a baked apple.

We set to notching, an act worked with chisels. The back of Bruce's pickup is like most carpenters': a jangled pile of tools. Generally all tools ride in this heap without regard to their cost, with the only exception being the delicate and precise 4-foot-long level, which traditionally rides in a rifle rack mounted over the pickup's rear window. In Bruce's case there was another exception. Carefully laid out in their own case were his chisels.

Timber framing has resurrected the once-dead long-handled chisels of the craft. The most impressive of these is known as the "slick," a 2-foot-long chisel with a blade running to 4 inches wide. Bruce has a slick and several smaller chisels, all from a single source, a man named Barr Quarton who lives in McCall, Idaho. Quarton hand-forges the high-carbon steel that is the heart of the chisel. To these blades he hand-fits either oak or walnut handles, starting again another cycle of shaping nearly as old as hands. He uses his chisel to shape the handle that makes a chisel that will someday shape a new handle. This, too, is a passing of culture.

Using diamond honing stones Quarton applies the skills he learned studying with traditional Samurai swordsmiths in Japan to give the blades their edge. To buy a Barr chisel, one calls his house and asks for one. He has an 800 number. MasterCard and Visa are accepted, but the phone rings in his house. When a chisel gets dull, the owner sends it back to Quarton and he sharpens it. This seldom happens, however, because their owners tend to handle them with great care.

One does not strike them with an ordinary hammer, out of respect for their hand-finished hardwood handles. Instead, they are persuaded to their tasks with blows from a sand-filled, plastic-covered mallet.

It was with some trepidation that Bruce let me use his chisels, because we were working over a concrete floor. He told me if I dropped the chisel point down on the hard slab he would kill me where I stood. Still, he wanted me to use the chisels; we were notching the joints of my house.

We started the hollows of the joints by drilling with a great, biting bit called a Forstner. The drill left a round hole for what would be a square peg, a splintered and chewed excavation that looked as if it had been made with a hand grenade. It was the chisel's job to square the hole and clean it up, to match the joint to its mate.

Big as it was, the chisel never did feel clumsy in my hands. I was wary at first of what its fiercely sharp edge could do when set against something as fine as the beams, but after a few tentative whacks with the mallet I found it matched to the task. It would slice across end grains, raising a plume of flat, nearly translucent chips. I let it carve and gouge along Bruce's hairline pencil marks. I pushed it straight down then pried it back just a nudge to break loose a satisfying chip. Down again, checking the plumb of the plunge with a small metal square, running a strip of metal the length of the notch to see that it ran true. Measuring, checking, and fitting, then again the mallet tapping at the walnut handle of the chisel.

Usually a building site is awash in a whir of electrical power, saws biting and whining. Our saws and drills now were mostly silent, clearing the air for the meditation of chisels. The quiet sent a trance over that afternoon. Tracy was there and tried chiseling. She liked it too. The radio brought in an old-time country and western program. We knew most of the songs and sang along with Patsy Cline, Merle Travis, and Hank Williams. We also talked some, Bruce, Tracy, and I. We spoke of the balance between force and finesse. Bruce confided a dream, that he would some day like to return to academia. He would like to use his training as a biologist to study religion as a biological imperative. He believes the call to religion is as innate in humans as a wolf's urge to hunt.

Somewhere during this carving I lost my sense of time. In the placid spaces between the singing and conversation we would fall silent and my thoughts would plunge deeply into the joint with the chisel. The carving was not at all mindless but demanded intense concentration. At the same time the chisel behaved as if it were a part of the intelligence guiding the process, drawing me deeper into the depths of this joint. For at least five thousand years carpenters have made such joints. Archaeologists in the Northwest believe Native people notched beams using adzes and chisels edged with clam or mussel shell. They probably used stone mauls and sheep-horn wedges. The use of post-and-beam houses in the Northwest stretched from present-day northern Oregon to the panhandle of Alaska. There are clues as to where the design came from or went, because the timber frames of this continent resemble greatly the wood houses of Siberia's Amir region and traditional Ainu homes of northern Japan. We believe we transmit culture with language, but chisels carry it too.

Among the four hundred secret joints used by traditional Japanese carpenters, the bedded dovetail must have existed, useful as it is. Maybe it is this Eastern path the chisel I'm holding seems to find as it burrows into the beam. Japanese carpenters referred to their tools collectively as *dogu*, which translates as "instruments of the way."

It rained that afternoon as it had not rained for months. We gathered up the chisels and power tools, stuffed them in the truck, and then took cover, the three of us, under a tarp I had strung between three nearby fir trees. We waited for the rain to stop, but it didn't that day, so we sat under the tarp and listened to it pour until quitting time.

*   *   *

I haul the concrete while my son, Josh, and Bill Haskins, one of the many friends who helped with the house, fill a pier.

CLOCKWISE FROM BOTTOM LEFT: I explain to Josh the technique of screeding concrete, while Bill stands by; a mixer rumbles through a meadow on its way to beginning the work of a house; Bruce Haroldson and I bolt fill atop the concrete walls while Tracy looks on; the essence of timber framing is hand-cut joints in massive, rough-sawed beams; the foundation rises around a grid of timbers that will define the surface of the house's main floor (the patch of fresh concrete at right will later be covered with wood to become the floor of the sunken living room).

The walls of the house rise from the foundation to hint at the
shape of the structure.

CLOCKWISE FROM BOTTOM LEFT: Bruce cuts a plank on the circular saw; the house continues to take shape; the wood stove stands in the finished living room; still lacking a roof, the house is nonetheless closed in—at this point, Tracy and I were residents.

TOP: Tracy and I in front of our finished house.
BOTTOM: The completed kitchen.

The Floor Plan
First Floor

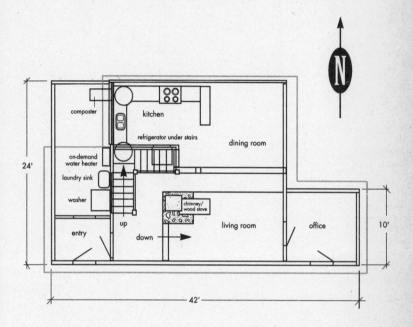

N

composter

kitchen

refrigerator under stairs

dining room

on-demand
water heater

laundry sink

washer

24'

chimney/
wood stove

living room

office

10'

entry

up

down

42'

Design by
Richard Manning, Tracy Stone-Manning, and Bruce Haroldson

Second Floor

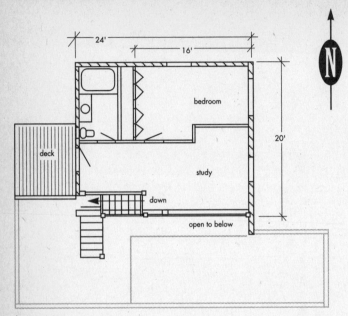

Cost: $50,000

Size: about 1,200 square feet

Bermed: first floor on north, east, and west

Insulation: walls to R-29, fiberglass and Thermax

roof to R-38, fiberglass

2–4 inches of extruded polystyrene insulation on exterior of foundation below grade

2 inches extruded polystyrene beneath slab

Framing: timber framed, post-and-beam first floor, stud-wall second floor, OSB I-beam rafters

Heating: passive solar, wood, electric backup

Water heating: on-demand, propane

Energy use: less than 200 kwh/month electric, less than 15 gallons/month propane

Solar surface: south wall, first floor glazed with 140 square feet of double-paned, low-E windows, 32 square feet of argon-filled skylights in south roof pitch

Exterior: rough-sawed board-and-batten pine, stucco over foundation insulation, steel roof

Construction: owner-built with subcontractors for framing, concrete walls, sheetrock, masonry chimney, and interior stucco

Construction time: one year

On the second day of notching Mike Dege joined the effort. Mike is Bruce's partner, an inverted mate to Bruce's half of the joint. He is wiry and quick; Bruce is ponderous and strong. He is confident; Bruce is skeptical. His unused master's degree is in wildlife biology; Bruce's is in botany. Both are consummate carpenters. I once speculated to them that if they ever dissolved their partnership it would be like a divorce.

"No, worse than a divorce," Bruce said, probably not something either of them takes lightly. They've both been through the real thing.

We finished notching the floor beams on the second day and began assembling them. We manhandled that massive ten-by-ten into place, resting it on top of the concrete walls. Then we used the pressure of screw clamps to draw the joist beams into the notches in the main beam, one by one. A deck's frame arose. From the bottom of the frame the dovetails are not visible, making it appear as if the joists butt against the beam and are held there perfectly square and matched, as if by levitation. No nail heads or bolts disturb the illusion. From above we could see a row of seven perfect dovetail joints, joists set to beam like piglets to a sow. At no point is it possible to so much as slide a sheet of paper between the halves of the joint. It was a wonderful display of craft, visible only for a few hours. The next day we sheathed the deck with fir planks, covering the joints forever. Only four or five people have seen the craft buried in that floor.

In the following days the house's timber-framed south wall arose. Ten six-by-six posts spaced on a line every 4 feet rise vertically 10 feet to support a six-by-six plate beam. This beam in turn supports the front edge of the roof, because the house slopes to a single story on its south edge. Simple mortise-and-tenon joints secured with hardwood pegs hold the posts to the beam. The mortise-and-tenon joint is probably as old as carpentry. Simply, the end of the post is carved down to a smaller rectangle, say, 3 inches by 3 inches, and that tenon is inserted into a similarly sized rectangle hole chiseled into the beam.

We chiseled the joints and slid them together, wiggling and mauling the massive posts into place. They came together hard, achieving a unity where post and beam behaved as one, with no movement. This would not have happened with a nailed-together stud wall, which always has some wiggle. The solidity of a timber-framed joint is unique. That notion of no movement, a strength that is deeply satisfying to feel, is sort of a mantra for Bruce. Ultimately it is his standard of quality. Often he would test a wall by heaving his bulk against it and then chant: "No movement." Solid.

It is a standard that can be quantified, but numbers do not explain how the feel of it echoed through my chest to reverberate in the soles of my feet. The concept is profound enough to be understandable only as a feeling. Measuring it is best left to poets, and as my front wall thunked together I remembered poems that had done so. Gary Snyder grabbed it, caught the heft of it all in the simple split of a once-compounded noun: Earth House Hold.

Walt Whitman, who supported himself as a builder between frequent firings from newspaper jobs and whose father was a carpenter, knew of solid. In *Song of the Broad-Axe* he measured the strength of joints in motion—so solid the poem could proceed without verbs:

> *The house-builder at work in cities or anywhere,*
> *The preparatory jointing, squaring, sawing, mortising,*
> *The hoist-up of beams, the push of them in their places, laying them regular,*
> *Setting the studs by their tenons in the mortises, according as they were prepared,*
> *The blows of mallets and hammers, the attitudes of the men, their curv'd limbs,*
> *Bending, standing, astride the beams, driving in pins, holding on by posts and braces*

Whitman's long narrative builds to a refrain:

> *The shapes arise!*

As we framed the front wall Bruce began to complain about the posts, specifically the wanes. A wane is a bit of bark that shows up on the corner of a post, a place where the diameter of the tree is not big enough to enclose the size of the post being cut so the saw's kerf breaks through the edge. This leaves a strip of bark on the corner of the finished post. It is more than an accident of the saw. Increasingly, lumber is filled with wanes, a sign of reduced circumstances, a sign of smaller trees. In the days of seemingly unlimited old-growth forests there was no need to be stingy with the saw, no close cuts. The old growth is mostly gone, so we squeeze our lumber from smaller trees.

A wane on the Finlays' post is not really an indictment of their skills. Rather it is a measure of their ability to pull a usable post from a small tree. That's how we go about saving what remains of the big, old trees. I have posts with wanes on opposite edges, meaning they pulled a single timber from a tree exactly large enough to support it, a maximizing of potential. With the bark left on, a wane will rot a post, but otherwise it causes no damage. We used a drawknife to remove the bark.

Then Bruce began automatically exercising a carpenter's skill of hiding blemishes. By using the wany posts in certain positions and turning them a certain way, say, toward an end wall, the blemishes would be forever hidden like the dovetail joints. "No," I said, "let them show, turn them to the living room."

A wane in a post is a living record of our place and times. A house is wood because of its obligation to record its time.

The shapes arise!

As we joined two posts to a beam, we'd tip the union into place and brace it temporarily until another such assembly was ready to join the line. In this fashion a wall grew, a series of solid rough lines, horizontal and vertical, backlit in the afternoon sun. Set against the curing concrete walls behind it that frame began to look like a sort of Stonehenge, attuned somehow to stars and solstices in ways we would someday discover. The heft of this mass tuned to the cycle of seasons suggested a timelessness. It occurred to me these lines were becoming something more than a house. They were a grid that would shape my view on the world. Their solidity and hints of immortality informed that they would outlast me. I read the grain of the wood in a post I was setting with my hands, the same grain and post now beside me in my study as I write these words—if all goes according to plan, the same grain I will read on my last day of light.

The shapes arise!
The shape measur'd, saw'd, jack'd, join'd, stain'd,

The coffin-shape for the dead to lie within in his shroud,
The shape got out in posts, in the bedstead posts, in the posts of the bride's bed,
The shape of the little trough, the shape of the rockers beneath, the shape of the babe's cradle,
The shape of the floor-planks, the floor-planks for dancers' feet, . . .
The shapes arise!
Shapes of doors giving many exits and entrances, . . .
The door that admits good news and bad news

With post and beams set plumb, we pegged the whole business together, leaving it to stand on its own among the living trees.

Framing that south wall and deck with the timbers pushed us to a new level on our house. It was Bruce's idea that the house be a hybrid, so the second floor would be mostly a conventional stick frame, once called a balloon frame. There we would shift from a technology at least two thousand years old to one only one hundred fifty years old. This was not, however, our primary motive. The switch to a stick frame was only a means to an even newer technology, one said to be easier on forests. The stick-frame walls would support sheathing and high-tech rafters made of OSB—"oriented strand board"—a material invented only recently but already ubiquitous in the construction industry. It and its derivative products are radically altering the way in which we build houses, although I am not sure if it is for the better. It depends on how it is used and how it is made.

Like wanes in rough-sawed posts, OSB is a measure of hard times, the sort of stuff we wouldn't make and use if we didn't have to. It is an adaptation to scarcity. Buried within is an admission of the central mistake of the American timber industry. We have been told all these years that wood can be grown like wheat. The timber industry said the nation was better served if loggers clear-cut the virgin forests and replaced them with tree farms of their own devising, faster-growing, genetically pure strains of vigorous trees to cover the fatherland.

These practitioners of biological engineering ignored a few dissi- dent voices in their ranks, some foresters who warned that tree farms destroy the web of life that sustains a forest: the decay and detritus, the invertebrates, arthropods, squirrels, and raptors. Consequently, tree farming wipes out a finely tuned ecosystem; in the long run, the only system that can sustain trees. One such dissident voice was Arnold Bolle, the dean of the University of Montana's Forestry School when he wrote a congressional study in the late sixties that raised the first alarm about the perils of clear-cutting. He called the dominant practice of the industry "Nazi forestry," but he was ignored and the practice prevails even today.

Now the necessity of OSB is the industry's admission that Bolle and others like him were right. True, the tree farms the corporations planted to replace forests have grown trees. Fast. That's the problem. By circumventing nature's patience they produced trees with large annular growth rings and a corresponding reduction in strength. Lumber sawed from these trees is not as strong. It twists, warps, and wanes, all qualities guaranteed to stimulate the use of a carpenter's complete vocabulary.

Writing in *Fine Homebuilding*, a sort of magazine of record for the building trades, editor Charles Wardell launched a discussion of the problem:

> Quality wood is becoming hard to get. Around the world, forests are disappearing; in the U.S. many once-vast stands of old-growth timber have been replaced by second- or third-growth trees of smaller size and lower quality. The environmental consequences of this dwindling supply is the topic of much heated debate, but the effect on the builder is certain: higher prices and lower quality. Just ask anyone who's tried to find a reasonably priced supply of straight two-by-fours lately.

A stick of quality structural lumber is not at all a "renewable resource," it turns out. A tree-farmed, third-growth Douglas fir, sawed into a four-by-four (if one can be found that large), likely will not support a ton at the center of a 12-foot span. The engineers' structural tables apply only to nature's trees, to trees that have been cut selectively, with respect to nature and the preservation of the integrity of the forest. Essentially, though, the nation has been clear-cut, not logged selectively and carefully. This process began in colonial times and is ending just now in Alaska and in the few remaining virgin forests of the Pacific Northwest. The big trees are gone, and now we are stuck with OSB.

Oddly, the product began as a replacement for plywood, the glued veneer already considered a bit artificial and high-tech. Yet plywood, in certain forms, has been with us at least since the ancient Egyptians. Further, it turns out that it takes fairly large diameter and high-quality trees to make the stuff. Those trees are gone, so we are stuck with manipulation.

To make OSB one grinds up weak trees and glues them back together to make them stronger. The forerunner of OSB was wafer-board, a name that succinctly describes its construction. Grinders reduce low-quality trees to chips ranging from a quarter of an inch square to the size of a sheet of notepaper. The wood chips tend to be flat, maybe the thickness of a magazine. At first, these chips were glued together randomly, as wafers, but it was discovered that by orienting them so that the wood's fibers ran in a consistent direction the board became stronger.

This trick was made possible by an advancing glue technology, some space-age organic chemistry. The bond is created when a liq-uefied resin flows into microcavities in the wafers and sticks to individ-ual wood fibers. The glues in OSBs are either phenol-formaldehydes or, in some cases, isocyanates, although manufacturers shy from the latter because it tends to poison mill workers. The former becomes not much more than an air quality problem in the communities where OSB factories exist, but then most of these factories are converted plywood mills and nearby residents already are used to bad air and paychecks. In any event, OSB's manufacture is an industrial process, so it must come from highly automated factories, not community sawmills like the Finlays'.

There is some concern about using formaldehyde in houses, be-cause it off-gasses—exhales volatile fumes—into enclosed living spaces. Most builders I know are leery of using OSB where it is exposed to interior space, using it only as exterior sheathing. Yet the manufacturers say we are not to worry about phenol-formaldehyde, the glue used in OSB. The real off-gassing problem comes from urea formaldehyde, the glue used in particleboard, a sort of cheap plywood that looks like what it is: glued together sawdust. Likely you will find particleboard in your kitchen cabinets or office furniture if they are fairly new.

Originally the industry developed OSB as a replacement for plywood. It comes in four-by-eight sheets and cuts and nails like the real stuff. As sheathing for exterior walls and floor and roof decks it is a completely acceptable substitute. More interestingly, though, engineering is pushing it into new forms that replace not just sheathing but those valuable and rare structural timbers derived from old growth. OSB is popping up as the foundation for a new sort of wood I-beam that replaces planks used as floor joists, ceiling joists, and rafters. It is glued directly to thick sheets of polystyrene foam as "stress skins"—panels used to erect studless walls and roof decks. I toured an experimental house that supports one deck without joists, OSB or otherwise. Instead it is made solely of large panels formed of a layer of honeycombed paper backed on either side by sheets of OSB. These panels, at least in this house, span distances as great as 17 feet yet are as solid as concrete: no movement.

Aside from the question of toxicity, the rise of OSB poses a dilemma for those of us who care for forests. On the one hand it offers an alternative to the structural timbers now mostly attainable only in old-growth forests. Good deal. This removes some of the pressure from the old growth, giving those people battling mightily to save them a new lever. The best OSB is made from aspen, not an old-growth species at all but a seral species that sprouts like a weed all across the Midwest in tree farms and old, neglected clear-cuts. A usable aspen will grow in less than twenty years; a Douglas fir of integrity in maybe two hundred.

I fear, though, that this technology cannot be penned in the tree farms. Like the manufacture of OSB, the harvest of the trees that produce it is a highly mechanized industrial process. The process requires no craft or care. It is a process that begs for clear-cuts. Because the sought product is chips, trees can be harvested without regard to age, species, quality, or size. The engine of this indiscriminate cutting is a device called a feller-buncher, which is a giant set of shears that grabs and slices off every tree in its path. It plucks up huge masses of diverse life and feeds them to the chippers, the homogenizers that reinvent the tree.

In Montana we are already seeing the effects of this technology. Timber industry officials no longer speak of trees; they speak of "fiber." They are attempting to cut in places once ignored, thick stands of lodgepole pine that are known locally as "doghair," skinny limbless trees that cover ridges by the mile. These lodgepole thickets are critical steps in the succession of forests. Where will our forests stand when their infant stages have been reduced to clear-cuts by this new demand and the voracious technology that allows it?

We have put Bruce's chisels away now. The tap of their patient chewing is absent. It is replaced by the scream of power saws and the background hum of an air compressor, a relatively new fixture of house construction. The compressor drives the nail guns that now perform most of the grunt work for old-fashioned hammers. The dominant fixture of a framing carpenter's tool belt is still his hammer, swinging like a pistol in a quick-draw loop. He uses it only occasionally, though, driving the odd spike in a corner brace or persuading a stubborn stud to its designated position.

Most of the nails of a house, the big nails, the spikes that hold the studs, plates, and headers in place, are driven by the air hammers, hand-held nail guns the size and shape of a small sewing machine. They are lightning fast, setting a spike in less than a second. In framing, speed and accuracy are the principle goals. (Their ranking depends on the integrity of the carpenter.) The business is competitive. People want affordable homes, so we build them fast.

The air gun also gives the carpenter a longer hold on his craft. While not completely a young person's trade, carpentry can exclude an aging person with carpal tunnel syndrome, a debilitating malady that afflicts the wrists that swing the hammers.

I got the hang of the air hammer soon enough, learning the light touch on the trigger that stopped me from accidently driving two spikes in a second instead of one. Mike showed me how to hold the two pieces of wood being joined. The idea is to keep one's hands away from the joint. Sometimes the spike will strike a hidden knot and ricochet out the side of the board straight through a carelessly placed hand.

A friend of Bruce's and mine who is a bartender once began his evening's shift by tacking an X ray of his leg to the mirror behind the bar. It had been taken that very afternoon and showed with nauseating clarity a profile of a 3½-inch steel spike resting neatly against his femur. This fellow had been working days for Bruce and had developed the bad habit of resting the point of the nail gun against his thigh between uses. Many bad habits in construction are self-correcting.

Mike and I were framing a rake wall, the term for a wall angled at the top to follow and support the pitch of the roof. The array of the angles would have kept me talking to myself, swearing and recutting botched attempts half the day. Mike, however, simply made some calculations and snapped the outline of the wall with a chalk line on the deck of the second floor. He cut plates and the two end studs to fit the outline, and then the rest of the studs came marching onto the deck in rapid succession. This is testimony to the elegance of carpentry's evolved internal logic.

Framers do not measure angles in degrees as does the rest of the world. Degree measurements are reserved for the miters of the finish carpenters. Instead most angles are expressed as "pitch," the horizontal run over the vertical rise. Further, the run is almost always given as simply "twelve," tying it neatly to the inches in a foot. A steep roof is a "ten-twelve," meaning for every 12 inches of horizontal span there is 10 inches of vertical gain. A gentle roof is a four-twelve. A roof climbing at a 45-degree angle would be a twelve-twelve.

My house has a ten-twelve south pitch and a four-twelve north pitch. The steep south roof makes the cathedral ceiling of the living room that bridges first and second floors. It also creates a surface of close to 45 degrees that is the ideal pitch, at this latitude, to catch solar gain from the sun's autumn and spring angles. The south pitch of my house would hold four large skylights for passive solar heating.

This system of expressing angles established a framework for the task. Simply, once Mike had set the top angle on the saw (its gauges also are calibrated in that same system of pitch), and once he knew the length of the longest stud, the length of each successive stud followed. The studs were two-by-sixes spaced 2 feet apart—2 feet of run or two twelves, which meant that as we worked down the rake of the wall, each stud was precisely 8 inches (two fours) shorter than the last.

The nail gun exhaled the spikes that stitched the wall together. I held studs, Mike nailed. First the studs and then the cripple studs, spacers, and headers that framed a door and a window. In the matter of a half hour the house's end wall was framed in pine two-by-sixes, ready to tilt to the light. And we did that, three of us hoisting, spiking the plate to the deck, setting a few corner braces until sheathing and the perpendicular walls could make the frame rigid.

The north wall was a rectangle and seemed framed before I had time to consider it. We sheathed it with OSB while it rested on the deck, an operation far easier in the horizontal because we did not have to hoist the heavy 4-foot by 8-foot sheets up a ladder. We tipped the wall into place and another space was defined. Another back rake wall grew, and then the front rakes, small triangles that tied the ends of the house to the south wall. In a little more than a day the house doubled in height.

Then came more timbers. We were able to go light on the stick framing because the main work of supporting the roof was to be handled by timbers, not the external walls. An eight-by-eight post went from the first-floor deck beams up to support a parallel beam that was the ridge of the roof. Back came the chisels for more mortise-and-tenon joints. Where the post met the upper beam we added two knee braces, small beams angled at 45 degrees away from the post to the beam to bolster the joint. The effect is much like a Y or, more appropriately, like branches—a sort of resurrection of the tree.

When we hoisted that post-and-beam assembly, the house scared me for the first time. Four of us, Mike, Bruce, Tracy and I, handled it alone, although we shouldn't have. The weight was unwieldy, all we could handle, but when Bruce issued the command to lift until the stars shot out of our eyes, we did.

We lifted the beams to teeter on the edge of a precipitous drop. They stand at the edge of the second-floor deck where it plunges straight down 12 feet to the sunken concrete floor of the living room below. One slip would have sent the whole gangly business off that edge. Barely had we tipped the beams and post into place—it still rocked and wobbled—when I looked up to see Mike standing atop it, 25 feet of clear fall above the living room floor.

"I have always maintained that carpenters will not be fully evolved until they have a prehensile tail," Bruce said. Bruce calls Mike "the gibbon," because he works the high spots. I've watched him stroll the 4-inch-wide top plate of a rickety rake wall as if it were a sidewalk.

Mike, on the other hand, says one cannot be a master carpenter unless one has sawed off at least a knuckle's worth of finger. Mike had performed this very act the summer before, so he probably said this simply to make us jealous.

We framed the short wall that spanned the gap between the two roof pitches, the clerestory, and that was it. The house had gained all its vertical. We were at the lid.

Tracy and I drove away from it that night and I had to stop on the road, surprised by what it had become. I had drawn it and dreamed it so long I thought I knew it, but it had grown beyond what I had suspected. It seemed alive, to be sprouting from the hillside. The sun caught its bare roof lines as it does the top of a hawk's wings.

The house took its roof line from an invention known as a TGI, a term derived from the name of the company that developed it. It is nothing more than a wood I-beam. TGIs are of varying heights, but mine were 16 inches tall. The web, or upright portion of the I-beam, is a sheet of OSB about a half-inch thick. The top and bottom is capped by a 3-inch by 3-inch strip of board made up of many laminations of plywood. They're light and seem flimsy, even though they're on the order of 20 feet long. Pick one up close to its end and it wobbles and shakes like a willow twig. Yet they replace what have traditionally been a house's most formidable planks, its rafters.

Until now the rafters were the big wood, 20-foot long two-by-twelves, the best of the saw logs. Aside from being scarce, traditional rafters have other drawbacks. They are heavy and so add to the load they must support. They are beautiful pieces of wood, yet modern construction methods bury them in the cavity between ceiling and roof, losing their grain forever. Because they were strong enough to serve their purpose as two-by-twelves, they made a cavity between roof and ceiling only a foot thick. This is not enough room to superinsulate the cavity. Plank rafters are artifacts, replaced first by engineered trusses built of smaller dimensional lumber and now by wood I-joists.

The four of us hung the I-beams on the roof in one afternoon. The house now bore a bit of technology that did everything I needed it to do, yet I couldn't wait to cover them up. They reeked so much of artifice, especially set against the rough-sawed timbers standing as walls below. They left the smell of glue and burned wood in the air.

The hanging of these high-tech rafters posed a dilemma in that they were the beginnings of a roof. Within a day or so it would be sheathed, and then the house would cross its first major milestone. At that point its shape would be complete. The form would stand.

Among building folks there developed a custom, probably in Scandinavia, probably as an outgrowth of atavistic tree worship that still and properly claims the attention of some carpenters. From somewhere on the site one cuts a bough, a green bit of living tree, sometimes a whole infant tree like a Christmas tree. This is hoisted like a flag to the highest point of the roof and nailed there, a sort of symbolic resurrection of the tree incarnated as house. It marks the topping of the house.

A couple of days before the rafters rose, Bruce and I had decided that the post rising through the center of the house to the branching braces at the clerestory ridge looked like a tree re-forming. It seemed appropriate to nail the bough to the roof ridge just above the post when the time came.

Our dilemma arose, however, from an earlier commitment Tracy and I had made to friends. We had to leave for a week. Bruce and Mike would work on, bringing our house across a significant line while we were gone.

I suggested to Bruce that he forego the hanging of the bough until we returned. He considered the suggestion heretical.

"Can't risk it," he said. It was not my house, I remembered. I understood how much of ourselves Tracy and I had invested in it, but we had been impressed during the past few weeks with Mike and Bruce's own level of commitment. In a real sense, it was not my house. We were leaving; they were staying. The house had grown enough to stand on its own, so it would, like an adolescent, undergo a rite of passage with parents absent.

We returned a week later to find the house transformed. Not much work had been done. There had been a lot of rain in our absence, but a little work had rendered big changes. The remaining rafters had been strung, and most of the roof stood sheathed, completing the lines of the main roof, lines I already had seen. At each end of the house, though, there are small rooms leaning into the main area like sheds to an old farmhouse. The east one holds my study, the other, a foyer and utility room.

I had planned for those rooms simple shed roofs pitched straight up to the main structure's walls, but Mike had another idea. He suggested, instead, small hip roofs flowing into the main roof. A normal roof, or gabled roof, is simply two planes tipped together, a sort of pup tent on top of a building. A shed roof is half of that, a sort of lean-to tipped to a taller part of the building, as in a shed added to the back of a barn. A hip roof, however, has four planes tipped to an apex, a pyramid instead of a tent atop a building.

In the case of my house, the effect was dramatic. The two little pyramids melded into the main roof, drawing in the sheds to become a part of the whole. They sloped toward the house from three directions to accent its reach to the sun. These new slopes cleaned the lines of the house and suggested an Aztec pyramid.

The house made a new statement, one I had not expected. To me its design was a practical enterprise of efficiency. I wanted it only to conserve energy and wood. I had drawn it with the pencil of an accountant. But now it rose with a heart of its own. It was still the basic design Trace and I had hatched, but it had grown in the hands of others. Its face turned to the light with the clerestory windows Bruce had imagined. It reached with the steep roof he had drawn. It softened and reached through time with the angled roofs Mike had devised.

On approaching the house Tracy and I realized that our fascination with the new lines had caused us to miss something. There was no bough tacked at the ridge. There couldn't be. A strip of sheathing was missing, so the house wasn't ready for its rite of passage.

It was a Saturday. Bruce and Mike were gone, but I set to work. The week's rain had been raising hell with a raw wood deck of the second floor, so I stapled the tarpaper over the roof's sheathing. I skipped the row of missing sheathing but soon sealed the rest from rain.

On Monday, Mike and Bruce returned, and we tied up some loose ends, finally finishing that row of sheathing. Then nothing happened, or an awkward nothing happened. No mention of a bough, but it quickly became clear that Bruce was taking leave of my house. For the first time, he admitted it was mine.

"I thought it wasn't my house."

"You've earned the right to call it that more than most."

He then picked up a scrap of lumber, a carpenter's version of a scratch pad, pulled out his pencil, and wrote a list of material.

"This is the stuff you need to finish the frame."

Ceiling joists and such. Work he had planned to do but was behind because of the rain, and besides, he had decided I could handle it. Then he left, not far off really. He and Mike only moved next door to begin work on the Moores' house. But from that moment on, when Bruce came to my house he knocked on the door, even before it had one.

He did so only a couple of days later, when he came around to present his final bill. He could have mailed that. There seemed to be something else on his mind, but what it was, Bruce never said. He was in street clothes and carried a camera bag. He said he wanted to snap a few pictures of my house, which was then not much more than a frame. He said he needed pictures now, before "it gets all covered up."

Then he rummaged around in his camera gear and found he had brought no film. So he simply walked around the shell, thunked a few beams, and stared.

It was September 18, Tracy's twenty-sixth birthday. She was there with me, the two of us inhabiting our land alone. As she set to some other task, I fished around in my tools for my cutting pliers, walked off to the front yard, and clipped off a foot-high Douglas fir, part of a thick clump that needed thinning. Someday one of the rest of that clump would grow to be a great tree, but that will be some other story. By then I will be gone.

With the fir in my hand and my tool belt swinging to my ascent, I stepped up the aluminum ladder to the roof's rear pitch, then walked to the peak, the vantage at the top of the trees. I nailed the bough to the fascia.

Back on the ground, Trace saw what I had done. When I joined her there we hugged and cried a bit, although I was embarrassed to have done so. I felt a bit silly weeping over something as mundane as the sheathing of a roof.

Filth

BRUCE SAYS A PLUMBER NEEDS TO KNOW but three facts: The hot water tap goes on the left, the boss is a jerk, and payday is Friday. This is only a slight oversimplification. Plumbing is not a horribly complex craft. Important, but not complex, and necessarily circular.

The concept of necessity registered clearly when we first faced a wooden shell we had come to call home. Literally, home. It was October 1, six weeks after the first timbers were set. To save money, Tracy and I had given up our apartment in town and moved in. Possessions susceptible to damage by the upheaval and grit of construction we boxed and stuffed in a storage garage. We were resident on our land, on our house.

In that latter phrase, "on" seems the correct preposition. There was not enough house to be "in." It had no doors or windows, not even the big windows between the timber posts of the long south wall. There were no internal walls, just the external skeleton skinned with OSB, ragged and coarse. No plug sockets. No kitchen sink. No bathtub. It was as airtight and as commodious as a picnic pavilion.

We had our backpacker's white gas stove to make coffee. Bed was our sleeping bags spread on the upper deck. Flying squirrels and wood rats took the run of the place at night, October nights in Montana, crisp, clear, and 20 degrees. Heat other than that generated and shared between bodies was still weeks away.

We did have lumber and tools, though; only work was necessary to make it a home fully wrought. So we worked, the two of us together, mostly alone. In the spirit of this high romance I had marked our first wedding anniversary a few weeks before with a gift to Tracy of a tool belt and a fine chrome-headed, hickory-handled trim hammer. It is the measure of our compatibility that she thought the gift appropriate and didn't immediately swing the hammer at me. At first, though, her swing couldn't have done much damage. Tracy's childhood was suburban: Volvos, dance classes, and theater in the city. Thus, she was deprived. We tried to overcome this poverty with training, but it didn't come easy. Her hammer did not always hit the head of the nail, and when it did it was not always effective.

To the uninitiated even the little acts of building come hard, even the tipping of a plank. The levering and lifting. The uninitiated believe the grunt work of construction is only that, that one grabs and heaves, but it is not so. I can still hear my father's voice to me: "Don't fight it, don't fight it," he'd scream as some plank got the best of me. Then slowly, over the years, the tricks would come, the finesse, the tip and counterbalance. Using the object's weight to the subject's advantage. The leverage, the arc, and the slide, a sort of dance, really, a forming of the body to its task.

Not long before the months of our work together, Tracy and I had gone back east to her former suburban home. I was buying a jacket in one of the endless malls, and a salesman sized me up. "You've worked for a living," he said, pantomiming the swinging of a hammer. Like I stuck out in this crowd. He wasn't saying I was heavily muscled, because weight lifters and steroid types are common sights in his store. He could just tell I had worked.

Do we really build houses, or do houses build us?

All the comforts absent in our primitive house deprived our bodies, yet in setting the priorities for our work Tracy and I decided we would like to have a toilet first. Further we decided we would like a simple toilet, which, in the reverse logic of the American economic system, required some complex thought.

Compared to the toilet the rest of the plumbing was simple. Imagine running a garden hose through walls to every place in a house that needs water. Now add a second hose for hot water and a third to drain everything away. The logic behind the system is not much more complicated than that. Instead of using hose, one uses copper pipe, or plastic pipe for drains. It is not screwed together; the copper is soldered, a skill that takes about a half-hour to learn. The plastic is cut with a handsaw and glued. These pipes together make up what is called the house's rough plumbing system, the part of the system hidden in the walls. Finish plumbing is simply the connecting of the fixtures: the sinks, the shower head, and all of their faucets. This occurs after the walls have been covered. Installing my house's rough plumbing system, a simple one, took me about half a day. I had never done it before, yet everything worked fine on the first try.

A plumber's job is simple and circular, an almost subliminal matching of form to function. Plumbers are the aquarians of the crafts. They bring the water. Water is not so much a natural and necessary compound as it is a cycle, a sort of moving history of change, the change that drives the earth: evaporation, condensation, precipitation, transpiration, erosion, flow. Water moves to shape the planet, but we forget this. We believe too often that water is a static slave here for our bidding, to be abused and forgotten. We forget that this water came to us through the cycle that drives all of our weather and, from our level, it will return to the oceans. Always. In this it cannot be stopped, only delayed.

The water in a house is a cycle too, so there are two halves to a plumber's job. There is a set of pipes that brings water into the house and a set that takes it out. Neither set does anything whatsoever to disrupt the grand cycle. Plumbing only adds a corollary loop, so this drain water in the end returns to the ocean. Sooner or later. Always.

It would be perfectly elegant to believe the connecting point of the two sets of plumber's pipes is our body. That would form a pleasant and justifiable equation. Pleasant to think our bodies flow intimately in the primal cycle of the sphere, literally plugged into the planet by water consumed in the maintenance of the part of our bodies that is water.

Yet our bodies consume only a few quarts of the average 250 gallons sucked up daily by the American family of four. Likewise, the water our bodies directly returns to the system also is an infinitesimal part of the whole that we call "waste." The average human urinates about a quart a day, yet virtually all of the 250 gallons that flows into a house flows out.

We can argue that the water used by bathing is a bodily necessity, and to a certain extent this is so. To a certain extent it is not. Our people's preference for a daily shower is a cultural bias, but say we grant it legitimacy. Showers don't use that much water and would use even less if we all adopted conservation devices such as flow restrictors. Showers, even wasteful ones, don't seem our most profligate use of water. Most of our squandering of water occurs elsewhere. As much as a third of the water used in our houses does not bathe us, it bathes shit.

It is a curious habit, the ritual washing of feces. In his introduction to Sim Van der Ryn's book *The Toilet Papers*, Wendell Berry considered it like this:

> If I urinated and defecated into a pitcher of drinking water and then proceeded to quench my thirst from the pitcher, I would undoubtedly be considered crazy. If I invented an expensive technology to put my urine and feces into my drinking water, then invented another expensive (and undependable) technology to make that same water fit to drink, I might be thought even crazier. It is not inconceivable that some psychiatrist would ask me knowingly why I wanted to mess up my drinking water in the first place.
>
> The "sane" solution, very likely, would be to have me urinate and defecate into a flush toilet, from which the waste would be carried through an expensive sewerage works, which would supposedly treat it and pour it into the river—from which the town downstream would pump it, further purify it, and use it for drinking water.
>
> Private madness, by the ratification of a lot of expense and engineering, thus becomes public sanity.

To me, the illumination of this point is the understanding that the madness is not universal but rather a disease particular to portions of the globe. Ours happens to be among them. The bathing of feces is a sacrament of the Western world, although it spreads now, as all of our good and bad ideas seem to do.

Just seventy years ago James Joyce could refer in *Ulysses* to the "cloacal obsession" of the British, largely because that's where the matter stood. He lamented the spread of British sewers everywhere as a mark of their imperialism, as a mark of oppression on the Irish. It is as good a mark as any. The British did not invent sewers. Their use had been earlier refined by predecessor imperialists: the Romans. The British, however, did evolve the combination of technology and repressive attitudes that today leave us flushing away nearly a third of our domestic water. They taught us to regard the product of our bodies as "filth."

In the nineteenth century a traveler to Hiroshima recorded what he regarded as an odd fact: If three Japanese folks rented a room, the combined produce of their bowels typically would be sold for enough to cover one person's rent. Toilets were dry then in Japan, and farmers emptied them. The proceeds yielded fertilizer rich enough to justify the price and trouble of transporting night soil to the countryside. Such is still the case in much of Asia, although Japan now flushes. The Japanese have become fond of the sound of flushing toilets to cover the immodest sounds of the bathroom. They developed the habit of flushing the toilet upon entering the john. Somebody finally figured this is wasteful, so now one can purchase in Japan tape recordings of flushing sounds to be played on special bathroom tape players.

Human excrement, especially urine, is rich in nitrogen. In *The Toilet Papers*, Van der Ryn says the average human "pisses away" about 10 pounds of pure nitrogen a year. Human feces are 5 to 10 percent nitrogen. He estimates the Los Angeles sewage treatment plant daily discharges two hundred tons of fertilizer that farmers would call "7-14-12," meaning its yield would be 7 percent nitrogen, 14 percent phosphorus, and 12 percent potassium. That is enough properly proportioned fertilizer produced each day to raise five thousand pounds of vegetables.

Technically some of this fertilizer could be recovered at the plant by simply removing it from the water that carried it there. Some of it is, but at an enormous cost. Yet even if the nation used all of the sludge from its fifteen thousand sewage treatment plants, a significant portion of the nutrients remain in the treated water to return to the rivers, streams, and oceans. There the nutrients become pollutants by upsetting natural aquatic and marine growth rates, a major factor in the premature death of natural ecosystems. Throughout the past few decades the federal government alone has spent roughly ten billion dollars a year in grants just to upgrade sewage treatment plants. The nation spends about fifteen billion dollars a year on sewage treatment.

One wonders with Berry how we ever came to this habit in the first place. Consider the notion of ablution, a ritual present in most religious traditions. Consider the use of water in rendering the unclean clean.

The halcyon days of the john came in the latter part of the nineteenth century. One writer pinpoints the target even closer, referring to 1870 as the "annus mirabilis" of the water closet. A flurry of developments led eventually to a patent in that year for J. R. Mann's "syphonic closet." It was a valveless flush toilet, so named because it worked on the principle of the syphon, the same principle that causes modern toilets to consume up to 5 gallons a flush. This development, though, only spurred a sort of democratization of the toilet and moved Victorian England toward the cloacal obsession Joyce would lament nearly fifty years later. Previously only privileged British backsides had benefit of the flush. Instead of the syphon, these earlier toilets employed valves to hold and then release the water on demand. Alexander Cummings recorded the first patent for a valve toilet in 1775. Even this was but a step in the trend, British all the way.

The French even recorded the matter linguistically. Until the eighteenth century the notion of a room reserved for relieving oneself had never occurred to the French. Like most of Europe they preferred instead a sort of glorified and encased chamber pot known as a "close stool." These were portable and were fetched by servants when necessary. French monarchs never considered this call to nature's business sufficient cause for disrupting other proceedings, and so they simply held court from these temporary thrones. The inventory of Versailles under Louis XIV included 264 such stools. When separate chambers finally did enter the picture in the mid-eighteenth century they were regarded with some suspicion. In what was considered a backhanded shot at the British they were referred to as *Cabinets et Commodities à l'anglaise*. The capitalization here preserves the original.

Meanwhile, the British had been retreating from public view to do business since at least the early fourteenth century. Castles had closets called "garderobes." (It meant wardrobe, so the euphemism came even earlier than toilets.) These closetlike rooms were on exterior walls and were connected directly by a sort of laundry chute to the moat, to water.

The great leap to all subsequent silliness came in 1596, when Sir John Harington, a godson to Queen Elizabeth, sketched detailed plans for the first flush toilet, the first ritual bathing of feces. He included the plan in his treatise "How to Reform All Unsavouray Places." This first water closet eventually was executed at the queen's palace at Richmond, where it sanctified the royal leavings. The telling aspect of Harington's essay was not so much the technology as it was a poem he appended. It recounted an incident imagined on the inventor's creation, a "draught":

> A godly father, sitting on a draught
>   To do as need and nature hath us taught,
> Mumbled (as was his manner) certain prayers,
>   And unto him the devil straight repairs,
> And boldly to revile him he begins,
>   Alleging that such prayers were deadly sins
> And that he shewed he was devoid of grace
>   To speak to God from so unmeet a place
>
> The reverent man, though at first dismayed,
>   Yet strong in faith, to Satan thus he said:
> Thou damned spirit, wicked false and lying,
>   Despairing thine own good, and ours envying,
> Each take his due, and me thou canst not hurt,
>   To God my prayer I meant, to thee the dirt.
> Pure prayer ascends to Him that high doth sit,
>   Down falls the filth, for fiends of hell more fit.

Lacking toilets and moats, common folks washed their feces to hell through a less direct route. In the earlier going, night soil was highly regarded in England, as in Japan, and was hauled to the countryside by farmers. As the cities became more densely packed and labyrinthine, everyday English folks took to dumping chamber pots in the streets.

There was even an officially sanctioned warning for this act, shouted much as a logger hollers "timber" or a golfer shouts "fore." The warning in French was *garde de l'eau*, which, by some accounts, survives in truncated form as the British euphemism "the loo."

The practice of pitching slops eventually was called into question, especially as germ theories of disease developed. The odd solution, literally a solution, involved people flushing the streets with water. The water did what it always does, drained downhill to rivers and streams. Eventually, instead of using streets the runoff was channeled to ditches, or open sewers. Those went underground and evolved into sewers as we know them. Down falls the "filth" to the lowest level of water, so by 1858 the British were actively considering moving Parliament. The stench from the Thames was disrupting business.

By the time theories of disease evolved to address all of this we already were committed to water as a key factor in the unsavory mix. No one stopped to consider the folly of stopping the spread of "filth" by mixing it with one of the planet's most mobile and mixable substances. We simply came to believe that good water comes from uphill and bad water goes downhill and away. We still believe there is such a place as "away." We believe that the way to prevent your disease from becoming my disease is to mix your feces, my feces, everyone else's feces, and several million gallons of water and then send the whole mess through a labyrinth of pipe that touches every single house in the city. This mixture eventually winds up at a big plant next to the river just outside of town where a suspect and creaking technology removes some of the feces and sends the rest downstream to the next town. People there repeat the cycle, first by drinking the water.

My house's quiet stand against four centuries of waterborne nonsense came by motor freight in a cardboard box, not much of a package considering its considerable burden. About the size of a doghouse, one person can easily lift and lash the modern composting toilet to the luggage rack of an aging Volvo. There it rode, a sort of final breath of fresh air for a device assigned a disagreeable chore.

The earlier generation of composting toilets were far more unwieldy, vaults bigger than refrigerators that took up half a basement and were fed by one or more stools upstairs. Known as the Clivus multrum, this earlier generation of composter is still available and expensive, around three thousand dollars. They are dependable and simple enough to be homemade and require little attention. Following readily available generic plans, owners can drastically cut the cost by building their own multrums out of common building materials such as concrete blocks.

The newer generation of composters uses only slightly more technology to achieve their compact size. Some even are designed as a single self-contained unit; composter, stool and all, built to stand alone in a bathroom. These units, easily installed almost anywhere, from summer cottage to urban apartment, give the user a unique and slightly lofty perch above the cooking, composting mass. In our house, however, we chose the discreet model, with a multrum or composter designed to be tucked away in the corner of a utility room or basement. The separate toilet is in the normal spot in the bathroom. This arrangement is the work of Sun-Mar Corporation of Burlington, Ontario, and is based on a design developed in Europe.

The toilet stool of this system is a common enough looking affair, originally designed for recreational vehicles. Although it does use some water, it has no tank. Instead, a valve connected to a foot pedal provides a sparse spray. It uses less than a pint per flush to rinse the bowl, compared to as much as 5 gallons per flush for the conventional variety of toilet.

The most important water savings, however, is hidden. Because the toilet's outflow is not hooked up to the general plumbing cycle, waste goes into the composter, not down the drain. This means we do not mix shit with the remaining hundreds of gallons a day that flow from the house from showers, sinks, and washing machines. This drain water, known as "gray water," is relatively unpolluted and easily filtered for reuse as irrigation water on the garden and fruit trees, something that couldn't be done if, as with conventional systems, feces were mixed with water. As Berry suggested, the solution to wastewater treatment is to not mix it with feces in the first place. Thus in summer the composting toilet saves hundreds of gallons of water each day, water that would normally have to be pumped from the well for irrigation.

Even without adding much water to feces, though, the first problem of composting human waste still is water. Human feces are about 25 percent water, and urine, of course, is wetter. The first chore of the composter is to drive this water away, a simple enough task. An internal heating element, an electric fan, and a vent pipe handle evaporation, preparing the mass for the real business at hand.

The more complex problem of composting is not the presence of water but the lack of carbon. Composting is a sort of magic biological process, really a digestion by bacteria that reduces organic wastes to simpler elements. The process is constantly occurring in nature; in fact, it can be seen as the engine of nature. It is the key link that completes the nutrient cycle. Life is a continuum, a storing of solar energy and then a conversion of nutrients to more complex forms of energy, most notably carbohydrates, proteins, and fats. These, when organized by genetic information, are what we call life, the raising of energy to growth, motion, and intelligence. Some of this life we kill and eat, some of it kills and eats us, but none of it is lost. What we call death, our own or our food's, is but the beginning of life again, a digesting or a tearing down of the complex elements life so patiently assembled. A bedeviling array of miniature plants and animals accomplish this, a whole half of life sorted by a range of specialists. This netherworld of undertakers, grave diggers, and sewer sweepers is the engine of life.

In the forest, for instance, the netherworld is a menagerie hidden in soil: invertebrates, mites, arthropods, bugs, fungus, and rot. In the forest this decay also is the work of bacteria, as it is in our guts. We think of bacteria in our systems as disease, and a few species, a handful, perform just that chore. But the human gut contains literally thousands of species of bacteria. Twenty percent of the volume of human feces is bacteria. Each of us flushes away about ten trillion individual bacteria a day.

In compost, bacteria do the work of digestion. Given time, all organic material will decay to its elements, but composting is a hypercharging of this process. Making it work right requires some tricks. Human waste is mostly nitrogen, but proper composting requires twenty times as much carbon as nitrogen. Luckily there are a variety of readily available waste products such as leaves, straw, or sawdust that easily correct the ratio. Most composting toilets, however, use common peat moss, about a cup a day per person, to balance the carbon-nitrogen mix.

My particular composter is a three-part device that sits in my utility room at one end of the house's first floor. The toilet is on the second floor in the bathroom and discharges through a short pipe directly into the composter. Inside there is a small plastic drum about the size of a beer keg that holds the peat moss and the offerings of the toilet, dispensed through a small trap door at the top of the drum. Every third day I use a crank mounted on the outside of the composter to rotate the drum about five revolutions, then I add the necessary amount of peat moss. This aerates and mixes the compost. Every month or so I rotate the drum backward to discharge some of the compost into a tray about the size of a case of soda cans that is located just below the drum. The compost sits in the tray to decay further until the next emptying cycle. The compost in the tray can be emptied directly onto the soil as fertilizer. In an ideal operation the composter produces a full tray every one to six months.

Below the tray the bottom of the composter's housing forms a sort of pan, the device's third element. Here excess water gathers; it is heated so that it evaporates through the vent pipe.

In theory these three parts work together to produce the magic. The bacteria go to work, greatly reducing the volume of wastes to rich fertilizer. The decay heat produces internal temperature in the mass of about 140 degrees Fahrenheit, which kills the pathogens. What water is present evaporates clean to the wind. In theory. Of course it doesn't take much imagination to see in all of this the potential for error with truly spectacular consequences.

As soon as the house's progress would allow it, we unpacked the toilet and the multrum and set the assembly to its task. This milestone of considerable significance largely awaited the arrival of Trusty Dave and his backhoe to install an underground water line from the well a couple of hundred feet uphill to the house. In due course, just as we were abandoning our apartment and moving in, this happened. Then we turned a tap on some pipes I had soldered together and our house stood plugged into the pressurized flow of a primary and sustaining element.

Of course we celebrated. Water is never appreciated properly until one goes without it, or has to carry it in 5-gallon plastic buckets. We drank some. We washed down some dust. We set the toilet to its business. I loosely followed the manufacturer's instructions as to the composter's start-up, then moved on to more agreeable chores.

In a matter of a few weeks a nasty stench settled on the house, so we called Burlington, Ontario, on our newly installed telephone and had a tense discussion with the multrum's makers. The theory relayed to me by the consultant on the other end was that my composter was not yet composting, even three weeks into its use. The consultant cheerfully advised patience. Of course his brand new house didn't reek like a Porta-John, so he could more objectively ruminate on the mysteries of unseen biological processes. I called him on this with some rather sharp criticisms. He finally hinted that maybe some of this problem was my fault.

I cooled, then had to agree he was right, that my casual scan of the instruction manual had overlooked certain steps that proved vital. I learned then that one does not so much manufacture compost as capture it, that the operative bacteria must be collected from nearby fertile soil and husbanded much as if one were preparing a sort of bacteriological zoo. Compost is not the construction, but rather the passing of culture. One does not simply plug a composter in like a toaster and assume it will work.

So I collected. With a shovel I gathered bits of soil from around particularly fecund looking plots in the garden, old black stuff with plenty of fat nightcrawlers and steamy rotted leaves. I stole bacteria from the garden's compost pile, some from beneath the nearby trees, and, just to be safe, some from soil in houseplants. It was a convocation of diverse envoys of the netherworld, a gathering of the forces of decay. The collection went to the composter along with a box of baking soda to absorb the fragrance of past sins. In a couple of days the stench died, and again I forget the whole matter. Big mistake.

Biological processes can be slow and subtle, unlike mechanical artifice. They come equipped with no warning lights. They are complex beyond our imagination, sophisticated and creative. Like the most elegant of computers they are self-correcting, at least to a degree, patching over disturbances with a wide range of tools. Sometimes they even hide the symptoms when we have badly screwed them up. Forests are particularly good at this. After an area is logged, new growth often proliferates, despite the fact that logging has greatly damaged the underlying web of life—the fungus, the bugs, the decay, the nutrient cycle—that supports the forest. Often this damage will not become evident for a century, when it is far too late to repair or even remember the original sin.

Evidence of screwups accumulates much faster in the case of a composting toilet. The biological reaction of aerobic decay requires a bit of carbon, a bit of nitrogen from organic matter, a range of digesting bacteria to do the work, oxygen, and just a bit of moisture. Just a bit. During the months when I neglected the composter, it built up way too much moisture. Despite my fresh addition of bacteria, my composter stopped composting, at least aerobically. Had I known what to look for, signs of this sad development were everywhere inside the drum, but there were two obstacles to my noticing the problem. First, I harbored the same squeamishness most of us do in dealing with feces. I simply was reluctant to pay close attention to whatever was going on in there, so I treated it like a machine. But second, the manufacturer apparently shared the same squeamishness. The owner's manual for the composter was inexcusably fastidious. It lacked a vivid description as to what the inside of a living composter ought to look like.

There is an alternative to aerobic digestion. Anaerobic decay, decay by bacteria that work in the absence of oxygen, which kicks in when aerobic digestion fails. Anaerobic digestion is slower and colder; it produces ammonia, methane, and hydrogen sulfide gas as by-products. Those who suffered through high school chemistry will remember these gases were highly regarded by adolescent chemists for their ability to clear the chemistry lab and, if the reaction was particularly vigorous, the whole school, of students.

The bubble built slowly in my composter. The mass cooled, the gases built undetected. Composting stopped, so the volume grew and liquids pooled slowly. I should have seen it coming but didn't. Then one day—Christmas Eve—the bubble burst. Because a drain pipe had plugged, the liquid, mostly stale urine, overflowed from the composter onto the utility room floor. When I attacked the offending mass inside the composter, stirring it to see what had gone wrong, it released the trapped rotten-egg gases, greatly augmenting the effects of the stream of foul water. I imagined the composter was nearing the proverbial point of total disaster: the contents had risen almost enough to become entangled in the ventilating fan.

Thus, on a hushed winter's night, my time came to overcome my squeamishness about feces. This was my problem to deal with. I was the only person I knew with a composting toilet. There was no one to call to fix it. On Christmas Eve I shoveled shit.

With a wheelbarrow and shovel, I unloaded the stalled composter and placed the offensive mass in an outdoor compost pile to slowly decompose. I will forego vivid descriptions of the chore, but I must note that I suddenly understood and sympathized fully with the Victorian use of the word "filth." With the composter empty, I sumped out the utility room, then disassembled and cleaned the plugged drain lines. None of these operations looked a bit like the photos in the manufacturer's color brochure, full of people in squeaky-clean street clothes standing next to gleaming, pristine versions of my own composter.

Then I installed a heater and thermometer next to the composter and monitored it until the ambient and now odorless air attained an even temperature. I mail-ordered a box of bugs, a commercial collection of bacteria known as a "compost innoculant." I insulated a pipe that had been causing excess condensation. For weeks afterward I measured the composter's progress as if it were the heartbeat of a sick friend.

Still I couldn't make the offending device compost, so eventually I called the manufacturer and we had an interesting chat. I described my situation.

"Oh, that's awful," said Mike Wilkinson, marketing manager for Sun-Mar. "What does it look like?"

What does he mean, "What does it look like?" It looks like what it is. It looks like shit. (Any notions of delicacy concerning this matter had long since evaporated with my last whiff of hydrogen sulfide gas.)

"No, no. I mean what's its consistency?"

I told him it was consistently foul and like shit.

"There's your problem. It is supposed to have the consistency of a wrung-out sponge."

Good god, there it was, a clean and simple descriptive phrase that changed the whole complexion of a battle I had now waged for two months. "Like a wrung-out sponge." I knew instantly what that meant and understood just as surely that the interior of the composter had never before achieved that state. Wilkinson then told me exactly how to achieve it, and I did. Since that day the composter has been performing well, mostly without odor. Now I can say I am glad I have it. Yet I almost abandoned the whole project because of a poorly written owner's manual, a problem Sun-Mar itself acknowledges. Shortly after I bought my composter the company rewrote its owner's manual. Wilkinson acknowledged that the earlier version was "terrible."

I guess there is some justice in all of this, a lesson in the value of craft. For lack of a cleanly written descriptive phrase a writer was forced to spend a day shoveling shit. It should happen to all of us writers. Work counts.

In England the guys hired to muck out privies were called "gongfermors," later "night men." Highly paid, and why shouldn't they be, they advertised their services on elaborately engraved cards, as if they were practitioners of a valued craft. They were. Now I feel an odd sort of accomplishment, as if I have been initiated into their ranks. I have survived the shoveling of shit, my own, and it's not that bad. I can make a composter work. I have no doubt now that I could start a new one working in a matter of days. I learned, and I urgently recommend anyone who will listen to undergo the same experience.

Look at the alternative. When the county health department made me bury an unneeded septic system in addition to installing my composting toilet, the officials were not being overly bureaucratic. They were facing a reality. Composters are fine, in theory, but they must be attended. They must be cared for responsibly, as if they mattered. Their owners must accept some obligation, something most people seem less willing to do. Composters can go bad, and when they do their owners generally fall back on uninspected and unreliable septic systems to pass their failings along, downstream or down into subsurface aquifers.

Even septic tanks can be reliable forms of sewage disposal. A septic tank system usually consists of a large concrete tank, generally at least 1,000 gallons, and several hundred feet of drain field downstream of the tank. The wastewater from a house goes directly into the tank, where solids settle to the bottom and decay anaerobically. The outlet is at the top, so only water runs into the drain field, really a long buried pipe punched full of holes. The water drains through the holes into the soil, which naturally filters the water as it percolates to the surface and evaporates or drains down to subterranean aquifers.

Problems can occur when owners fail to have accumulated solids removed from the tank, causing solids to enter the drain field and overtax the filtering ability of the soil. Also, poorly designed drain fields often allow wastewater to escape to nearby wells, streams, and lakes. Septic tanks often fail. They are, in most rural areas, the leading threat to water quality. They pollute water with their excess load of nutrients, both from human wastes and from the phosphates from detergents. They are fed by flush toilets, so water is wasted and water is polluted. Septic systems malfunction from neglect, but their maintenance is difficult to enforce, far-flung, buried, and diverse as they are.

The solution our society chooses for our individual neglect is centralized sewer systems. One hundred million households daily bathe their feces in 80 billion gallons of water and then send it to a septic tank or one of 15,000 sewage treatment plants. The grossest of the pollution is removed, but never all, so the nitrogen, phosphorus, and carbon flow downhill to kill our rivers.

The alternative is to trust individuals to attend to their own shit, and remarkably we are not up to the task. The government is right about this. Given the evidence, the bureaucrats are justified in keeping us as dependent as we are on a centralized sewer system, a nation of individuals diapered by a central authority. In this light the care and feeding of a composting toilet, no matter how wretched the learning process, becomes a matter of pride. I am a night man proud of my craft, a turdmeister, a gongfermor of the first water.

I am not sure the composter ever really was fixed, but I think it was. I am almost sure of it, but by now I have learned enough from the house to allow for other possibilities. Perhaps it was I who was fixed. Perhaps the house and I simply entwined our knowledge and prejudice until we grew together. I cannot honestly say. I understand only that my judgment has changed, so I have no confidence in reproducible results when evaluating something seemingly as objective as a smell. Sensations become subject to a new sense of one's life.

I am pretty certain that the toilet started to work, though. The liquids began evaporating. The foul odor disappeared. Its internal mysteries, depths I now probed with curiosity, not revulsion, began to steam and cook. Its contents underwent transformation. I no longer consider the toilet a necessary burden, a sacrifice to save water. I actually like the thing.

I cannot pinpoint exactly when it happened, but the fetid, acrid burn of filth faded. In its place came the fecund aroma of rot, the very smell a farmer knows as moist and promising soil. Life cycles transform decay to growth. Bacteria transformed my shit to something I value.

This is what becomes of my life's leavings, so a part of my life no longer goes away. It is here with me, so in a new way I inhabit my home wound back to the cycle of it all. The compost goes to the garden, then I eat and round it goes. Rot smells like soil, so I uncover a long-buried truth, lost to our culture like the ancient wisdom of craft. This truth is buried in language. The words "humus" and "human" spring from the same root, the same as "humble." Our language encodes the circle of our lives. Our lives can again break the code to live it.

I am low, coarse, and humble. I shit and shovel shit. I am of the soil. Daily I spring from it. Daily I return to it. Like building, this is how I reclaim my life, by reclaiming control of it.

Power

At Union Station in Washington, D.C., there are six statues honoring what were regarded at the time of their building as the earth's greatest inventions. The homage to electricity says this:

> Carrier of light and power. Devourer of time and space. Greatest servant of man. Thou has put all things under his feet.

October's weather went easy on us. The rains left. Usually fall rains come here only in the first week or so of September, then it's dry and easy until winter sets in. Each day dawned crisp blue, the very sort of days to comfort the owner, builder, and occupant of a roofless, windowless house. The windows were on order but were delayed, so there was not much we could do about the vacant holes other than a temporary fix. One day Tracy stapled some clear plastic over a couple, and until the wind blew it off our nights were a little warmer. Mostly we wanted the plastic windows to seal out the dust pushed everywhere out of the bare gravel around the house's hole. Grit in our coffee. Grit in our sleeping bags. Grit to remind even our nights that our days were strange.

Otherwise progress was coming fast. Trace and I spent all of our days, every day, attacking the long list of obstacles between us and a house. Here and there the shell had become criss-crossed with the studded skeletons of internal walls. Because the structure had been timber-framed there were no internal, load-bearing walls, so we could frame the interior with almost whimsical abandon, quirky jigs and jags relieved of structural burdens. The bedroom wall did not even run all the way to the ceiling, the better to let heat and light from the clerestory windows careen through the space.

But light and heat and the attendant conveniences would come later. Now our nights were dark and on the edge of cold. At the end of work each day I unplugged the 50-foot extension cord from the table saw or drill and plugged it into the house's only lamp. There was no wiring inside the house yet, so our electricity came from a temporary service box the power company had installed near the house. At night we carried this lamp about the house lanternlike, as the need arose. Mostly it was dark, and we ignored the squirrels and woodrats running through our bedroom. We had a phone, running water in a makeshift sink, and a refrigerator. We lived on sandwiches or camp food or an occasional burger at the Piney Woods. Life was much like camping out.

With the windows on hold, we attended to the roof. We had ordered a roof that is deep forest green. The color was permanently manufactured into the roof material: long ribbed sheets of steel. Both color and substance spring from the forest nearby. The color matches as closely as possible the green of the needles of the ponderosa pine that are the real shelter of this home. We wanted our house to fade into the trees that made it, an illusion as necessary as most, an illusion we achieved with a forest-green roof.

We chose a steel roof—a sort of modernizing of old-fashioned steel barn roofs—because it is a virtual certainty that the nearby forests will burn at least once every couple of decades. In dry-land mountain forests a roof with a meaningful thirty-year guarantee must be fireproof. If one were to overlay a map of the forests of Montana with maps of each year's forest fires, year by year, piddling fires most years, raging infernos in drought years, every three decades or so, then eventually the maps would coincide. We live in forests so forged by fire that their continued health has become dependent on allowing, not suppressing, fire. It is a measure of our species' advancing wisdom that we are coming to understand that fire suppression is ultimately of no consequence. The will of these forests to burn far outstrips our ability to prevent it, so, despite the billions of dollars we send to the task of fighting fire, these trees will burn.

The human residents of these forests have no choice but to design a house to withstand fire, just as residents farther west design them to withstand earthquakes. One learns to roll with this particular punch. It's a relatively easy matter of installing a steel roof instead of shakes or shingles and minding the buildup of brush and dead trees immediately around the house. Besides, the steel sounds nice in the rain.

I remember the morning of laying the roof because of the day's sure colors: the green of the roof and the trees; the faultless blue of the sky; Tracy's flag of red hair furling around shafts of sunlight. She was shaky at first, nervous about ladders and heights, but soon she got her roof legs. She wore an apron stuffed full of the hex-headed screws that cinch a steel roof to the deck. I tipped the 20-foot-long sheets of steel into place, squared them with the world, then checked that they sat properly capped and lapped to the last sheet, watertight. Then Trace walked the lines of the roof with a hand-held drill, setting a screw every foot, stitching the steel.

To most, closing the deal on a house is a real estate ritual held at a bank downtown, but in a real world, houses would be closed by laying a roof tight.

In our mythology a house is shelter, a necessity, but this seems less the essence of the matter all the time. So much has been layered on the core of necessity that this central purpose has become invisible. A house is shelter the way a car is transportation. It seems more accurate to tie a house to convenience than to necessity. Our modern notion of house evolved with the relatively new idea of comfort, not necessity. We build houses that make us comfortable. A house is simply a bundle of conveniences. Heat is not necessary. Our species survived without heated houses for thousands of years in climates far worse than Montana's. Running water. Electric lights. Stereo systems, dishwashers, doorbells, and trash mashers.

Hidden behind virtually all of these is the notion of power, or, by its other name, electricity. Literally hidden, a fact that dictates part of the logic of the progression of a house. Before one hides its bones with the skin, one threads wires among the bones.

Household electricity is a simple matter, artless really, a construct of unrelenting logic. This realization first served as an open invitation to me, because I am stubborn and cheap. Electricians are expensive. Like wizards, they behave as if they guard a series of secrets, arcane and inscrutable. The institutionalization of this is a document known as the National Electrical Code, a tract properly regarded as religious. It is designed to insulate not electricity but the electrical priesthood by obscuring a series of relatively simple rules in obtuse language. It excludes and then enforces its distance with fear. Electricity is invisible, a terrifying god that can leap from wires to punish infidels with pain and harm. Better to call a priest than to mess with this.

Happily, there is a movement of electrical protestants. There are books written to translate the electrical code into English. The rules are straightforward, simple, and consistent, so anyone with a reasonable grasp of the language and logic can become an electrical lay priest. Montana, bless its iconoclastic, cussed soul, even recognizes this in its electrical codes. To pass an electrical inspection, construction projects need the blessings of a licensed electrical priest who must be paid for the dispensation. There is, however, an explicit exemption in Montana for the owner-builder. Here you can wire your own home, legally blessed by the state.

One wires a house by hiding power in walls.

Power is straightforward and without ambiguity. A simple matter of going from point A to point B. Any issues of judgment are settled by the code, which lays down a set of conventions and rules designed to limit the possibilities to the ultrasafe. Kitchens have two general circuits. Major appliances get their own circuits. Outdoor outlets and those near sinks and tubs require ground-fault protection. Twenty-amp circuits take number 12 wire, and green is ground the world around. Stuff like that.

The task of designing a house's wiring system begins with an understanding of the basic circuits. Think of a number of lamps plugged into a single extension cord. This is analogous to a circuit. Knowing the number of lamps and the current drawn by each lamp allows one to get a big enough extension cord to handle the load without overheating, a factor determined by the diameter of wire in the cord. One could calculate all of this by precisely pinpointing and assessing each appliance and circuit, but this is unnecessary except in highly specialized cases. Electricians have over the years developed standards for wiring designed to accommodate the average house so that designing a house's wiring system is a matter of looking up and understanding these standards. Cole and Wing provide a thorough discussion of the issue in their book *From the Ground Up.* For my house I used a pamphlet-sized guide called *Wiring Simplified*, by H. P. Richter and W. C. Schwan. Such guides are available from most building supplies stores.

Once the broad outline of a house's wiring is understood, then installation simply becomes a matter of drilling holes in studs and pulling the wire through the holes. Most residential installations require no conduit, special pipe designed to contain and protect wire. The wire is sufficiently sheltered in the walls. Mine is a small house with few electrical gee-gaws beyond the basics. Still, it required about 500 feet of wire. The national average is 750 feet.

The wire pulls to junction boxes—once metal, now plastic—about the size of two packs of cigarettes and mounted so their open faces are flush with the surface of the finished walls. The boxes will contain either a plug socket, a switch, or a fixture, which determines the array of incoming and outgoing wires and subsequently how those are tied together. Once the function of a box and its relationship to the rest of the circuitry is understood, there are three ways to wire it: wrong; right but inefficiently; and right. In the last case the circuit works, is safe, and uses the least amount of material to get the job done.

Experienced electricians can wire a house in a day. I had never wired one before, so it took me two. My work passed a safety inspection, though. I turned it on, and it was ready to do its work. Like most people, I was ready to bury it in the walls and forget the whole business.

On paper, the wiring of my house did not begin as a mundane matter. I had planned the job in winter before the first shovel turned. Spurred by some alternative energy catalogs and the earth-saving fervor that months of hard-core dreaming could bring, I planned a solar electrical system, New Age and clean, free energy from the sun. Such systems can work for the average home owner, especially in the West where sunshine is abundant. The underlying technology is that of photo-voltaics, the process of directly converting the sun's light to direct-current, low-voltage electricity, the sort of electricity that powers the systems in a car or in a simple flashlight.

Direct-current, or DC, power is immediately usable in a house for such loads as lighting, fans, and specially made appliances. Many household uses, however, require alternating current, or AC. Devices called inverters bridge that gap, converting DC to AC so that all of a house can be powered by the sun. One supplier, Real Goods of Ukiah, California, sells complete packages containing all an average home needs to convert to solar power. The package for what most Americans would consider a modest electrical load costs $5,500. There is no free lunch.

Such an enormous outlay for power, a commodity we take for granted, actually makes sense for some people. In rural areas, some houses are forced to pay enormous costs to extend power lines to remote sites. Often, solar is cheaper. Even in some sunny areas where power is exceedingly expensive, solar can make financial sense. The calculation for the rest of us, however, generally comes out the other way, at least at current rates. Real Goods, which now has about 300,000 customers and is considered one of the fastest-growing companies in the nation, lays it out this way: Amortized over a reasonable life of the equipment, a solar system yields electricity at about 35 cents per kilowatt-hour. In my neighborhood, we pay 5 cents per kilowatt-hour for power from the grid. What do I do?

The answer is not as straightforward as it seems. It is specific to place. Further, if I am to formulate a responsible answer then my questioning cannot stop at the meter.

In many ways the question of electrical power would be more clearly drawn if I did not live in the Pacific Northwest. If I lived elsewhere I would go solar, costs be damned. This because I hate coal, and in most of the nation a toaster plugs into a junction box into a wire into a meter into a bigger wire that ties it straight to a coal-fired plant.

In many ways this issue of assigning blame to energy sources according to where one lives is a meaningless exercise. Virtually all of the nation is now linked together on what is called "the grid." This means that power generated in one region of the country can quickly be transferred to another if there is a shortage. We are, in effect, one big system. While it happens to be true that most of my power comes from hydroelectric dams, there is still a huge transmission line near my house that "wheels" coal power into that hydro system, as the need arises. Still, the day-to-day uses of coal power are much higher in the rest of the nation. Further, because of the nation's unwillingness to fire up new nuclear plants and because of the unavailability of new hydro sites, most of the nation's new power, power to meet growth, comes from coal. As it stands about 57 percent of the nation's electricity comes from coal. No matter where you live, but particularly outside of the Northwest, you run your blowdryer and stereo with some coal.

Local radio newscasters in Montana issue boosterish cheers at reports of increased coal sales. Great stretches of the eastern part of the state are given over to strip mines. When sales rise, so do tax revenues, so schools and such have more money, hence the cheers. We are engaged in friendly competition with Wyoming, which generally outstrips our production, but only slightly. Montana has about one-fourth of the nation's coal reserves.

Because of this, Montana is one of the few places where a solid alliance has formed between genuine, tree-hugging, sandal-wearing environmentalists and genuine, snoose-chewing ranchers, lean of bone and red of neck. The ranchers' minds have been wonderfully concentrated by the prospects of strip mines chewing up the open range. The strip mines are winning. Their advance is driven by urban political power, people who have never seen Montana but can clearly see their toasters and all else that plugs into the flush-mounted electrical junction boxes.

Once, though, we were blessed in this exchange in that the coal was not burned here. We loaded it on trains and sent it east like a rail-borne black plague. There plants burned it and visited upon the immediate environs the sulfur dioxide, the acid rain, the soot, and the thermal pollution. The band of acid rain–killed forests, largely the spawn of coal plants, begins in the Midwest near Chicago and stretches to the populated eastern seaboard. This is the nation's coal-burning belt. There is no justice in this for the trees, but for the people there is. It was that population that plugged in the toasters in the first place.

But now the population centers are demanding that air be clean. Pollution is defined in relative terms, so the polluters are eyeing the clean air of the West as an untapped reservoir of consumptive license. The practice of exporting the coal is giving way to the practice of exporting electricity. The idea is to "site" coal-burning plants in areas with now clean air, giving the polluters wide latitude before violating urban-derived clean-air standards. One such farm of coal plants is planned for northern Nevada. In Montana we have Colstrip, Montana Power Company's coal-burning sprawl designed to wheel power out of the state.

The joke, of course, is that ultimately this sooty shell game matters not at all. It makes no difference where the coal is burned. There is no such place as away. The sulfur dioxide, nitrogen oxide, and particles are only minor irritants compared to the real menace of coal. Combustion necessarily produces carbon dioxide. It is a product, not a by-product, and cannot be filtered out. Invisibly and inexorably, carbon dioxide gathers in the atmosphere like a ghost. Now it warms our planet.

The credible body of thought emerging from the scientists studying global warming is this: We will pay for this upset of natural systems unlike any paying and pain we have heretofore considered. Coal-fired electrical plants emit more carbon dioxide per unit of energy produced than any other source of energy. At present the nation derives about a quarter of its total energy diet from coal, a percentage that is expected to rise as oil supplies deplete and abundant coal reserves pick up the slack.

Were my house burning coal I would know it, mostly by price. Coal power, especially new coal power, is expensive. My power is not. I pay roughly half what most people pay. This blessing is a gift of the federal government and of the precipitous drop to the sea of lands lying west of the continental divide. I use public power, hydropower, arguably the very power that has forged the nation's international position today. My power comes from damming rivers.

From my land I can see Lolo Creek about a mile down the gulch. It flows to the Bitterroot River and on to the Clark Fork River, Montana's largest, then to Idaho's Pend Oreille Lake, which drains to the Pend Oreille River, and finally to the Columbia. Just downstream the Columbia gathers Idaho's Snake River, so the veins of the Northwest twine for the final roily sprint to the Pacific. Not so long ago these waters were asked only to behave like veins, freighting the flow of the life of these lands. The warm Pacific air brought the rains that fed the forests, and then the rains trickled back through the living soil, through fish, rocks, and towns to weave us all together on its way to back to the sea. These waters were rife with salmon for all of their near-thousand-mile stretch through Washington, Oregon, Idaho, Montana, and British Columbia.

Then came the Great Depression and the social engineering necessary to lift it from us. One of the schemes of the FDR administration, then widely regarded as crackbrained, was the damming of the Columbia system. Considered so crackbrained that it was necessary to sell it with propaganda. We greet the spectacle of Woody Guthrie in the employ of the federal government. Guthrie—populist poet, malcontent, communist, hard traveler, father of folk music, one of my heroes—drew the task of selling the dams with song. He made up one or two songs a day and went around the Northwest singing them, stuff about honest working folks and cheap power and "Roll on, Columbia, roll on."

Roosevelt and Woody got their way, and now we have the world's largest hydroelectric system, comprising fifteen dams operated by an independent federal agency, the Bonneville Power Administration. Some historians argue it single-handedly granted the nation its present status of superpower. The rationale for this assertion lies in the timing. Some even argue that Roosevelt's motive for the dams had nothing to do with the Great Depression, more to do with a gathering storm on the Pacific rim.

The first dam, Rock Island, was started in 1933. It was followed by a string of others that gave the Northwest far more power than it could use. The solution was to attract the budding aircraft industry with the lure of dirt-cheap power for the smelting of aluminum. Just a few years later, when war flooded the Pacific, it was the aircraft industry that eventually beat the Japanese. Hydropower backed air power.

Today one can fly across this region, say, from my home in Montana to Seattle, and see this legacy evident from the air. Just out of northern Idaho the clear-cut mountains peter out to a great arid plain, now squared, or more commonly circled, to accommodate irrigation lines. Cheap power and dammed rivers allowed farmers to colonize what was a desert. On across the Cascades comes the urban sprawl of Seattle, at night seen as lights. This city grew up around cheap power and aluminum, but from the air it looks like most cities. It looks just like most, because escaping heat is not visible to the human eye.

We of the Northwest have done with cheap power what our culture does with cheap anything: We have wasted it. Most houses have radiant electric heat, arguably the single most wasteful form of heat. Many houses, especially those of the last generation, are not insulated, despite the severe climate. The power has always been too cheap to justify the expense of insulation. We waste power. So what? It doesn't come from coal. It's from hydro—cheap, clean, and forever, or so we used to think.

This is the legacy of my home and the sort of thinking that steered me away from expensive solar-generated electricity. This is what first allowed me to consider electricity simply as a bundle of conveniences pulled through the wire in my walls. I rejected my elaborate plans for photovoltaics. This problem's solved, now on to the next. And yet in the shell of a house, as I drilled holes and pulled wires, the wires pulled hard, as if tied to a large weight. Then I remembered Pat Ford.

I had known Pat for years in my ramblings about the West. He is part of a determined but small group of environmentalists waging war in the Neanderthal political world of Idaho. The thinking of the state is prodevelopment, rock-ribbed Mormon and brutally conservative, yet the state contains some of the nation's most pristine lands. People like Pat fight for them, a bit like daily wading into a bare-knuckled street brawl for virtue in a red-light district.

I first met Pat under odd circumstances. He and I were both enrolled in the same writing seminar. Career ladder stuff. For a budding writer it was a big deal, yet Pat did an odd thing. He showed for the first night's social activities, chatted with folks as expected, and then simply disappeared. He said he had to leave, left almost in a claustrophobic panic, with the urgency one sees in a life's watershed decision, and it was. Pat said he couldn't go on with writing and pursuing that line of work, that he felt compelled to return to Idaho. He couldn't think of writing and his career when he knew all the salmon were dying.

To the cultures of the Pacific Northwest, the Native peoples, the salmon filled the same niche as the buffalo farther east. They were the foundation. Time was measured by their migrations. Spiritual metaphors were cast in their bodies. They were food, god, and art. Their annual migrations—salmon live in the ocean and migrated through the Columbia's web of rivers to spawn—took them well into both Montana and Idaho, sometimes 900 miles. They no longer run in Montana. Dams built even before the federal Columbia system emerged shut them out long ago. In Idaho the runs remained, largely because of Rube Goldberg–type measures that now seem only to prolong the agony.

Once I was wading a small creek high in central Idaho's Sawtooth Range, a creek you could jump across, and a salmon splashed, a fish as big as a pig. It was near Redfish Lake, named for the salmon hordes it once sheltered, an alpine lake set in sharp mountains. In 1989 a biologist spotted one single redd, that is, a salmon nest in Redfish Lake. No adult fish, just one nest. Redfish Lake is where they spawn, and careful counting that year had found only two sockeye salmon pass Lower Granite Dam, the last of eight dams sockeye must pass in their 850-mile run up the Columbia system. In 1988 twenty-two sockeye passed the dam, then the pair in 1989. In 1990, there were none. Another salmon, the chinook, is only slightly better off. The life has gone out of the Columbia's headwaters.

Crash-cart biologists called to the scene, some of the same people who are pulling the California condor back from the edge of the grave, say that it is too late for the salmon of the Columbia system.

The dams killed the salmon, studies confirm. True, the dams were built with fish ladders, devices to allow salmon to migrate upstream. Some fish don't make it up the ladders, but some do. Incredibly, though, no one thought to complete the cycle. While adults make it upstream, there they naturally die after spawning. The juveniles, however, can't make it back to the ocean: They are ground up in generating turbines at dams, or they succumb to the disease, high temperatures, and introduced predators in the slack-water reservoirs behind the dams.

Writer Timothy Egan has defined the Northwest as anywhere a salmon can reach, a satisfying definition rooted in biogeographical reality. Yet by Egan's definition the Northwest has ceased to exist. Just so. It is this very definition of a place that is at stake.

People like Pat Ford are pleading with the federal government to recognize this sad fact by affording the salmon the protection of the Endangered Species Act, and yet the political resistance is enormous. It was relatively easy, for instance, to disrupt segments of the region's economy by listing the spotted owl as endangered, because that only curtails timber harvest, an important part of the economy, but just a part. All of us understand that the demise of the salmon is wound up in *all* of the region's economy. Killing salmon is the cost of cheap power, and cheap power made us what we are. The salmon could be returned simply by leaving those dams open during those days of the year when the juveniles head downstream, by returning a part of the year to the life of a river. Such a move, however, would cost us power, lots of it, just as the region is running short of electricity. Both Seattle and Portland, Oregon, are growing by great leaps, so new houses must have wires. So the salmon die.

I write this to the hum of a computer ultimately plugged into Lower Granite Dam. The people running the dam never will read or hear me say that I would pay twice as much for power willingly if they would only open the dam and let the salmon pass. They won't read this. They will read my electrical meter and hear me ask for more, so I cannot speak to them as I speak to you. I must speak through my meter. If I ask for more power, they will send it. That's the way America works. They will grind up the salmon, strip-mine the coal, poison the planet, and send power through the wires.

Wiring the house provided an odd refuge. The rest of the project had become frustrating. Although there was rapid progress, the work was perplexing. The house had begun to assert a sense of itself, almost as if it were developing its own set of standards and holding me accountable to them. It wasn't as if there were a right or wrong way of doing things. It was as if everything I did I knew could have been done better. The house always stood before me, almost like a kid in the second-hand clothes that were all a down-and-out father could afford. Like a beautiful kid whose gift was being squandered in the hands of the wrong father.

At the same time, our lives were hard. Trace and I had been working ten- and twelve-hour days for months, most of them strung together weekday and weekend, no days off. It was not drudgery, nor was I held to this schedule by anything other than my will and the onrush of winter. Even if nature had not imposed this deadline I would have worked this way, simply because there was nothing else I would rather be doing. It was good and necessary work. Still, by this time, by late October, both of us were through and through tired.

Mike and Bruce had left us with something of a shell, a sort of exoskeleton of a house. We had to fill in all the details: framing interior walls and doors, hanging and bracing details like ceiling fans, bathtubs, and shelves, finishing the sheathing of exterior walls, sheathing them all over again with a special insulating board, covering all of that again with pine siding, framing braces of kitchen cabinets—all jobs that become virtually invisible in the final house. I barely remember doing them now, but then it seemed like a thousand chores, most involving heavy pieces of lumber held in place by long, hard-fought nails, most driven in awkward positions.

Many times I would find myself falling into a fit of cursing, hanging upside down by a rafter someplace, trying to drive a spike at an angle as the dust and dirt fell into my face. Then the spike would hit a knot and bend, and I'd start all over again.

There was no escaping the work or the shell of it each night. We slept in it. Hard days. Nights dark and cold.

A wiring job either works or it doesn't, and if it doesn't, you fix it. When you fix it, you fix a small, easier corner for your life. It is so richly satisfying to send home the final screw in a switch carefully plotted and wired. You flip the switch and for the first time a light glows. The lights came on in our house like this, one by one, and our lives got a bit easier. We could consider luxuries such as sitting at night amid the sawdust piles and rubble to read, quiet time to let the brain unjangle. Or in the middle of the night we could make our way to the bathroom without carrying a lamp and a 50-foot extension cord tether, like spacepeople.

The house was a mess; the remedies for all of its problems were fuzzy in my mind. But a light switch flips crisp and cocksure. Here in these lights was something I could fix. I am programmed to fix things. It is what I mean by being male.

Maybe this is what my father finds in his work as an electrician. I hear tradesmen today call electricians "sparkies," but I learned to call them "narrow-backs." My old man wasn't a common sort of house electrician, a trade regarded by him and his peers as the equivalent of a house pet. He was a lineman, one of those guys who hiked up 80-foot power poles walking on short steel spurs, bucking off with a scare strap up top, and handling 13,000 volts in his rubber-gloved hand. He ran the wires from the houses to the dams. "Narrow-backs" is a derogatory term.

Today he doesn't have much money, probably not enough to retire, so he works now and again as a narrow-back. Sometimes. He has a big I.Q. and seems drawn to the convoluted and arcane logic of the trade. I talk to him on the phone a couple of times a year. When I last did, I said I had built myself a house, and right away he wanted to know if I'd wired it. I said I had.

"Good for you. It's not so hard."

I was raised to understand that to be male is to fix things. When switches are broken or lives are broken, then you get your tools and you fix them. That's your job, particularly when what is broken is hurting someone close to you. The job is to make lives easier. If you have to string a power line, take over a corporation, run for office, or build a dam to do it, if that's what it takes, you do it. If winter is coming and people in your charge must be protected from the cold, you do it.

Tracy tried hard to learn to hit a nail. She would take the hammer I bought her and swing and swing and swing, but somehow she never got it to look just right, and the nails would mostly bend or go home only after a dozen or so swats when two should have done the job. She'd get mad as hell about this at first, near tears. I know she wanted to blame it all on male conspiracy, that somehow we had built these hammers in the manner of a secret handshake to prevent women from using them, and then finally she said, "I've decided construction is really a male world."

She's right. It is, and she's not angry about this anymore, more philosophical. She doesn't think it's okay for house building to be a male preserve, but she's accepted it. I'm not sure we should accept it, but it seems to be remaining that way. Much of this has to do with an odd snobbery of our people. Parents do not encourage their daughters to enter the building trades. Fathers do not even encourage their sons to do so. Always there is that notion of doing something better with your life. I was raised among people who built houses, and still the trades were always held out to me as a job to fall back on when all else failed.

I find this odd today. I have spent my life working with writers, preachers, congresspeople, executives, doctors, and lawyers, some fine, some honorable, some performing necessary work. And still I believe one of the finest statements to be made about a person is, "He is a good carpenter." It is craft. It is discipline. It is art. It is a calling so consuming that mainstream society hears little from them, that they are absorbed and independent enough to form a subculture, still a male subculture.

During the last decades, when women began asserting their rights, their target was the mainstream culture and the notion of "advancement." Such are the biases of our culture, and the trades have suffered because of it. The subtleties of building require a grasp of the sublime, a grasp that does not come easy to the men I know. The trades need more feminine sensibilities. Men are more comfortable in fixing things. A switch is either right or wrong; most of building is not that way, but wiring is.

One cannot learn to swing a hammer. I cannot fix Tracy's swing. She of all people should understand this. She was trained in dance, and to hammer is to dance. At some point when you're a kid a hammer gets stuck in your hand, and you flail away as kids will do and then you cut your peace with the thing. Then you're a gangly near-adult working your way through school on summer jobs and you one day find that the hammer swings clean, comes from clear over your head in a fluid unconscious arc that finds the head of the nail full-force like a smart bomb. A 16-penny nail goes home, so the dance is done. No applause. Just a paycheck, carpal tunnel syndrome, and a job done workmanlike.

We are artless and linear and male in our fixing of things, so each generation fixes the fixes. Now we are left with a patchwork of patches we call technology. When our rivers become polluted with sewage, we design ever deeper layers of artifice to treat sewage, to extract the water from the shit. It never occurs to us to stop bathing feces in the first place, as if we have inherited from our fathers the rules by which we must proceed.

So it is with electricity. When we need more, we make more. When that begins to poison us, we design devices to "scrub" the resulting pollutants. When some of us see even that as a problem, we then turn to "clean" sources of electricity. We buy expensive solar panels and believe we have solved the problem. I headed in that direction when I thought of Pat Ford's salmon, so early in my planning notes there are pages of calculations of expected electrical load matched against a fitting array of photovoltaic panels, storage batteries, charge controllers, and inverters.

The people who sell photovoltaic systems report a common event: A potential customer demands a solar system on grounds that he is sick and tired of paying $100 a month to some utility. Never mind that a solar system to meet such a load would cost more than ten thousand dollars. The illumination from this story comes in our identification of the problem: that the evil lies in utilities and their greedy or mysterious methods of generating electricity. We believe the problem has nothing to do with our own use. If a household's power bill exceeds $100 a month, that's not the fault of the utility. The household is using too much.

Although we like to think of our difficulties as a series of ever more complex threads, all current problems that plague the planet, the problems we label "environmental," distill to two simple facts, the multipliers in a filthy and oppressive equation. First, there are too many people. Second, some of those people, those in the developed world, particularly those in the United States, are mindless hogs of those commodities humans use to sustain life.

According to statistics compiled by the Worldwatch Institute, per capita energy consumption in the United States is about six times as great as in countries such as Mexico, Turkey, and Brazil. The average American consumes thirty-five times as much energy as the average Indian or Indonesian, 140 times as much as the average Bangladeshi. Yet this is not simply a factor of standard of living alone. The average American consumes almost twice as much energy as the average West

German, much more than twice as much as the average Japanese. The emphasis here is not so much on "hog" as it is on "mindless."

The giver of electric light in our world was from the beginning and still is the cheap incandescent light bulb Edison invented. Yet it is only incidentally a giver of light because it is a primitive device far more suited to giving heat. Eighty percent of the energy consumed by the average light bulb wafts away as heat. Further, the heat is destructive to the bulb itself, making it relatively short-lived. One wonders why they are still with us, particularly because alternatives are now so readily available.

The logical replacement for the common incandescent bulb is a device known as the compact fluorescent. It is a simple downscaling of the large fluorescent tubes used for office and factory lighting. Models are available, however, that use fluorescent material that yields a warmer, incandescent-like light, not the cadaverous hues of office lighting. Coupled with a small, built-in electronic ballast, the ancillary device that converts electricity to a form fluorescent lights use, the compacts are not much larger than the standard light bulb. They are designed to screw directly into incandescent sockets. Several brands and varieties rest on the shelves of hardware stores in Lolo, Montana, and most other small and large towns. Mail-order sources abound.

Each bulb costs from fifteen to twenty-five dollars, a shocking figure, but there are calculations to be made. To begin with, the bulb uses about a quarter of the energy of an incandescent to yield exactly the same amount of light. This is a matter of conservation, not of sacrifice. Because of their lower heat, compact fluorescents last longer than incandescents, much longer, about 10,000 hours of burning time, compared to 500 to a 1,000 hours for an incandescent. Together these factors yield a savings on the low end of about twenty dollars per bulb over the lifetime of the compact fluorescent. The low end is my end, where power generation is cheap unless you are a salmon. On average in the country the savings would be more like forty dollars per bulb, compared to the cost of buying and burning incandescents.

Social savings are more spectacular, considering that about one-fourth of all electricity generated goes to lighting. Over its lifetime a single compact fluorescent offsets the burning of about 528 pounds of coal and its attendant release of a ton of carbon dioxide. Energy expert Amory Lovins suggests that simply replacing one incandescent with the new bulbs in every American household would immediately shut down one nuclear plant. Over its lifetime, a compact fluorescent saves the equivalent of a barrel of oil. If we converted the five hundred million light bulbs in residences in this country, the United States would instantly become an energy-exporting nation.

All of this is speculation, though, and likely will remain so. These problems are not on the national mind, nor seen in our houses. The dead salmon and coal plants are elsewhere, objectified and removed by the power lines, the hidden umbilical cord.

At first the energy carried by the wires in my house was my own. That 500 feet of wire pulls hard through the holes in the studs of the walls. Sometimes on a long, convoluted run, I'd thread the wire through and then sit on the floor, brace my feet, and pull for all I was worth, trying to free enough wire to reach the next box, all the time counting wires and working out the logical loops in my brain. Then the plasterboard came and the wires were buried in the walls. Then I followed with a belt full of tools and a box full of switches and plug sockets, tying the whole system together, testing logic, and then tying the system to the bigger system: the grid. Doing this invokes the rare thrill of probing a metal screwdriver around live wires bigger in diameter than a thumb. These big wires, the main leads to the house, were hot and fused at 200 amps, a potentially deadly dose of power.

I already had run afoul of lesser circuits from time to time, the 20-amp stuff. I'd poked a screwdriver carelessly or forgotten that the invisible power, the unseen tyrant, was present and awake. Then there'd come a bang and a great spark, the smell of ozone in the air. These accidental shorts always scare me witless, although they're usually harmless. The pyrotechnics occur when a tool completes the connection from a hot wire to a ground, which is a sort of built-in safety in most circuits. The short makes smoke and sparks, but the idiot who triggered it gets no shock. Still, it focuses the mind, especially when one's tools are tripping among the high amperage power. I like it.

I like the intensity and finality of all of it, the surety of making lights work and fixing things. I like the warm glow of compact fluorescents in every socket in my house. Our heritage is of comfort and technology, and I will not shy from it. At the same time there builds in one an awareness of where those wires lead. A life lived close to its sources is a contemplation of the trees and all that they protect. This contemplation teaches a broader notion of comfort and makes the invisible visible. In it I can see Pat Ford's face, the dead salmon, and the coal smoke stinging the air. This too is about comfort. I am uncomfortable with the killing my life has done, even when it occurs in distant rivers behind dams I never have seen. Uncomfortable.

I mean to claim no virtue or moral high ground in this discomfort. At times I wish it would go away, that I could sedate its incessant beating with drugs or diversions or even the American drug of choice, the most highly evolved tool of the tyrant's wires: the television, the device for making an unreal world visible. This is the world most Americans see. The average television hums away seven hours a day, chewing through 40,000 watt-hours a month (color set, solid-state circuitry). I find no comfort in this sedation, so I and my house muddle through in fluorescent glow, happy, for a minute at least, that some things can be fixed, that I have power over some problems.

But just for a moment. The conservation measures I had chosen drastically trimmed the power consumption of my house and still cost me almost nothing. We spent a few hundred dollars for light bulbs, but then to save power we have no clothes dryer. The money not spent on a dryer bought the bulbs. We have no television. Heat is from the sun or wood. We have saved money, yet my life is as convenient as before. So far, conservation has cost me nothing, but this is not enough. I will be uncomfortable until I actually pay to offset some of my damage to the salmon. Now I find myself retrieving those lost plans for photovoltaics and scheming ways that I might raise the money to buy them. Scheming, as in genuinely desiring and longing to have them, as one would long for a sleek, new car. At night I kill lights and think of ways to curtail my needs. Tracy, the environmentalist, is even more adamant. Conservation is not something we believe we must do; it is something we want to do.

Suddenly what has long been a mere slogan as hollow on my ears as on most others, seems to ring. The simple sentence "Less is more" resonates true. I really want this, not out of any sense of altruism but because I believe the act of using less will make my life better. A through-and-through American, I have somehow internalized a profoundly un-American notion.

Asceticism is anathema to our culture, yet it appears we do so need it now. Many of us have believed this for decades but seem to have gotten nowhere in our attempts to crudely graft self-denial to the rootstock of the American soul. We are not by nature mat-sitters and skinny eaters of tofu. We are fixers and tinkerers. Frequently we are mistaken for hogs, but mules would be a more accurate anthropomorphism. We are stubborn and loathe to yield to power. When we can see it.

In this light, there can be an American asceticism, but it does not derive from self-denial. I have thought long now about what sent me back nightly to thumb through catalogs of high-tech, stingy light bulbs like a teenager with a stroke book. Why do I still want these things? I want them because I have seen the power and I wish to be free from it. The invisible power of the grid is control. It is participation in a system that has become corrupt and destructive. I do not wish to deny convenience to myself. I wish to deny them. The struggle is for independence. If this means I must live in a smaller, darker, harder house to deny this system any pounds of my flesh, it is a small price—really, no price at all. The alternative is to admit complicity in the killing.

There can be an American asceticism, but it must learn to accommodate a raised middle finger.

Light

IT IS MID-OCTOBER, WARM AND PLEASANT, but the weather hints of an early, tough winter. The empty reach of the night sky sucks each day's light and warmth into the null. The woodpile stacked near the rising house seems small when I look at it, and I often do. My mind is on heat.

The house has windows but no source of heat and no way to hold it. The temptation during those shivering mornings was to attend first to the former and turn some heat on. That's the custom of our people, but in this house we hoped to circumvent such customs. Holding heat is more important than making it.

Insulating a house used to be considered the grunts' work, work of no account. If it was done at all it was done while the skilled trades took a break, with an attitude of hurry up and get it over with. Two dollars and fifty cents an hour, then back to the real work. Insulation is buried in walls. It has no aesthetic. At any given minute it is difficult to tell whether it performs well or whether the job is riddled with little faults, so subtle are its workings. The blessings of insulation are felt only over the long haul.

It is a job that was grudgingly done, respecting a few vague thermal theories and then on to the next task. Or at least this is how it used to be. More than almost anything else in construction, our attitudes toward insulation are changing.

The house was ready for insulation, a milestone we had pushed toward with a rush stimulated by the cold. The wires were in, the windows hung, pipes placed and soldered, roof on, rafter ends blocked, exterior walls sheathed, internal walls framed, drains stubbed, soffit and fascia cut and nailed down.

My friend Michael Gallacher figured he owed me a day of work, and I figured a day of insulating was just the way to collect. The chore doesn't take great skill, although Gallacher had some. A photographer by trade, and a fine one, he had worked his way to a white collar by summers and weekends of dirt work, railroad work, construction here and there, as a helper to a mason. He had been a grunt, so of course he had insulated.

The delivery truck had unceremoniously plopped the bales of fiberglass next to the house the day before he and I began the chore, great fat batts compressed by machine into plastic bags. When we'd cut one open, the contents erupted like coiled paper snakes from a magician's can. Insulation is a magic of sorts, but a simple one, nothing more than a giant blanket in which to wrap a house.

Insulation is made from a variety of materials, all performing the same trick. The materials have a great resistance to conducting heat, a notion engineers express as the "R value." The higher the R, the better the insulation. Most of the materials act by imprisoning small pockets of air, almost as cells. Trapped air has enormous resistance to the flow of heat, as long as it is held in pockets small enough so the air won't circulate—not cup-sized pockets but beer bubble–sized pockets. The trick of insulation is to do this in a relatively thin space, so R is generally expressed in thickness—R value per inch. The more expensive insulating materials, like polystyrene, provide far greater insulating value per inch. Accordingly, a house's design can cut costs and still get the job done by allowing for thicker cavities in walls and ceilings for insulation. That's what allowed me to get by with cheap old fiberglass, $5\frac{1}{2}$ inches in the wood-framed walls and 14 inches in ceilings.

Fiberglass is cheap, but it's hateful stuff. Usually bright pink or lemon yellow, it looks like monstrous mounds of cotton candy. It comes in strips sized to fit between rafters or studs and glued to kraft paper. It looks effective. The people who install it do not. Because it really is glass spun to fibers, it irritates and stings any skin it can find, so installers wear long-sleeved shirts buttoned tightly at the wrists and neck. A pair of jersey gloves, a hat, and a paper respirator worn like a dog's muzzle complete the ensemble. Nothing protects the eyes, so the fiberglass and the already accumulated dirt, dust, and sawdust among the rafters rises to sting like a cloud of angry insects. Fiberglass installers are rarely of good humor, even those who are minute by minute gaining the benefits of a blanket flowing over their house.

Gallacher and I worked fast. From my ladder I barked down a measurement, just the length of the batt I needed. He measured out the piece and whacked it, usually with one slick slice of a razor-sharp utility knife. That's all there is to it. I'd take the batt and unfold the strip of kraft paper creased along either side. These tabs overlapped the studs that cradled the batt and are meant to hold the staples that fasten the batt in place. Whap, whap, whap from a staple gun that swings like a hammer and another bit of blanket is hung. Later, the surface material of the interior walls will cover the insulation. We worked our way down the walls, up the ceiling, around windows and doors, and over cracks.

Then the house began to change. The hard ring of the OSB sheathing slowly faded from our echoing voices. Sounds grew soft and close, tones settling to the calm of dead air in closed corners. The house learned how to whisper. It learned to give comfort. We worked fast.

"Goddamn it, you missed that last piece by an inch and the rake was off by a mile."

That was a message sent from atop my ladder to Gallacher's cutting station just below. It was the sort of sentence builders of houses use to convey constructive criticism. But Gallacher's reaction made it clear he had been away from construction for a while—too many hours among the desk-bound—so he sulked and began to slam things around.

"It's close enough."

"Bullshit. Look at this. Look at this gap between these two pieces. You can throw a cat through here."

"Don't tell me about insulation. I've insulated twice as many houses as you have, and from where I come from an inch off is close enough."

"No such thing as 'close enough.' This job only knows about 'right on.'" I realized how I must have sounded to my good friend, that the job's hours and inches had made me something of an insufferable prick, but I didn't care. If it came down to not doing this right, then I didn't need his help. I'd do it myself.

"Don't talk to me like that," Gallacher said. "You're not my god-damned ol' man."

That was serious. He meant that, so I figured I'd better lighten up. Gallacher and I are both forty, and still he speaks and I listen in those terms. We're both still mad about the way our fathers and their surro-gates treated us on the job. The depth of Gallacher's reaction made it clear I had become a crank.

In a curious sense, we may credit the past's profligate use of energy in the Pacific Northwest with today's scrupulous attention to standards of insulation; that, and some wise action by an arm of the federal govern-ment.

In 1980 Congress created the Northwest Power Planning Council, in response to the demise of the salmon in the dammed reaches of the Columbia River drainage. The council was a weird federal arm, a creation of one federal hand meant to slap another. That is, the council was to check the excesses of the federal Bonneville Power Administra-tion, the dam builders.

The new council quickly evolved a curious worldview completely contrary to the standards of the 1980s. To address the killing of the salmon it did not look to alternative sources of generation. It didn't seek to save fish by making coal smoke or nuclear waste. Nor did it adopt a second course: the Luddite view caricatured by the proposal that we solve our problems by freezing to death in the dark. For the council economic growth, new houses, the American dream, and all that sort of business were a given, as was the survival of the salmon.

The mediator of these two poles—positions we often see as opposites—was conservation, not a great leap in logic. The council, however, added a new spin to the idea. The reasoning went like this: A given utility has a choice. It can satisfy growing demand by generating new kilowatt-hours, or it can meet that same growth by cutting the use of that same number of kilowatt-hours in existing houses and busi-nesses. Further, new generators are enormously expensive, while steps such as insulating homes are not. Wouldn't it make more sense to spend money on insulation?

That's what the planning council did. During the 1980s it spent about $1.1 billion of ratepayers' money insulating houses in the Pacific Northwest, offsetting the need for 350 megawatts (the production of a medium-sized coal plant) of new power. The cost of that "new" power from insulation was about 1.8 cents per kilowatt-hour. At the time, new power from coal plants cost about 10 cents per kilowatt-hour.

Interestingly, it was the federal government, not bound by a profit motive, that had the flexibility to dabble in this program. The economic logic, however, was completely amenable to profit, so the scheme spread to the private sector. By the end of the decade private utilities, particularly those in the Northeast, were beginning to examine conservation as an alternative to new plants. The trick was a revision of the rules governing rates to allow the utilities to recover the money spent on conservation. Regulators simply had to allow utilities to charge a higher price per kilowatt-hour for power they did generate to create the economic incentive for both producer and consumer.

In the Northwest the program worked in a unique fashion, in that the council made no assumptions about how insulation or conservation works. Instead of accepting conventional wisdom the council built houses using a variety of methods and closely monitored performance. The behavior of the people living in those houses became a part of the equation. Once it had developed a raft of tricks to save energy, the council took a vital step. It went soft on regulations mandating the standards. Likewise, it shied away from selling the idea of those standards to consumers. When people buy houses they think very little about what is beneath the veneer of the walls.

Instead, the council went to builders and taught them insulating tricks that added very little to the cost of the house but increased its efficiency enormously. It coupled the education with an array of rebates and financial incentives. The result was a quiet takeover by conservation in the Pacific Northwest. It became unpopular in the region to build a wall without a vapor barrier or with only 3½ inches of fiberglass insulation. The latter practice was the standard of the nation before the 1980s, only because those 3½ inches happened to fit inside a two-by-four stud-framed wall.

We understand how to insulate now. Further, we understand that steps such as thermal integrity and installation of efficient appliances and light bulbs can and does cut the energy use of a house by as much as 70 percent. No hardship. No freezing in the dark. Pressing the practice of conservation to its fullest potential could offset the threat to the salmon. So far, however, we have not pressed nearly that far.

Early in 1990 I sat in on a meeting in Portland, Oregon. Gray-suited bureaucrats from the Department of Energy in Washington, D.C., had come to visit with the staff of the Northwest Power Planning Council, by then a bunch of field-tested energy wizards. The bureaucrats had heard a rumor of great doings in the Northwest and had come for an accounting of the potential conservation. They heard several days' worth of discussion and pronounced themselves impressed. This could work, maybe even in a federal energy policy, long sought by environmentalists and said then to be grinding through the gears of the Bush administration.

Long-time combatants of the energy wars suppressed some smirks at this development, in that the feds were reinventing the wheel. The earliest pushes for conservation came from that very Department of Energy created for just that purpose. The drive for a sane federal energy policy was a keystone of the Carter administration. Reagan scrapped it all, so the DOE assumed the position shared by a whole range of federal agencies as lapdogs of the industries they were designed to reform. Now, just a decade later, the DOE was listening to a restatement of its fundamental principles as if they were new ideas.

As I write this it is early in 1992. My house is warm and light. It is cheap to heat. Insulation works, but no mention of this is made in what has become known as the federal energy strategy. Now the keystone of the Bush administration's strategy is opening the Arctic National Wildlife Refuge to drilling rigs (—folly that might have ended with Clinton's election).

I know what heats my house. I know where my wires lead. I know something of the wonder of the caribou migrations in the Arctic National Wildlife Refuge, of the great bears that thrive there. All of this makes me a bit of a crank and unpleasant to work around when I am insulating. I'm not sorry for this. An inch between pieces of insulation is just too much. My house is only one house in the battle, and it cannot make much of a difference. True enough, but it is the only house over which I have some control.

This is not a parlor game or academic exercise. This is a house. It is real. It counts. Its walls shall be insulated to R-29, its ceilings to R-38. They'll be airtight. That's the standard. That's how it's going to be.

The technology behind my active heating system is simple. If one is to burn wood inside a house, one needs a way to transport smoke to the outside: a chimney. Simple, but a long time coming, Primitive smoke holes have been around, presumably, as long as fire, but it never really occurred to anyone until the eighteenth century that smoke holes should perform as advertised and actually remove smoke. Before 1720, when builders began making improvements, chimneys were not sufficiently insulated to keep the smoke warm and therefore ensure that it would, like all hot air, actually rise. The big development was to make fireplaces smaller. (Until then fireplaces were used mostly for cooking; heating rooms was not a goal.) Although the Germans had developed the airtight porcelain stove about two centuries earlier, they weren't widely used until about the middle of the eighteenth century.

Meanwhile, the Brits were still wheezing smoke until well into the nineteenth century. The American-born Count Rumford suggested a series of modifications to the chimney in 1795. His influence produced a flurry of patents, but real progress was slow. As late as 1860 writers were still bemoaning lingering problems of smoke.

The chimney I proposed for my house was a simple metal pipe connected to an efficient wood stove in my living room. Bruce Haroldson, by then absent from but still mothering my house, forbade it. Metal pipes lose heat rapidly, causing a decay in their draft, which in turn causes smoke. Metal pipes are also ugly. Further, the heat they lose can spread to adjacent wood walls and cause a fire, especially if the pipe is poorly installed. This means lawyers have become involved in their design, which in turn means a metal chimney pipe costs nearly as much as a stately, reliable, sound, and tight masonry chimney.

I don't know how to lay concrete blocks and wasn't about to learn on a structure that would rise in my living room. Bruce advised I would be a fool to try. Bruce's partner Mike advised it would be even more foolish considering rumor had it that Karl Marcus was both available and in a mood to stoop to the laying of a simple masonry chimney.

I called Karl. All rumors were confirmed, so we chatted a bit about roof pitches, various varieties of lightweight concrete block, masonry sand, Byzantine brick, and the contribution of Roman baths to the development of the Swedish masonry stove. Small talk mostly. Actually, he talked, I listened. I had been warned about this, that mortar and bricks are to Karl what the cosmos is to Carl Sagan, that with but the slightest provocation Karl will recount the billions and billions of facts at his command.

Further, hiring him to lay up a simple block chimney was the equivalent of commissioning van Gogh to slap a couple of coats of green enamel on a bathroom door. He is an artist with stone, specializing in the collection and laying of natural stone walls and fireplaces, massive works around which an entire house is built. He routinely lays fireplaces that cost as much as my house.

To collect the stones, Karl has become amateur geologist, his education largely gained by accosting real geologists and engaging them in arcane discussions of upheaval. He can recount the entire geologic history of the Rocky Mountains as a play-by-play man might announce the second half of a Minnesota Vikings game. An acquaintance once made a mistake of accepting Karl's invitation for a Sunday afternoon ride to collect rocks. Three hours later Karl finally shut off his pickup truck in a deserted valley in Montana's remotest corner, a place where one could reasonably expect to find moon rocks. The acquaintance quickly found some rocks he liked for his chimney. Karl was dubious.

"Are you sure you want something from that early in the Precambrian?"

He'd do my chimney, though, no matter how mundane it seemed to me. It was all work, and work was all interesting to Karl. Nine hundred dollars for 30 feet of chimney. A week's work, and he'd supply the material.

Karl's pickup showed at the job laden with chimney blocks, clay flue liners, insulation, sand, mortar, and sections of scaffolding. The blocks, nearly 2 feet square, stack in a column to form the chimney; the clay liner, much like clay tile, lays up inside like a pipe, the real conduit of the smoke. The void between is filled with insulation to keep the chimney hot. That's the secret. Hot air rises, and insulating keeps it hot and rising. This simple allowance removes the smoke by creating the draft that so eluded seventeenth-century Europeans.

Karl is slight and wiry, maybe forty with small and intense eyes and a full black beard. Another aging hippie in a long string. That has been one of the joys of building this house. It's as if this building process put me back in touch with all the friends I lost track of after the sixties died. To hear the press tell it, the counterculture folks of those days all sold out and became yuppies. There have been stories to this effect, mostly written by counterculture types who have became yuppies. In lavish lifestyle articles we have been taken into these people's houses to learn that the decade of excess was fueled by their consumption.

What we did not learn was that the other half of the generation helped build houses. The long-hairs are alive, well, and practicing craft. I would cheerfully build a house every year just to see them again.

As Karl worked on the chimney I helped him a bit, but mostly we kept to separate projects. At least I tried to work elsewhere, but every time I'd wander within shouting distance of Karl he'd launch into a dissertation on such topics as the wonders of thirty-thousand-dollar masonry stoves as developed by Scandinavian masons; the development of the chimney during the Norman conquests, at first a device for sending heat to wall-top guards of the castles; the misunderstood intricacies of Jerry Garcia's music; thermal mass; berming; chaos theory; heat pumps; and Arabic transmission of Aristotelian logic.

And the chimney rose straight up 20 feet to the ceiling, and Karl cut a hole in the roof. The work then moved outside. The front pitch of the house's roof, the south solar pitch, is ten-twelve, too steep to walk, so scaffolding went up, a tall tower of Pisa in front of the house. Karl laid planks from the tower across to the roof and the chimney, a working platform 20 feet up. Then the chimney rose some more. I helped with the grunt work, running the well wheel, a device that is nothing more than a big pulley and a long rope with which one hoists blocks and buckets of mortar skyward, as if running a flag up a pole. Slowly we loaded the scaffold, a block at a time, then clay flue liners and mortar, until there was maybe a ton of concrete blocks, clay, mud, and Karl on the platform.

My phone rang and I walked away from the scaffold to answer it. I suffered the nuisance call not long, hung up, and then heard more than the phone's click—something more like a crack. Then I heard what sounded like an avalanche. It looked like one, too, as the scaffold, blocks, and boards collapsed like a dynamited skyscraper, a puff of dust and a roar. The whole business tumbled in a great cloud straight down the slope of the roof, through the air, then down the slope of the hill coming to rest as a pile of rubble in the trees 60 feet in front of the house.

As the dust cloud first rose on the roof, I saw Karl's head and shoulders rise above it for a second, then he tumbled off the scaffold, just to one side of the crashing mound of concrete. He fell just a couple of feet to the steep roof, clear of the path of the avalanche. There he executed a quick tuck and rolled down the roof, off the eaves like rain, and dripped the remaining 10 feet to the ground. When you fall, to stay down is to believe you are hurt, which is the same as being hurt. Karl wanted to make no such admission, so he was on his feet instantly, as if his fall had landed him on springs. He was mad. He was shaking, and he couldn't talk. He couldn't talk the rest of that whole day. He only seemed to shake worse and worse as the afternoon rolled on, and he figured how close he had come to a real fall.

Mostly I think he was mad at himself for building a bad scaffold. We had overloaded it. Because one end rested on the inclined plane of the roof, the downward pressure of the extra weight also tended to deflect the whole scaffold sideways and tip it over.

Karl shook as we ripped apart the twisted, tangled scaffold, then levered it between trees to straighten it. We rebuilt the tower and this time lashed it to the house with some aircraft cables he had. Lost concrete block and lost time to rebuild all the scaffolding meant he had lost all profit on this job, but he seemed mostly mad about falling. By the time he could talk, he scolded himself. There was a ding in a dollar's worth of cedar trim, and he apologized at length for the damage to my house.

Then, still shaking, he climbed back onto the rebuilt scaffold, headed higher, and laid the block of a quality chimney to the top. He finished it with a poured concrete hat. In the wet mud, he signed his name where no one would ever see it.

*   *   *

There are no universal solutions to environmental problems other than the broad directive "Use less." Rather, the paths we ought to follow arise from context, from the specifics of place. Finding these paths is not a matter of reading maps drawn by others but of discovering them personally. The goal is not so much following the rule as it is participating in the process of discovering the rule. This search requires the attention of our minds or, better, a tuning of our lives to the places that hold them.

For this reason, most of my house's heat comes from wood. This must sound very strange to some of my neighbors, because they are choking on wood smoke, as is much of the West—smoke from small wood stoves heating small houses. In the mountain West there are no hardwoods, no seasoned, twisted old knots of oak to burn clean and hot. We burn conifers, fir, and larch if you can get it. They're the best, but we also use pine now and then. All these species, but the pine especially, are full of pitch and resins that smolder and leave a tarry creosote on chimneys and in the air. The tar is as beneficial to human lungs as the tar in cigarettes.

Just over the ridge above my house one can see the small city of Missoula on a winter's day, assuming Missoula can be seen on a winter's day. Usually it cannot. It is like most Western towns in that it rests in a small bowl of a valley, a hammock suspended between protecting hills. Cold air builds in the valleys and then is trapped by warmer winds sliding over the top of the hills. This is a phenomenon called an inversion, really an isolation from purging winds, so the valley must suffer its own smoke and fumes, like falling into one's own cesspool.

On the order of twenty days a year, usually in December or January, formal bad-air alerts issue from health officials. The wood smoke has thickened until it is too foul to breathe. Don't drive. (Auto exhaust is a problem, too.) Don't exercise outdoors. This sort of advice one would expect in Los Angeles or Tokyo, but not in a high mountain valley. Yet here it is.

There is worse news. We are coming to understand that the mysteries of the forests hinge on death and decay. Biologists hereabouts have done some counting and now understand that the web of life is spun around big, dead trees. Most dead little ones won't do. Some forty species of invertebrates and a whole range of birds, damned important ones, depend heavily for nesting and food on big standing dead trees called "snags." Normally a Douglas fir will survive for three or four hundred years, then spend as long as five hundred years present but dead, first standing then falling to rot in the soil. In this rot is the accumulation of decay that will hold the moisture and nutrients that bring the next generation of forest.

The biologists here say they are not so much worried about the snags, the standing dead trees, falling to the timber companies. Loggers do cut snags. They consider them hazards, but a bit of explanation seems to impress the loggers quickly, and they leave the snags to go on with nature's work.

Firewood cutters are another matter. They favor snags, standing dead and so partially seasoned. Big snags. Sometimes big cross sections of a trunk, called "rounds" hereabout, are displayed in the backs of pickup trucks as if they were trophy elk or deer, with the same air of conquest and capture. On the public lands, the federal lands of the West, the great areas of forest reserves in Montana bigger than some Eastern states, the snags disappear. Biologists have even taken to marking the trees with signs calling them "wildlife trees." Often Forest Service agents find these signs splintered or shot full of holes and laying next to a stump.

Tracy and I found our wood stove used. Some people had added onto their house, so the old stove was too small, almost too small for our house, but we wanted that. We wanted to rule out the possibility of fixing energy leaks—shoddy insulation—in the house by simply burning more wood. We limited our choices to efficiency or shivering.

It is small, but it's a pretty little stove, made of solid cast iron by the people of Vermont Castings. It is known as the Intrepid II. Properly filigreed and doodaded to earn the name "parlor stove," it sits hooked to Karl's chimney in the middle of the living room, looking like a smug little anachronism. It is not.

Its joints are finely machined and sealed with gaskets to make the little stove airtight. This is a refinement on the idea the Germans started in the sixteenth century, but in the late twentieth we do mean airtight. A thermostatically controlled little trap door at the rear of the stove lets in the only air, just enough for combustion, not enough to allow the flames to suck out all of a room's heat and send it up the chimney.

A wood stove is basically a metal box for burning. An air inlet allows it to breathe in the oxygen it needs for combustion and a short pipe connects the stove to the chimney, its exhaust vent for smoke. If the stove were not sealed to be airtight it would not only burn air, it would also heat air, causing it to rise up the chimney. This exhausted air would be replaced in the house by cold air from outside, meaning the stove would tend to cool, not heat, the house. The airtight seal of the stove limits its consumption to only the amount of air necessary for combustion.

To enhance the stove's stingy air intake I installed a piece of plastic pipe running from the stove under the concrete slab and outside. This means combustion air comes from outdoors. It always does, but if it weren't for the pipe the stove would suck its air through the doors and windows, meaning the cold air would travel across the room and so become a draft in the house. Isolating the intake air in a pipe removes the house's heated internal air from the stove's combustion circuit.

The real technical leap of the stove, though, is a sort of hump on its back, a device called a "secondary combustion chamber." Simply, this box burns smoke. The solids, the creosote in smoke, are almost as combustible as wood. In fact, about 40 percent of the energy in wood is in smoke, the stuff sent up the chimney to foul the air. Burning it is not that hard. It simply requires that the smoke travel in a serpentine pattern to pass near the hottest part of the fire but still remain isolated from the flames in a separate chamber. If the chamber is hot enough— about 1,100 degrees Fahrenheit—and if that chamber is supplied with a second blast of oxygen—air separate for the main fire's draft—then fuel, heat, and air mix in the chemical reaction we call combustion. Heat, not smoke, is the result.

The problem with all of this, particularly in the West, is that the woods we burn seldom heat the secondary combustion to 1,100 degrees. More technology intervenes: a catalytic converter. This causes the smoke to pass over a special metal element—usually platinum. The converter cuts the minimum temperature of secondary combustion to as low as 500 degrees Fahrenheit, easily achievable even with pine. The afterburner kicks in, burning the smoke. Almost none leaves the chimney. The woodpile lasts nearly twice as long but delivers the same amount of heat. What could be the matter with that?

Still Missoula chokes. There are about 15,000 wood stoves in this city of about 80,000 people. Only about 250 stoves have catalytic converters and so are allowed to burn during days when air alerts are issued. On any given bad-air day, an estimated 5,000 inefficient, polluting stoves burn illegally.

Stoves with catalytic converters are readily available and are not expensive, especially when weighed against the cost of wood saved. Given all of this, the resistance to them is difficult to understand. To an outsider it must sound even grossly irresponsible, as we Montanans foul our own nests. But better ours than someone or something else's. Is it better to burn wood and breathe one's own smoke or burn oil and forget in a few months the decimation flowing from the *Exxon Valdez*?

I have the odd notion that choking on the smoke of one's own life, day after day, year after year, keeps the smell of responsibility acrid and sharp in the back of one's throat. It stiffens the resolve every day to do something about it.

When we whack a tree's trunk to stove-sized chunks—the process is called "bucking it up"—we create a pile of rounds. Elsewhere, these sections are called "billets," but I prefer the local term, resonant of a deeper significance. The rounds are small symbols of the act, in that woodcutting is a craft of circles. It is a ride on unique and specific cycles.

It begins with the cutting, which everywhere deserves—on one's own land it demands—fidelity to the life cycle of the forest. In woodcutting there are no universally applicable proscriptions. In some climates, on some sites, in some states of mind, the cutting of wood is simply wrong in all senses of the word. In others, it is benign, even beneficial, in that it eases pain already inflicted.

In my place, man has meddled mightily by suppressing forest fires. The fires can't run freely now, because we put them out. So the young trees choke each other. I thin them. All winter I watch them, walk among them, watch how the sun favors and disease, bugs, and rot punish individuals, and then I thin them. Mostly I cut live trees, leaving the snags for the woodpeckers and all that comes in their wake. Mostly I cut young trees.

I try to behave like fire rushing through the trees, leaning on them hard in the dry spots, striking without regard to any aesthetic values I set to particular trees. Here and there, though, I cheat, cutting a tree on wholly anthropocentric grounds, because it shaded a solar window or because its absence might make a peaceful sitting spot in the center of the woods. Sometimes I leave a tree only because of individual beauty as I perceive it.

Mostly, though, I try to reason how the capricious hand of nature would behave, and I try to ape it. Paradox, I know, but what choice do I have? The trees are there, they need cutting, and mine is the only hand present to do it. Besides, I must have wood. I have made that choice and now will not shy from it or from its implications. I have made a choice that entails killing. All of us do. I will do this killing with my own hands.

My tool of choice in this act of playing god is a primitive crosscut saw. I used to use a chain saw but grew tired of its clatter and the greasy blue smoke streaking the sunlight that filters into the forest. Crosscut saws are long-bladed, gap-toothed antique tools. A carpenter I know calls them "grandpa saws." The wilderness rangers of the Forest Service call them "misery whips." The Forest Service must use them in backcountry areas where federal law prohibits the use of motors. I knew this and learned from that agency that the remaining supplier of such saws in the nation is the Crosscut Saw Company of Seneca Falls, New York. My saw came UPS, along with its file and spider for checking the "set" or angle of the teeth, which determines the width of the kerf.

It took a while to get the hang of it. This saw asks a full commitment of the sawyer's body, not so much a push of the arms but a roll of the back and a heave of the shoulders. It's all work, good work.

Felling a tree is the hardest. The saw is designed to cut perpendicular to a horizontal tree trunk, but in the cutting of a standing tree the target is vertical. I compensate with a few bites of a sharp, double-bitted ax, leaving a clean, open notch in one side of the tree. From opposite the notch I angle the saw cut down to the notch. When force of falling outweighs the dwindling resistance of the tree's stem, a creak speaks from deep in the tree's trunk. Sometimes I feel the snap in the ground, a shudder down through the roots and up through the boots. Comes a whoosh of limbs grabbing air, and then a tree falls.

It stops breathing. This fact hits home first. Just when we so need trees, I have killed one. Plants are our opposites in respiration, mostly breathing in carbon dioxide, exhaling oxygen. This is why we have given them new notice, realizing, slowly, but still realizing, that excess carbon dioxide in the atmosphere is about to ruin many lives through global warming.

Trees store the carbon in their trunks. By burning them, I release it back to the air. Yet the same carbon escapes when a tree dies and decays. All trees die. Not all coal is dug. Not all oil must be drilled. The carbon in trees is only temporarily stored. That in oil and coal can be permanently stored if only we had the will and wisdom to do so.

The tree I have cut stores no more carbon, but I cut small trees, mostly shade-stunted by more vigorous trees nearby. Its absence gives the survivors more minerals, sun, and water. They breathe faster and fuller now. Carbon gets sucked up all the same. Still, all this talk has the mealy ring of rationalization to it, as I see a green tree spread flat on the forest floor.

I take my ax and limb it, then buck it to long sections, drag the sections to a sawhorse, then whack them into firewood-sized chunks. In a half hour I can cut about a day's supply. The woodpile builds. A real and pleasant way to measure the passing days. Not these days— next year's days. The cutting and stacking of wood is an act of faith, removed from the actual burning by the demands of water, weather, and combustion. A tree cut now won't burn well for at least a year. The rounds must sit a summer under the sun until the water cooks out. They shrink and crack. The word for this has an obvious etymology. The act is called "seasoning." Not just aging, a passing of time. Rather, the wood gains value by passing through the cycles of seasons. Warm, cold. Wet, dry. The ups and downs.

Once a round is dry, I split it; then the wood goes in the wheelbarrow and on to the house, where at least a week's worth is always stacked dry under the stairs, a few feet from Karl's chimney. Thus we heat.

Our nights were already cold by the time Karl signed the chimney and pronounced it ready for hot smoke. We already had the wood stove on the scene and ready to fire up at first opportunity. It had sat for a bit in the previous owner's garage, which only worsened a rust spot on its lid. Trace had at this blotch with some naval jelly and then we oiled the stove from one end to the other, seasoning it too, like a cast-iron fry-pan.

I hooked it up, fitting it with the short length of black sheet metal pipe that connected it to the chimney. I cut the last piece of pipe with a spray of sparks from a carbide saw blade, then hammered it home in its hole.

The stove stood rickety on four rocks, surrogates for the someday-stone floor that would rest beneath it. We fired it up, loading it with building scraps, pieces of fir from beam ends, and a couple of rounds of pine from the forty-year-old tree I had cut from the middle of the future living room. Presently there came the cricks and cracks of thermal expansion, cast iron on the move. Then the smell of heat, hot-dry, black-iron. The stove has a windowed door, and it glowed. The heat rose to billow against the still open-faced walls, to confront the insulation that would contain it.

The heat was meager at first. We lost a good bit of it to the cracks we would find and seal as winter winds elevated them from irritants to threats. It took us a while to learn to operate the stove, to make it wring the calories from a piece of wood. But now it sets the rhythm of our winter days and nights.

In late winter, when the sun isn't up until well past eight, the house is cold in mornings. Not unbearable, but cold. That's as it should be. I shy from control of climate and metered, even heat. It distances us so from the cycles of our days, from the forces that surround us. This distance is the disease of our times.

A house ought to be cold in the mornings. It ought to entice one to linger sinfully in bed, to savor the body heat that is the only real antidote against the depths of winter. In morning's cold you ought to have to pull on long johns and shiver, then find your mind focused on nothing so much as breaking up a few shards of kindling, sticking them among the coals of last night and huffing and puffing the pile aglow.

Then come the first crackles, bigger wood goes in, and heat flushes the room. The smell of hot iron rises to mix with that of the morning coffee. Just outside, last night's snow hangs in the trees that flow through it all, flow together with the days of satisfying work, the real work, the work that holds lives together. On lucky days, the sun rises to illuminate all of this.

This fact first must be understood in approaching the business of using the sun to warm a home: The phrase "solar-heated house" is redundant. The sun heats everything, so the sun heats all houses. In the early days of the energy crisis when the word "solar" served as a sort of mantra, we more or less overlooked the omnipresence of the sun. Instead we set out to capture it with technology. I toured some of those houses back then, strange affairs with complex arrays of flat-plate and hot-water collectors mounted on tracking devices, wires, conduit and pipes, heat exchangers and basements given over to great piles of rocks. Mostly contrivances. Gradually these machinations came to be understood as "active solar houses," a notion that has fallen from favor. That family of devices is generally too complicated and unreliable and costs more than the energy saved.

A quieter idea has lasted, a soft-path technology. It is guided by the understanding that the sun heats all houses and that our job is to make the most of this. We do this by orienting the long side of houses to the south, and by providing large areas of properly tilted glass for the sun to fall through. Inside we provide large volumes of thermal mass—a substance such as concrete—that absorbs the heat, preventing the house from overheating and retaining heat for release at night when the sun disappears. Finally, the walls and ceiling need to be superinsulated, to retain as much heat as possible and to compensate for the poor insulating value of the necessary windows.

Behind passive solar heat is a wry sort of joke, that the operative principle, the activating law of this alchemy, is our destroyer, the greenhouse effect. Both light and heat are forms of energy. Light oscillates at a certain wavelength, one that happily passes through glass as if it didn't exist. Once through the glass, though, the light strikes solid objects in the house, which absorb some of the light energy and reflect it back as heat energy or as infrared light. Infrared waves oscillate at a different wavelength and cannot pass through the glass directly. Some is lost indirectly through heat transfer: a warming of the glass and then a warming of the material next to the glass, a slow and inefficient way to move heat. Most of the heat, however, is trapped, so there is a net gain of heat inside the house.

Layers of carbon dioxide and certain other gases with the proper molecular structure, compounds we have come to call the "greenhouse gases," behave just the same as glass. This is why the carbon dioxide from the coal we burn is slowly but certainly warming our planet.

For years I have chased around calculations about solar energy as if drawn by a sort of magic, and to me it was. I never really believed any of this, but considered it only a phenomenon of the abstract world, a subject of elegant equations but of no real bearing in my life. Solar energy was the capture of fairies in glass bottles, and these calculations simply explained how many of them could be made to dance on the head of a pin. Solar energy was for the paper world. Heat is real stuff and is made from real stuff by work. Heat is a woodpile built with a crosscut saw. Solar energy can't be earned by work, and I did not believe in grace.

I got my backing in this from some hard-headed folks, my gurus in the whole project. John Cole and Charles Wing walk through the calculations and then advise builders to steer clear of passive solar, because they can achieve a lot more with superinsulation and a good system of wood heat. The costs of even passive solar simply do not return in heat saved. I read this and then once again put the whole business away from my mind, filed with sprouts, granola, and Birkenstocks.

But then new stuff kept coming up. Argon-filled windows for instance. The biggest objection to passive solar is that the necessary windows lose so much heat that they almost cancel solar gain. That problem is real. The average double-paned window is about an R-2. The insulating standard in my area for a wall is R-28. You see the problem. People, however, keep coming up with new ideas for windows, such as filling the cavity between the two panes of glass with inert argon gas, doubling the insulating value of the windows. Amory Lovins said this new generation of windows cracks the passive solar nut. Research has shown that an argon-filled window captures more energy than it loses, even on the north side of a house on a cloudy day.

More calculations. There are pages of them in my planning notes, long penciled equations of seven-digit numbers, BTUs, angles, and mass. After reading Lovins's advice I found a set of insolation tables, which are month-by-month accounts of solar energy averages observed in a given location. They are available now for most cities in the United States, including, specifically, Missoula, Montana. I ground the numbers through the specific design of my house as a passive solar house, including south windows and skylights. For every month except December I showed a net gain from solar energy. During December, our gray, dark, cold month, the energy balance was zero—no net loss. Overall, the few windows I planned would save the equivalent of two and a half cords of firewood each winter. I saw that wood stacked in my mind, year on year, saw the trees falling and the smoke rising.

And then in my mind I saw a house flooded in light, the fairies in a bottle, and I went for it.

The key, it seemed to me, was to so integrate the passive solar in my design that it would use the basic aspects of the house. It would rely on features I would need anyhow and therefore create no added costs. The superinsulation was necessary in any event, no matter what heat source I chose. The necessary thermal mass I would create with concrete walls. Those are cheap and a necessity in an earth-sheltered house such as mine. No incremental costs. All houses need windows. My idea was to drastically curtail windows in the north, east, and west walls of the house; in effect, to shift the glass to where it would do the most good.

Further, the biggest expense from windows is not glass (a trick I learned from Cole and Wing). Windows are one of the most expensive parts of a house, typically costing about three thousand dollars. The expense, however, is in the mechanics, the hardware necessary to make a window open to let air in. Windows don't need to let air in; they need to let light in. Vents and doors can more efficiently and cheaply provide fresh air. One can greatly reduce the cost of windows simply by buying panels of glass and mounting them directly in homemade fixed frames. These cost much less than factory-made windows.

Having thus rationalized my fascination with the fairy world, I set my design. Call it passive solar, or call it a well-lighted house that heats cheaply. It doesn't matter. The windows are there as I planned them, a south wall of glass framed between vertical timbers set every 4 feet. Our south wall is a window wall. This opens our house to a meadow below and a thin belt of stately pine trees. I did not expect it—my carefully penciled calculations did not communicate a full sense of it—but the effect of these windows is real. That first winter, it all came together slowly and subtly but as real as a fire's glow.

Our living room, the room bounded on one side by the wall of windows, is small. Yet it doesn't seem so. There is an illusion as we sit in it, as if the boundary between outside and inside does not exist, as if we live in the forest. Our vision and thoughts walk freely out and among the trees. The light filtered by pine needles just as freely makes the opposite trip.

The only thing that breaks this illusion is night, or more accurately, the artificial light that night brings. We discovered this early on, even before the inside walls were covered. At night when the lights were on, our window wall went black and opaque. If we turned out the lights, the wall disappeared. It vanished, and we were outside again, sitting among the stars.

As our time in the growing house stretched on, we found ourselves in a new habit, that of rising early and with the sun, just as the first gray bled through the dark of the east. We'd make our coffee and drink it in the living room. By January we had stopped marking this ritual by the crack of the wood fire, preferring instead to leave the room a bit cold and the stove dark and silent. Then the sunlight would come first in pastels, then a more confident orange, then flushed nearly as red as Tracy's hair.

On the living room wall there is a thermometer, indoor and outdoor, digital readout to the tenth of a degree Fahrenheit. On mornings like this I can't help but watch it, watch the sunlight reflected in LCDs. I can almost hear it tick off the sun rise, up a steady degree at a time. We are warmed. It's real. It works. My house is enlightened.

After a few weeks of working in our shell of a house, of grit, dust, dirt, insulation, and cold, Tracy decided it would be a good thing if we had a bath. The idea hadn't occurred to me, but when she mentioned it, it seemed sound enough. Besides, the house was nearly ready to afford this luxury. I could have the tub ready for operation in a day or so of work.

We had a tub already. It came from Fred and Susan's goat pasture.

Fred and Susan Reed are our neighbors, although we can't quite see their house, which rests at the end of a ladderlike road to the top of a sharp ridge. Their front windows open to miles of air backed by two mountain ranges, offering a view probably slightly better than that of the gods. Fred teaches sociology at the university and is a woodworker. Susan is the county's auditor and a potter. Both avocations require shops, so their property is dotted with neat little pine-sided sheds, a reflection of Fred's philosophy that one can never have enough buildings.

The goats have their own pine-sided building down in the valley floor, although it was not altogether clear why the goats needed a bath-tub. But there it was, not a beat-up or antique bathtub at all, but a modern and spacious cast-iron fixture, the sort it takes four people to lift and would take five hundred dollars to replace, if you could find one. When they learned we were building a house, they gave the tub to us.

That was the beginning of a habit. Later I found three pieces of oak I couldn't use and gave them to Fred. He treated them like he had found gold and fashioned them to a fancy railing on a stairway in his house. Their house is trimmed one end to the other in oak, including their bathroom where they can sit in the tub and watch elk that wander into the yard. The Reeds were so proud of the railing that they invited us up to dinner to look at it. We drank a bottle of wine Tracy and I had given them earlier. Now it appears we have sort of a potlatch going, that ritual of Northwest Indian tribes where the object is to give away pretty much everything you own. It seems a fine way to build a house.

We dragged the tub to our property even before there were signs of a house. There it stood, it and the woodpile, for weeks. Passersby must have understood that someone had ideas about this property.

Before we tipped up exterior wall frames, we moved the tub onto the deck where it would eventually go. None of us wanted to lug the behemoth up steps and through the doors that would come later. By the time Tracy was ready for a bath, we had pretty much jockeyed, beaten, and levered it into its final position, there to be double- and triple-braced against its own considerable weight and that of the water it would carry.

The rough plumbing was already in, so in late October we bought faucets and I spent an afternoon sweating them to appropriate fittings, then assembling washers, spigots, and knobs. I turned on the water to pressurize the assembly. Nothing leaked. Much. Then I let the water run until it flowed hot. This was the core magic of our baths. Hot water.

Both the propane guy, a sharp-faced fellow with darting eyes, and *The Washington Post* were on record as opposed to my hot water heater. The propane guy would eventually get his comeupance. I still plot revenge on the *Post*.

Americans heat domestic water in a truly curious fashion. There is virtually no variation on the theme, other than the choice of energy sources; electricity, propane, or natural gas. Beyond that, almost all water heaters work the same. There is a large tank—about 50 gallons, sometimes larger—filled with water. Either a gas burner or electric resistance coil heats the water to the desired temperature, about 110 degrees Fahrenheit. As soon as this is accomplished, the water cools. Then the element heats it again. Then it cools. This process goes on until somewhere in the house there is a demand for hot water, and there it flows.

The problem lies in the cooling and reheating, always to keep a supply of hot water at beck and call. The process has been compared to leaving one's car idling in the driveway around the clock just in case one decides to travel. In the rest of the world, where energy is more expensive, domestic water is not heated this way. Both in Europe and Japan the common method is an on-demand or tankless water heater. As the name implies, there is no tank. Instead, when a faucet is opened, water circulates in a nest of pipes before a propane or gas flame, heating it very rapidly. When there is no demand for hot water, none is heated. The device may sit idle for hours or days, then respond when ordered with just enough energy for the task.

The savings achieved by this system can be substantial, depending on how one uses hot water. Lesser savings accrue to large families that pull a fairly steady flow of hot water throughout the day. In this situation, not much energy is spent keeping water waiting and warm. For relatively infrequent users of hot water, such as Tracy and me, an on-demand heater can run on about a quarter of the fuel used by a conventional heater.

The *Post* sniffed at these heaters because certain smaller models have a limited flow of "only 3 gpm." Never mind that a perfectly brisk shower can be had at less than 2 gallons per minute, hot and cold water mixed. And never mind that some models of on-demand heaters will supply close to 5 gallons a minute. There are weightier issues involved. What if, the *Post* reasoned, one wished to run one's dishwasher and take a shower at the same time? Not being able to do so would constitute an unacceptable deprivation. And what if one wishes to live one's life and preserve the Arctic National Wildlife Refuge at the same time?

I bought one, a French model readily available from alternative-energy mail-order houses in this country. It cost $475, about $150 more than a conventional model. Installation was as simple as the similar process for a tank-type heater. The *Post* said I could expect to pay $250 to have one installed. Following the instructions that came with the heater and using simple handyman's tools, I installed mine in about an hour.

Before it could be fired I needed propane in the tank. In rural areas, propane replaces natural gas as the fossil fuel of choice. It is like natural gas, relatively cheap, clean, and plentiful, a reasonable substitute for those living away from gas pipelines. Instead of an underground pipe, rural folks have sausage-shaped tanks about the size of a picnic table. In some places they are called, appropriately, "pigs." I had my tank but no fuel. Litigation being what it is, my supplier refused to fill it until he had inspected my system, a useful safety check to my amateur plumbing job. A single gas leak can undo a great deal of work.

The propane guy pressurized the system, then cast his beady eyes up and down my pipes for the merest hint of a leak. He worked his way methodically down the line until he came to my water heater, then stopped and stared as if he had just discovered a dead Norway rat floating in a punchbowl. What the hell is that. French, you say? Great. A frog heater.

And then his screwdriver came out, the heater's cover came off, and he prepared to peruse it with extreme prejudice. He checked internal safety switches, thermostats, vents. He hated it. It all worked perfectly, so he filled my tank.

In midwinter this same guy returned with his delivery truck to refill my tank. By his calculations, enough time had elapsed for me to need fuel. He dragged his hose to my pig and cracked the cover, took a look at the gauge, and then dragged the hose back to the truck, unused. Then he came to knock at my door to advise I needed no fuel, that I had not used enough to justify refilling. How was that frog heater working? Fine, I said. He shuffled his feet a bit and then asked if I might be so kind as to provide the address of that catalog. Tracy and I had used less than a quarter of the propane his other customers used to heat water. His own house needed a water heater, and he would like to buy one just like mine.

About the same time, our second electrical bill came and we performed some calculations. Our 1,200-square-foot house, fully lighted, refrigerated, stereoed, coffee-grindered, and blessed with two perpetually running computers had used an average of about 200 kilowatt-hours a month. The average residential use on our system is 1,100 kilowatt-hours. Propane and electricity were our sole external sources of energy.

Our house is as warm and bright as most, our water as hot and plentiful. The devices that achieve all of this at a considerable savings added maybe three hundred dollars to the cost of my fifty-thousand-dollar house. Even with our cheap power rates in the Northwest I'll recover the added costs in a couple of years. Sitting now in this house, living with it, I can't imagine why anyone would do otherwise.

The work done, it was now well into the night before we got around to drawing that first pool of hot water into the tub. Fully dark, there were no light fixtures yet to offset the night. The walls were still without sheetrock, so there was not even a touch of white to reflect what light there was. We rigged up a small table lamp in the middle of the bathroom floor, an effect like a candle in a cave. The shadows played along bare pine studs and the logo of the paper-backed insulation.

Still it was a bath, the first in gritty weeks. Trace slid into the pool first, emerged a good while later, still pink, to pronounce it fine. I followed her and wondered whether the goats had appreciated the tub as much as I did. Normally I hate baths, but the plumbing for the showerhead was a month away, waiting for sheetrock, tile, and sliding glass doors. A bath would have to do, and it did just fine. Both of us still glowed from it as we climbed into our zipped-together sleeping bags, leaving only noses sticking into the chill autumn air.

Art

LATE IN OCTOBER THE ROCKERS CAME. LARRY and Rick. The hanging of sheetrock is not delicate. The job proceeds in a panic, with the sense of a river rising, water breaking, or winter coming on. It requires not so much a broad range of tricks as just a few done over and over again until they can be executed with the mindless speed of an assembly line. The job of hanging the sheetrock all around my house would have taken me weeks. Rick and Larry did it in a bit more than a day.

Sheetrock, otherwise known as gypsum wallboard or drywall, is an industrialization of house building, whole chunks of walls sold in 12-foot by 4-foot plaster sheets, one-half or five-eighths of an inch thick, perfectly flat and square, bound between paper. It is the interior wall surface of virtually all modern houses. The sheets are simply nailed to the studs, leaving as little gap as possible between them. The gaps then are filled with a special plaster called joint compound, a sort of mortar. This is layered with paper tape, plastered again, and sanded smooth until the joints disappear. Then the whole surface is painted. Fast and cheap.

In the order in which tradesmen peck, rockers take one of the lowest niches. They are not highly paid or regarded. Their work is widely believed to proceed more rapidly with chemical assistance, and so, at least in some circles, there is a taste among rockers for speed or cocaine. Not on my job, though. Rick and Larry seemed fueled by nothing so much as hustle.

Beat-up pickup trucks arrived late one afternoon to disgorge the pair: Larry, the boss, the journeyman, slightly shorter than average, T-shirt and prodigious beer gut; and Rick, tall, dark, and cool with a bit of a baby face, but a tough guy. They unloaded a stash of tools but no boom box, a notable absence. Larry explained: The two could never agree on a station, with Larry partial to rock and roll and Rick a devotee of country and western, so the only workable compromise was silence.

Right off there was a fight, but not between Larry and Rick. The rockers luckily arrived just as the lumberyard crew was delivering the material, an act that, for good reason, is called "stocking the rock." The price a contractor pays for sheetrock includes not only its delivery but placing it inside the house at the most convenient location. By the time Larry and Rick arrived the delivery people had shed nearly half their load in what Larry regarded as a less than convenient location. This was no small matter, because accepting it would mean the hangers would have to lug a couple dozen sheets of rock an extra 40 feet, up a flight of stairs. Rockers work on tight margins, and this bit of extra work might kill any profit they would have.

Larry was irate. There was a frank exchange of views between the stockers and the rockers that ended only when Larry framed the issue as one of professional pride. He pulled rank.

"Look," he said, now nose to nose with the trucker and livid. "I hang rock, I don't stock rock."

The stockers submitted to this alpha male behavior, and Larry and Rick hung rock. In a flurry of dust and a whine of routers our house was transformed. Quick, hard, crisp work. Still a craft. If their work is lowly regarded, Larry and Rick hadn't yet heard the news. Once finished, they took time to strut around my house as if it were their own.

"That's what I like about what I do," Rick said. "When we're done, a house looks like a house."

Larry said his dad was coming soon to visit from Seattle. Larry liked what he had done to my odd little house, and would it be alright if he brought his dad around to show him?

Actually, Rick and Larry were the preliminary event in the finishing of the walls. They were employees of Tipi Steve, so named because he once lived, winters and all, in a tipi pitched on a mountainside near Missoula. Steve is the artist of the operation, the master of the finishing coats. Working with a stunning variety of pumps, stilts, sprayers, scrapers, and sanders, he and a partner spent about a week taping and sanding the joints, masking all of the beams, priming the walls, spraying them with a special paint that gives them the texture of an orange peel, then finally painting them with three coats of latex. Together with the hanging of the rock, this was to be one of the most expensive steps in the building of the house, a total of $2,700.

The irony of this expense was it ran counter to what began as the guiding philosophy of the house. All this rocking and painting were cosmetic, simply veneer. In the world of hard alternatives, this is money I could have spent trimming energy costs or buying wind generators and such. True, something had to cover the walls, and sheetrock was the cheapest way to do that. It's also the easiest method, so I could have hung the rock, taped and painted it myself for about half the money, maybe less. Yet when Tipi Steve's estimate came in even higher than expected, I didn't blink for a second, I just said, "Let's do it." I no longer could face the nights of depression. The house was getting to me. I was beat and needed desperately and soon to sleep through the night.

Sheer physical exhaustion was the biggest factor. The work had gone on hard and unrelenting for two months, no weekends off. It was about this time I noticed my jeans were perpetually sagging deep down into my tool belt. When I investigated I found my frame had shed 20 pounds. And this was the first I'd noticed it.

But there was more at work than my need for a rest. Sometimes I would sit nights in the dark, squatting on a dusty, littered concrete floor, and the house's hollow shell would engulf me like the black hood of a demon. The house came alive in a sense I had not predicted. I meant for it to be mine, to flow from my hands in perfect replication of my notions, ideas, and values. The house's job was to be an extension of my life. Instead it had taken a life of its own and was making demands I had not expected. I had meant for the house to be efficient and sparse. It was that, but I had not considered the possibility that in achieving this it would become beautiful. It did, and in its beauty it made demands.

Each night these demands would pound in my head as a review of each of the day's mistakes. My craftsmanship had progressed to a painful point. My skills as a carpenter now were utilitarian and adequate, but they were building to a more sinister phase. The first step in this building is training the eye to discern quality. This is the step that brings us to do things better, the negative phase—criticism—never more vicious than when it is vented on one's self. The eye's ability to see errors soon outstrips the hands' ability to correct them, so the eye nags. At the end of each day I saw only mistakes. These I took with me into the long nights.

I had rocked, taped, and painted before and had always botched the job. I never had the patience or touch to render clean, crisp lines, so the house needed Larry, Rick, and Steve, and it got them. They came and went. The dust settled, the paint dried. Trace and I stripped the masking tape, high on the smell of new paint and the new life of the house. Then we had a house, white walls one end to the other set against the rich brown and rose tones of the rising posts and the beams.

One afternoon while fitting a piece of trim, I found the first twist in a post. No longer set straight, plumb, and square as we had left it, the internal pressure of its drying had canted it just a touch; not enough to cause structural problems, but enough so that the eye could tell it was not conforming to linear standards. It was a touch of rebellion from a piece of wood surrendering its life force. A twist in wood is supposed to make a carpenter mad. All his days he works against just such capriciousness, toward a linear perfection. This twist, though, gave me a giggle, a deep-down satisfying, impish laugh. It was not perfect. It was alive, and that was better.

Bruce Haroldson says the job of a carpenter is to bring order to chaos, and so it would appear. The very first act of man's hand against wood is sawing the log, the taking of the round and making it flat and square. And so it goes until a tree is a house. We kiln-dry wood to make it behave like iron; we plane it to render it flat, perfectly flat; we joint it to exorcise warps and twists. The act of framing a house is a constant process of disciplining wood. The uninitiated think of carpentry as hammers and saws, but a mark of a good framing carpenter is his inventive use of levers and braces. Planks and framing members are constantly being pulled to the level and plumb with all manners of come-alongs, straps, grasshopper clamps, pipe clamps, C clamps, levers of all three degrees, and simple brute force.

Always a sledge hammer is at the ready for the truly stubborn cases. In this application, the sledge or maul is called "the commander."

Smash.

"How's that?"

"Once more, easy, just a titch."

Smash.

"How's that grab you?"

"Any closer and we'd have to change it."

"Nail it."

This is chaos ordered, and a good carpenter need understand only this. But just practicing this side of carpentry would build houses exactly as we expect them, and that would be getting what we deserve. If that's all we wanted, why build houses of wood, a living thing? Why treat it like concrete and steel?

A good carpenter brings order to chaos, but good carpenters do not necessarily build great houses. A builder of houses must work both sides of the street—he must respect chaos.

Almost every day Bruce repeats the punch line to the same story. It concerns a friend of his, a biologist, doing field work in Alaska. For a time this friend lived in a village of Native people. The village had a new community center, just finished; but when the time came to paint it there was no money or paint for the job. To deal with this the residents scrounged around their houses for any paint they might have and assembled at the community center. The search solved the problem of quantity. There was plenty of paint, but there also were plenty of colors. The people of the village sat around for a bit pondering this situation, until Bruce's friend, a white guy like Bruce and me, finally solved the problem.

He grabbed a big bucket, poured all the paint into it, and stirred it even. Then he announced. "There's your color."

An old Indian woman considered this for a moment, then said, "T'inking, t'inking, t'inking. That's the problem with the white man, always t'inking."

If Bruce had told this story only once, it would be because he saw only the white point of view. Instinctively, that's where Bruce's sympathies lie. He is like that guy. So am I. So are the men who were raised to solve problems, to be always "t'inking," because people are depending on their solutions. But Bruce tells this story repeatedly, and then he always grins the same way afterward, like the joke is really on him and he knows it. In our solutions we have stirred all the paint to one monotonous color. We have lost the rainbow.

Carpentry is the art of telling this joke on yourself over and over again.

With my walls standing white and clean, it was time for me to change hammers. My coarse framing hammer, the wafflehead, was not appropriate for the work that was to come. After sheetrock and paint, after the wood that does work is covered, it is time for woodwork, for the veneer, for the trim. This point is the crossing of a significant line in the building of houses. On commercial jobs it is a line that divides carpenters from hammerers. The framers go away and in come the finish carpenters, precise, quiet, and patient fellows who miter clean joints.

My wafflehead is a stout hammer made for framing, for slamming big, fat nails deep into timbers and planks, for setting their heads down deep where they will stay for the ages. Its counterpart, the finishing hammer or trimmer, is a much lighter tool, fine and clean. The head is ground smooth, nearly polished like glass, so that it will not mar the surface of trim wood. Strength is not an issue here, beauty is, and so the job calls only for a fine stroke sufficient to drive a wiry casement or finishing nail.

Ahead of me lay many hours of work: the baseboards, door casings, doors, bookshelves, balusters, rails and newel posts, and the cabinets, especially the cabinets in the kitchen. For these I would need a finishing hammer. Yet as I took it down from its hook on the wall and hung it on my tool belt, I couldn't help but think of the post and beams and the joke they were making of this ritual changing of hammers. Their presence blurred the line I was crossing and so charged me with a greater task. I had set out to make the house practical and strong and did that, but then it began to assert itself and I wanted to make it beautiful. And then it beat and insulted me, informing me that my abilities were so far short of the task. Then, as I began to summon the tools and determination to try anyway, those beams, rough as an old carpenter's hands, brought me back to the beginning of the circle.

The veneer of sheetrock usually covers a house's insides in unblemished planes of white. Nothing is allowed to break the illusion that the sheetrock stands alone like a blank slate. Utility—the studs, wires, and pipes—hides within. But on a timber frame, the sheetrock rests between, not over the framing timbers. The structure, the skeleton, protrudes with the formless sheetrock accentuating the hard, confident bone of the house, like a silk robe draped on a taut body. Its strength is its beauty. This house struts on bare limbs. It lives.

It lives—an odd notion for an inanimate object, but during the days, then months, spent with this house one idea kept coming back: Make it live. It is not enough to build it, to assemble a shell of wood, wire, and metal so that they converge according to a design rendered on paper. The building of a successful house seems more an act of integrating our lives and its rhythms.

How does its light flow? How does it take to the outside? Does it reach to the trees? Do the stairs creak? If they do, is it a creak that satisfies? Does it sleep right? Does it seem to hold us tight yet bend to feel the wind? How does it spread the smell of wood fire and fresh-baked bread or spring rain? When I shout, do the walls ring hard and righteous with my anger? Can it hide me to let me cry alone? How can I frame the room where I write so that it will hold my thoughts? Can a house spread sunlight across my wife's warm face? How can I build all these things with my hands and a hammer?

I keep coming back to wood, drawn as it is from the life of the forests. It is twisted because it was, and is, in a sense, alive. A life force, desiccation, created the internal pressure that created the twist, now a permanent cant of maybe a half inch. This twist would drive most carpenters nuts, but timber framers work with green wood as a rule. In their techniques and joints they make allowances for the shrinking and bending of the drying process. They sheath the frame so that any gaps from shrinkage are covered by the skin. After a year, my posts and beams were each maybe a half inch narrower than when we first set them. In drying, Douglas fir shrinks about 5 percent. Still, all this motion, greatest during the first year, has created no problems, no air leaks. The house settles. The joints let the frame live and it is strong. It is the frame.

Lately, however, I have been drawn not to this post's strength or its twist but to its face. A few days ago Tracy sanded it. Not smooth and polished like furniture, but just a quick pass with very coarse sandpaper, enough to knock off the dirt that still remains from construction and the splinters. Then we oiled it to preserve it, always a rewarding task because oiling highlights the grain and draws out the eccentricities of the wood. The annular rings lay row on row, their roundness crosscut by the flat plane of the saw. Against the post's straight vertical lines flow the twists of the tree, the cambium and the darker heartwood, here and there the nipple-brown of the knots. The native beauty of wood everywhere is valued and sought. It is important that these timbers will support Volkswagens at their centers, but it occurs to me that wood is even more valued for the beauty of the grain, because it is a record of life, capricious and unique, art we cannot re-create.

Once I saw a documentary film in which a number of Native artists were interviewed. They were from a variety of tribes, all with separate regional ideas about art: sand painters from the Southwest, carvers, and potters. Yet there was a common attitude that was best expressed by a carver from the Northeast.

His art was the making of ceremonial masks, warped ovals shaped like the half tree trunks they were. His first step in the making of the mask was to find the proper tree. As the camera followed him, he rejected tree after tree only to choose one that appeared completely identical to all those rejected. In the prescribed traditional manner, he cut the tree and carved it to a mask. The interviewer complimented him on his work, a flattery he dismissed as white man's silliness.

The Indian explained simply and as a matter of fact that he had not made the mask. The tree had made the mask. If one looked carefully one could see the mask clearly resting inside the tree. His job was not to carve the mask so much as it was to let the mask out of the tree.

The finish work went slowly and deliberately. It usually does, but this was going slower still because I kept getting distracted. The house was cold. In part I could blame this on a few cracks not yet sealed, infiltration here and there. I had begun to think of the building process as erecting a frame, which is, in a sense, a rack of holes. The job is then to fill all the holes, starting with the biggest ones and working down. Most of the filling had been done, so as the months passed, the house should have been tighter.

I didn't see how the few remaining holes would make the house as cold as it was. Not uncomfortable, really, but cold even before the truly bad weather. Outside, the night temperature was dipping only into the twenties and teens. Ten below was but a month or so away, and then what? If the house is cold now, what would it be like then? Ten below is no trifling matter. If a house isn't right when such weather strikes, all hell breaks loose. Pipes freeze and burst. Life gets miserable.

I spent my nights rechecking my calculations. Surface area and volume, heat loss through windows, R factors, and all of the abstractions that were supposed to add up to my comfort. The numbers all said the same thing, that the house should have been warmer. I kept thinking about ten below and whether I had, in my inexperience and ignorance, made some horrible, damning mistake.

I poked the tiny wood stove and stoked it harder, then stared into its coals wondering why it wasn't doing what it was supposed to do. Fred and Susan stopped by one night to inspect progress. Such is the neighborly gesture in the country, to admire a person's sheetrock and the fact that a door had been hung since the visit a week ago. Fred is something of a connoisseur of wood stoves. He has four of them and is constantly fumbling and tuning their behavior. I knew this, so I explained my concerns about my cold house. As a matter of pride, not all of my concerns, but some.

"I wouldn't worry about it," said Fred. "A house is kind of like a ship. Every one is different. You have to get to know it before you can learn to sail it."

An apt metaphor. Fred and Susan left. Trace and I were alone in a house floating on a stretch of cold, dark woods that seemed as big as an ocean.

My error in constructing the house, and it was nothing if not a process ruled by error, was that I thought of it as simply constructing a house.

From the very beginning it was a house pitched against, and still defined by, the wild, a house among the woods, and yet I had been observing only a narrow sense of that idea. It was made of wood and so it was obviously drawn directly from the woods, of this I was conscious. The grain of a wood is information, a living record, if you will, a patient recording of the cycles of a year laid down in annular rings. My house drew its art from this information; it was informed by the woods. Yet this was but a beginning. Anyone can simply buy or even imitate the grain of wood. So what.

We fool ourselves in thinking our works are distillations of nature, but nature is not distillable. Nature is The Other, that which educates by advising us what we are not. It teaches we are only a part, not the whole, of nature.

From its conception, I understood that the character of my house would derive not so much from its taking from nature but rather from its attempt to ride the line, the crease of tension between what we call nature and civilization, between order and chaos. My mistake was to spend all my time building the house on the side of civilization and not enough wandering among the woods from which it came. A walk was needed.

The last time I had simply walked had been the Fourth of July, even before holes were started, when Tracy and I took a day away from the picnics and crowds to roam the perimeter of our 38 acres. It sounds not at all like a full day's hike, but the land is mountainous to the point of being nearly unwalkable. Land area is measured, in our straight-ahead linear world, on a perfectly horizontal plane. Therefore, 38 acres in mountains, mostly vertical, covers much more surface area than 38 acres on the flat. The ups and downs of the perimeter of our land make for a long walk.

Besides, we stopped often, learning the names of things. We found the whole range of midsummer wildflowers—horsemint, yarrow and showy daisy, crazyweed. We stopped and smelled the sagebrush (two species) and the juniper. There was clarkia in the few old ponderosa pine at the hilltop, owl clover along a fence line, and then, way up high and in a forgotten meadow, the light pink, bowled flowers of bitterroot, the flower for which the nearby mountain range is named, once plentiful and a source of food for the local Salish Indians. Now it is mostly gone from the region, but it lives on our land unmolested. In this I find some hope. We sat in the sun and watched a kestrel, a pocket-sized hawk, hover and hunt the field. A nesting pair of bluebirds perched on the fence.

This hike in July, however, was not a real walk, just a day's stroll. In the fall I tore myself away from the house for the walk I really needed to take. Long before we had started building, we had promised Michael Gallacher and his wife, Jo, that we would take a week in the fall for a trip in the Bob Marshall wilderness area. This is something Tracy and I do most every year, to save our lives.

The Bob Marshall is sort of the flagship of the nation's wilderness system and the very opposite of a house or any other bit of artifice. It is nature not in the sense of a national park, not of scenery and paved footpaths, handrails, scenic lookouts, and interpretative signs. Rather, it is simply wild, meeting the strict definitions of the 1964 Wilderness Act. It is roadless, in all senses of the word "road." No motors of any sort are permitted within its more than 1 million acres. To cross it, one rides a horse or one walks. We walk. Grizzly bears live there. Once Tracy and I confronted three of them within a half hour, one from a living room's width away. We have been married ever since.

On the trip with the Gallachers, we climbed a high pass to an alpine lake. It rained on our first night, 7 miles in. Then we walked in damp silence for two days, down a gentle drainage to a lake 6 miles long, where there were no other people. There was frost at night but the sun shone on mornings. We watched a pair of loons and a family of beaver and caught countless cutthroat trout, fat for fall. One day it snowed and we walked 15 miles until our talk was delirious and silly.

We were out of control, and that was just the point.

When I tell people of wilderness I can see their minds' eyes seeing elk and pristine sweeps of mountain ridges, snowcaps and clear lakes in gentle, forgiving sun. These scenes are there, true enough, but they are not all of the images of wilderness. Wilderness is first sad, and that is why I go. The entry, the first days of walking for me are always just the same, winding up in gentle wet valleys of old-growth forest. This is the forest so often rhapsodized about but so rarely seen by our people, a place of gloom. Here the trees grow with an aching timelessness that speaks of nothing so much as our human insignificance. They grow tall and deep green reaching for what little sun penetrates the canopy maybe 100 feet above.

The forest floor is impenetrable here, a tangle of centuries of its dead. The living are a specialized lot of creatures, evolved as specifically as weird deep-sea fish. Micelike voles that spend their whole lives at tree-top. The goshawk, with clip-tipped wings of agile flight to maneuver among the trees. Fungus and timeless rot.

In human terms, the only terms I have, it is a place of grief, maybe why we hate the forest so and have cut almost all of them. Some say we are doing the forests a favor by cutting them. It lets in the light, breaks the governing hand here, which is death and decay. Yet we need their death. The life cycle is only half of what we call life; the other half is the recycling of life we call death. We need the grief. We need to see it to settle our own lives. The forest runs on the chaos that made us and will take us.

I come to the wilderness without a house or even a reasonable copy of a house. Trace and I even have stopped carrying our tent, preferring instead a wisp of a nylon tarp. Sometimes this makes us cold and wet, which is the point. Through the years we have learned not to care. Now I remember why we travel this way. There comes a time, after the grief of entering a wilderness, that I can describe only as the summit experience. Usually there is even a real summit, a great open vista out of the trees when one can begin to understand flight. These times are a revel in surrender. The grief of the dark forest canopy is a necessary prerequisite. We have surrendered control. Control is a house or tents or motors, and here there are none of these things. Control is a resistance to natural forces. Control is a fear of death. After days of climbing a twisted trail there comes a mountaintop and the illusion that I see all there is to see. For a second, for a brief liberating moment of light and flight, there is no need to control, to bring order to this chaos. On this realization, one builds a life or a good house—it is all the same.

Before we had started building, I was bicycling through Missoula one day and saw a pile of beat-up old lumber in front an apartment building. On it was a sign: FREE WOOD. In panic, I found a friend and posted him at the pile. Don't move. Tell anyone who stops that it's taken.

I got a pickup truck and scooped up the lumber. It must have been the private stash of some old woodworker, forgotten in a garage for generations. I surmised it was forgotten, because it was dry, seasoned by years. I guessed it had once belonged to an old woodworker, because the wood was eccentric as hell. It was rough-sawn planks, some 4 inches thick with the bark still on two edges, some a full 2 inches thick, most planks a foot wide, 16 feet long. It was the sort of lumber someone would stash with no specific goal, simply letting it season and wait for a purpose. Mostly the planks were pine, but buried in the pile were five 10-foot-long rails of solid oak, expensive wood. Ignorance piled that lumber here, which is why I assumed the original collector was gone. Anyone who had taken the time to collect it wouldn't have given it away like that, piled curbside like trash.

It was the same oak I later gave to Fred and Susan for their rail. The planks we used over and over around the house, scaffolding and such. Some of it went into the scaffold that dumped Karl Marcus. (The planks were faultless in this.) Rick and Larry stood on the planks to hang sheetrock on the steep living room ceiling. I ripped one piece to form the skeleton of my homemade front doors. Some of the lumber had weathered like barn wood, so I used it as paneling in the house's entryway. Some of the planks I have set aside for Tracy's desk and bookshelves. One particularly rotund plank became a countertop.

Back in the days of framing, Bruce had cut the stringers for the house's inside stairway, so he needed treads. The stringers are the saw-toothed inclined planes that support the stairway. The stringers hold the treads, which support the steps of the person climbing the stairs. Bruce eyed my free plank pile and in it found suitable specimens. He ripped them to size, whacked them into twelve 2-inch-thick by 12-inch-wide treads, and temporarily screwed them into place. A two-by-twelve is virtually unobtainable these days, let alone a dry two-by-twelve that will not warp or twist. Bruce considered the treads quite a find.

When Tracy and I first saw them we considered them rough as cobs. At that stage, so was the house. The treads were beat-up, rough-sawed planks that looked like they came from a barn floor. Never mind, Bruce said, they'll plane out fine. And so I forgot them. They were a sore thumb, but they were hidden on the sore hand that was our unfinished living room. Through the months the living room grew more finished, but the planks grew rougher, and not just by comparison. The sheetrockers packed them full of dust, then grout, then paint. We never took them seriously, so we didn't protect them. They gradually became embedded with dirt, dust, and nails.

Then the time came to finish the stairway. Bruce was gone, but I remembered with some skepticism that he had said the planks would clean up fine. It was worth a try. By then I had built the cabinets and worked with a lot of finish wood, and I knew something about planes, jointers, and routers and the magic they could work.

The planks were too wide to fit in Bruce's power plane, so I took them to an old friend of Bruce's, a strange fellow with a workshop that appears to be a legacy of the gods, a sort of woodworker's Valhalla. He planed my planks, cut the cups—a U-shaped warp of the wood—out of them, and suddenly I began to see possibilities.

I hauled them back to the house. Bruce happened to be there, and I showed them to him. We talked about the fellow with the plane, and Bruce said there had been some terrible troubles in his life, but he was still the best woodworker there is. Then I learned that Bruce had apprenticed with this woodworker, but there had been a falling out. Bruce didn't want to talk about that. He told me how I should cut a rounded edge on the treads. And then he told me in blunt commands how I was to align and mount them, drill and plug them, match them to risers so that everything comes together just so.

Alone, I took my planks into the house. I was supposed to be writing that day, but I was too excited by the possibility of these planks. I set to work with my table saw, drill, and finishing hammer, a bag of hardwood plugs to fill the counterbored screw holes. The treads felt right in my hands, the saw cut as if it had eyes, and the joints matched cleanly. I felt as if all of this was not altogether my doing. I felt only a part of the process. Before me, rising ever up, grew a stairway that appeared to be the work of a craftsman.

I sanded it all, four times over, working down to a quick lick and a promise with 400 grit polishing paper. In stocking feet, I worked into the night varnishing the wood.

Bruce came by the next day and read the wood. On the face of each pine tread is a smear of blue stain, a naturally occurring blue-black blotch that is evidence a tree stood dead a while before it was sawed.

The blue is really a fungus introduced by beetles that attack the dying tree. I can only guess as to how long ago that was, or who cut it, or how it found its way to the mill and how long it sat forgotten in a garage before it was piled streetside where I found it.

Bruce began reading the planks as a botanist, sure they were ponderosa pine, probably from hereabouts. The deep brown streaks in the white of the pine is simply the tree's way of storing its energy. Some of the treads were pierced here and there with small, oval holes, the work of beetles that probably had killed the tree or infested it after it stood dead. I did not fill the bug holes with putty; I have not covered the record.

One of the planks had a deep brown burl of a grain along one edge, the plank I thought the prettiest. I had mounted it at center of the stairway, eye level from the living room. Bruce said the burl was a fire scar—not a fire that had killed the tree, but a trouble it had survived.

I remembered then that these were the planks Bruce had laid last summer, the planks that had brought me the frightening realization that this house would outlive me. If I am lucky, I will see these stairs and this grain on my last day of light and life. I imagine these are the stairs I will climb to die, but now that I see the scars of their life, the thought doesn't seem so bad.

I first met Steve Loken at the lumberyard. Missoula is a small town, and word had spread of what I was up to and vice versa. He recognized me and walked over to introduce himself. Mostly he wanted to extend an invitation to tour the house he was building. I jumped at the chance; in fact, I had been meaning to call Loken to wrangle the same invitation. Both the house and Loken already had achieved a national reputation.

Steve is a carpenter and unrepentant environmentalist. His apprenticeship in the latter calling was served as most are here in the northern Rockies: battling the timber industry. Still he battles, but along a very different front. Like some, he saw a diminishing return in throwing oneself in front of log trucks and so began the exploration of yet another path of protest which made full use of his skills as a carpenter. His company is called South Wall Builders, and he has through the years dabbled in all manner of energy-efficient homes: earth-sheltered, passive solar, and superinsulated. When the Northwest Power Planning Council developed its five-state program for the superefficient home, Steve built one of the prototypes.

His latest project, however, leaps straight into the next generation, a fact that is not at all obvious when one approaches its hillside perch in a toney neighborhood on Missoula's north edge, a sort of country club Republican ghetto. The problem with this house in this neighborhood is that it looks as if it belongs. It is no hippie yurt but rather a distinctive and appealing suburban house, with the sort of architectural detail that honors the art.

Yet some underlying numbers tell its unique story more clearly than its lines. The most revealing is this: A conventionally built house of these dimensions could be expected to consume about 10,000 board feet of timber, but this one used 3,700 board feet.

The root problem of construction is that our nation is running out of trees. Our houses are to blame. The timber industry's public relations hype about renewable resources and their replanting of trees is wasted on people like Loken. He is a carpenter and he knows better. Like all carpenters, he has held in his hands the best evidence of the degeneration of our nation's timber supply. The quality of lumber on the mass market today is appalling: knotted, waned, twisted, and warped. The remaining good stuff comes from old-growth forests of the Pacific Northwest and is as costly as sin, but harder to find. Those of us who live here have a hard time sleeping if we use it.

Loken's solution to the inevitable is a step into a new world. The house's stingy use of wood comes from innovative engineering and cutting-edge use of recycled materials. The house is a sort of a three-dimensional catalog of building materials. Loken scoured the nation to gather all the weird stuff he could find, some products barely off the drawing boards or in testing. The result is state of the recycled art.

The skeleton of the house is all worked in novel applications of oriented strand board, the plywood substitute made of ground-up tree-farmed trees. Floor joists and rafters are OSB I-beams, the same as used in my house. Some of the floors, however, have no joists at all, but are simply clear spans of a recycled paper honeycomb sandwiched in between sheets of OSB. The exterior walls contain no studs, but are stress-skin panels, laminates of insulating foam, OSB, and sheetrock.

The house's siding and shingles are lightweight cement. Painted, the siding looks like wood or wood-fiber clapboard. Ceramic floor tiles are made of ground-up fluorescent light bulbs. Insulation is recycled newsprint. Carpet underlayment is tires; carpet was once plastic milk bottles.

The house, a two-story suburban sprawler, is passive solar and earth-sheltered. It uses new windows from Owens-Corning that achieve an R-8. I weighed this against double-paned windows of R-2, or argon-filled windows of R-4. A simple technological leap such as this window could revolutionize energy conservation.

No doubt, Loken's house is where we are headed and, in a sense, where I wish to head in my suggesting that our houses ought to be held accountable for our abuse of the earth. And yet it is unsettling to me, because it is so different from where I wish we were going.

One of the house's numbers keeps sticking with me, and I push it back at Steve. Why did he choose to demonstrate the new world with a house of 2,400 square feet?

"I know, I know," he says. "If I had my way, it wouldn't be that big, but I don't."

This house is about 400 square feet larger than the national median, a standard that has itself risen by 20 percent in the last decade. This technology cuts use of trees, but wouldn't it cut it further still if it were smaller? Doesn't our future lie in recognizing limits just as much as in using technological fixes in futile attempts to circumvent those limits?

"I know, I know," says Steve, but he also understands consumers. He has been building houses professionally for a long time, and he knows what will sell, what the bankers will finance. He would like to build this house smaller, but what good would that do as a demonstration of the technology if no one would buy it?

Yet there is an air in this house that suggests the price of this size is great. The materials are efficient, there is no doubt of that, even attractive in the predictable, controlled, and sanitized sense of the word. All of the materials are recycled, which means remanufactured, and there is no way to remove "manufactured" from that term. Manufactured. Manipulate. Man's hand. To achieve its size it has foregone the art of living trees.

In Steve's stash of salvaged lumber—every carpenter worth his jack plane has one—there is a fine old fir door raised by the old school. Steve says he's going to knock it apart. A good wood door is not a laminate, it is parts: rails and stiles and framing panels. He's figured a way to use the parts to make the stairway railing in the recycled house. The parts will have in them the dowel holes and screw holes that held it together as a door. Steve plans to leave these blemishes, just to remind this house of the circumstances surrounding its arising. This is how carpenters make political statements.

"I know, I know," says Steve of this brave new world. "I'm a carpenter, and I hate this shit."

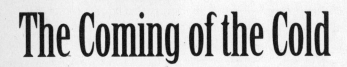

The Coming of the Cold

OUR WINTER BEGAN WITH WIND. I WAS in the house alone, wrapped in my tool belt and work, when I heard a crush of wind slide down the slope behind the house, air rumbling and rolling like Karl Marcus's concrete avalanche. I wanted to say that wind was evil, but I knew better. Nature knows no evil, just the wind.

I should have been working, but as the storm built head I had to watch it, rapt. I dropped my tool belt and simply sat as the mass of air—it had mass, I could feel it—hurtled down the canyon and spilled across the valley, a runaway freight. It crashed into the trees on the opposite slope, punishing the fir and larch. In this part of Montana a single blow of wind sometimes sweeps a whole mountain's face of standing trees. This I expected. It was that sort of wind, so the scene was as riveting as gunplay.

Nature here works in bold and histrionic sweeps of creativity that sometimes pivot on megadoses of death. So be it, for I am a fan of nature's excesses. Let her rip. I simply sat ringside to this bout of wind, thrilled. But then another boom of wind slid the slope and took a bite of the debris around my house. Suddenly sheets of plastic, styrofoam, fiberglass batts, table-sized pieces of sheathing, and cardboard boxes all took leg. They ran like ghosts chasing the wind out across the valley floor. I ran after them, or maybe among them, a coconspirator in this flight.

Eventually, though, I rounded up what fugitives I could and returned them to the yard to imprison them beneath stout rocks and planks. The successful escapees I left pinned by the wind to trees across the way. I would gather them when the wind left.

The blow built force, and I worried less about the litter; I was worried more about the house. A part of me needed to call the wind evil. It threatened to send pieces of my house fleeing like the debris. This realization gave me an accountant's mind, reviewing and assessing every nail, beam, screw, and bolt. Would they hold against this assault, this armed and dangerous psychopath of a wind? Over the months my house had come to stand for so many things in my life, for art, for love, for discipline, for responsibility, and for humility. But now the wind came to strip all these anthropomorphisms and leave only the elemental fact: A house is just shelter against winter and wind. Would it hold?

All around me nature raged; chaos ruled. Against this stood a 42-by 24-foot island of order, a contrivance. A part of me is nature, and so I root for its capricious hand. Yet a part of me is order, more so now that I have built myself into this house, and so I root also for the strength of my artifice, for my house. No matter how much nature may abhor it, I root for my survival. Even in its manifest futility I still muster this seminal human hope.

That wind seemed to go on for days, to punish or to warn, and then too soon it brought the snow. The first brush of it came on October 27. On Halloween it was 6 degrees outside. We weren't ready for this weather. The house was not yet sided. Here and there pieces of its walls were missing, to let the cold blow in. The building scraps that were to be part of the firewood supply for the winter were strewn all about, not yet gathered into neat, safe piles, and so they were lost to the snow. Inside, the house was still a shell; no cozy corners where one could retreat to and watch the weather.

I had designed the house to work as a whole; its heating system was integrated into its skin. Incomplete as it was, there was no way the system could work well, so in this first rush of winter we were cold.

We had sensed the snow's coming, even in that first wind, and then we awoke one morning early in November to find ourselves in a different world. It had snowed nearly a foot, cloaking the pines and us in a silent, shadowed world. That morning I stole a few minutes just to walk among the trees and hear the muffled whumps of winter under my feet, and then the work went on. Harder. All summer and fall we had worked in T-shirts, but now we had to wear gloves, layers of coats, and big hats with ear-floppers. Every move was a calculated battle against the cold, a real battle now with an enemy that was real and present. Slowly the house grew tighter and held.

November 13, 1991.

Yesterday I laid a tongue-and-groove floor of fir, a fine and necessary preface to writing this book. The coincidence of flooring and the beginning of writing was first a practical matter, as were many of the details herein. It was a physical prerequisite of writing, and probably more than that, but I cannot tell how much more. I find I now am unable to sort the details of a house into separate rows containing the necessary, the practical, the aesthetic, the personal, and my responsibility to community, both natural and human. The floor is just a floor, so let's keep it that simple. I needed it to write.

Although we commonly ignore this fact, writing is a craft, a physical act that requires tools and a place for its conduct. In this it is not that much different from the rest of the activities of our lives. It needs a venue, a shelter; in particular, a quiet corner with a desk and a phone, cabinets for books and file folders, electrical outlets for computers and printers, a chair, a desk lamp, a window to serve as diversion from or as an indirect path to the task at hand, a place to rest one's coffee cup, a wall to hang a favorite photo or a map or chart or two, and beneath all of this a floor. Hence I officially mark the beginning of this writing with the laying of the floor. All of the details of this house, months of hand-held labor, flow now to this single pinnacle.

This act occurred on a pleasant day. Most of the days that made my house were pleasant, despite the deprivations. I was called to this particular day's meditation by first light that breaks here at this time of year at about 7 A.M. The light shows first as a glow through the sinfully large east window hung at the head of our bed. This glassed profligacy was Tracy's idea, and I opposed it until the day I nailed it in the rough frame. I thought the window was too large to be energy-efficient, especially on an east wall, but she favored it on points of art. She says there is value to rising each day from the marriage bed illuminated by a glow from the eastern sky. Tracy wanted a clear vantage when the planet turns us to the light. Months later, a small black bear would pound his paws and smear his slobber on that same window.

When I arose the sky was clear, and so daybreak came as a faint rose flush filtered through the airy boughs of the few ponderosa pine just outside the window. Venus was the morning's planet, a sharp and crisp white earring piercing our valley's lobe of sky. I am glad now that I lost the argument about the window. There are few days left to me, and I want to see them all begin like this.

Downstairs I brew a cup of coffee, drawing water from a cast-iron sink propped a few inches above its intended hole in the counter. It won't be lowered to its final resting place for a week or so, until I can get time to face the aggravation of laying the ceramic tile around it.

As the coffee brews I split a few pieces of dry pine and fir for the wood stove. Friends are expected for an evening celebration, and so I whack up a chunk of venison and set it to simmer in a kettle of beer. The venison will be the foundation of a large pot of chili, so it must stew all day, a pungent harmony to my carpentry.

The fire begins to crackle, and the coffee pot sputters good news. I pour a cup and sit quietly for a minute as the sun begins to spill through the south windows, directly lighting the space where tonight there will be a fresh floor.

Presently I begin carpentry. I have learned (stubbornly, painfully, slowly, and awkwardly, but I've learned, damn it, I've learned) that carpentry is, in its initial and all other stages, a meditation. Carpentry is not so much a skill as an attitude, a discipline, a full-body commitment to the level, the square, and the precise. A task of building seems to flow best if it first flows deeply through the head and then the hands.

Just inside the house's south wall is stacked 720 lineal feet of tongue-and-groove fir, each piece planed precisely to a thickness of three-quarters of an inch. The boards are evenly split into three piles containing lengths of 6, 8, and 10 feet. I sort them into an apparently random pattern so that butt joints never line up, a coincidence that wouldn't harm the strength of the floor but that would be a terrible jar to the eye. Normally I also would need to grade the flooring so that the odd knot or rough board would be hidden, but I know in advance that this pile contains virtually no rough boards.

I know this because a couple of weeks ago when I bought the boards I was granted a rare privilege at the lumberyard. It was a Saturday, and business was slow. A fellow I had dealt with often during the course of the house's building happened to be on duty, and we talked about the flooring. Apparently I had done enough business with him to earn a favor, so he let me back my pickup to the yard's entire stock of fir flooring. Unescorted and unwatched I picked through the whole pile, culling the stock, board by board. It was an hour pleasantly spent, sighting down boards, reading grain, smelling the tree in them, feeling them, getting to know each one. I felt as if I had been given free passage to Midas's counting house.

When I finished I took my own tally of boards back to the office, a little more than four hundred dollars worth, where the clerk transferred my numbers to an invoice without verifying my count. Business still is done that way here.

Since then the boards have been piled on the concrete slab where they would eventually rest. They spent a necessary period of acclimation that allowed them to absorb or expel the particular vapors of my house, to feel the wood stove and react, a final drying and shrinking. The waiting period, I hoped, would prevent later shrinkage, which causes the floor's joints to gap just a bit, a blemish on a carpenter's honor. My precaution, though, likely was futile. Fir is strong and hard but a notoriously mobile wood, as if it refuses to die. Even the people at the lumberyard had counseled me against using fir. They said every such floor in their experience grew gaps, except one installed in a bar downtown frequented by a rowdy student crowd. The lumbermen theorize there is enough beer spilled on that particular floor to prevent its drying.

My alternatives to fir, though, were oak or some other exotic hardwood. I live in the West. No oak grows in Montana, but next to the ponderosa pine just outside my bedroom window there is a Douglas fir. Furthermore, a lumberyard's designation of a "fir" floor is structural, not a biological specific. Mixed with boards sold as Douglas fir are those from Western larch. A trained eye can spot the larch in a finished floor, more a coffee color than the rose of the fir. Larch has a tighter, straighter grain. A trained hand can feel larch as the flooring slides together. The larch joints snap cleanly, as if machined, unlike the stubborn joints of the fir.

As I look to the southwest, across the narrow valley that holds my house, and up the adjacent ridge of this gulch, I see a verdant spread of Douglas fir punctuated with a dusting of larch. You need no trained eye to pick out the larch in autumn. Unlike most other conifers, larch are not evergreen. Their wispy green needles turn gold in the fall, transforming trees to candles on otherwise green ridges.

My house will be a house of place, a house in context, and so it will have fir and larch floors, just as its framing members come from the same two species. Its trim is ponderosa pine, a soft and forgiving lumber carpenters call "whitewood."

I finish my coffee and switch on the radio, "Morning Edition," but hear little of it. Meditation deepens. My thoughts are not on the broader implications of the laying of the floor, those will come later. I am engaged in the details, in the minutiae, facts carpentry has taught me to hold as profound. The first boards must lay tight against uneven concrete walls and so will require scribe cuts, lines traced from the wall to the board to mediate between the unevenness of the once-fluid concrete and the linear precision of straight-planed wood. The first row of flooring must start as two rows in two separate rooms, broken by an intervening wall, but when the rows meet at the door that connects the two rooms, they must match perfectly to become one row. This assignment reduces calculations to the sixteenth of an inch that competent carpentry requires. Just a couple of months ago I would have botched this detail, but this work comes toward the end of my house's building. I have learned much from the good carpenters who helped me. I have made and repaired hundreds of mistakes, have hidden the irreparable ones. I am a better carpenter now.

I pull a chalk line from my leather apron and prepare to bring order to the random chaos of the floor. Calculations are made and checked against the 30-foot measuring tape that through the months has come to seem like my third hand. I square the unreliable factory-cut end of the first board on a Hitachi chop saw, a menacing little banshee mounted on a tooled-steel slide. I wish I owned its precision, but Bruce loaned me this enormously expensive tool. I flip the board and cut the other end to length, allowing the saw's kerf to exactly halve a thin pencil line for a tight, butt joint.

Now I get the feel of the floor-nailing machine the lumberyard has loaned me. It is a sort of brace loaded with a row of special barbed nails for floors. The brace is angled so that the head rests against the edge of the floor board to drive the nail at a 45-degree angle through the wood. It's called blind nailing, meaning the head of the nail lands in the edge of the board that is then covered when the next board butts up to it. When the floor is finished, no nail heads are visible.

The machine's angle also forces the board against the previous row, thereby tightening the joint. To drive the nails, the carpenter smacks the nailer with a lead hammer that weighs about twice as much as a normal hammer. Struck with the right force, trajectory, and spin, this mallet sends the nail home in one swat as it tightens the joint to unity. It's fun, and soon I am into the rhythm of this deft nailer, racing the length of each board, setting a nail every foot, whack, step, whack, step, another 4-inch-wide strip of floor in place for all time, or at least for all my time.

I am working in stocking feet to avoid marring the raw wood floor. The lead mallet glances off the nailer, smacking my foot. I dance and curse, knowing I will limp for a couple of days, the latest in the hundreds of aggravating injuries rendered by this house.

I cut more boards, laying them out in rows of staggered patterns across the floor, ready for nailing. I tap each into place, tighten the butt joints, then follow with the thump of the lead mallet. As darkness begins in earnest, about 5 P.M., I power up the table saw to rip the strip that will rest against the front of the floor. I wedge it into place, nail it, and now I have a floor laid wall to wall. It is clean, straight, and simple. It is solid. Somehow it gives the illusion that my house has just crossed a critical line, that it finally is the place where I live. It is not finished yet, but it seems so, and I am stunned by the transition.

Four months ago Tracy and I turned the first spade of hard-pack glacial gravel just a few inches below my feet. Since then we have done little but work here. I am exhausted. My hands are beat, scabbed, cut, slivered, and, I believe, permanently sore. They are stiff and clumsy on this keyboard. I only now am beginning to learn to sleep the whole night again, learning to silence the deafening convention of details that have now come to support these walls. I have spent more money than I've ever spent in my life. I have made egregious mistakes on an hourly basis. And now, looking at this floor, I am sorry the building is nearly over. I have the illusion that I have come to the end of my story, but I want it to go on.

As Thanksgiving approached, I took a break to kill a deer. I shot one on a hillside in sight of the house, then hung it in a tree, using an old sledge hammer handle for a gambrel pole. Tracy and I buy no meat, so what we kill is all we eat, a part of our bargain with the land and with winter, like cutting wood. This killing is really no different than the building of a house. I take the trees and deer against the winter, simply to sustain our lives. That's all there is to it. Yet winter comes and comes, and one of these years it will require that we cease taking and give back, just as the trees and deer have done.

There is solid progress in the house. Now sealed against winter, I am allowed the luxury of again working on its amenities. All along I had promised myself I would build the kitchen cabinets, but it scared me to say it aloud. Cabinetwork is the neurosurgery of carpentry. Cabinets require a consummate craftsman, and I wasn't. Still, I persisted in my hubris and once confided the plan to a carpenter and friend.

"Oh hell, go ahead and build them. They're nothing more than boxes," he said.

And so during evenings all during the building of the house I studied *Cabinetmaking* by Paul Haynie, a dated textbook I found in a used-book store. I stashed pieces of clear fir the Finlays had saved for me. Clear fir—that is, Douglas fir boards without knots—is hard to come by, but every now and again some would flow from the Finlays' saw. They had taken an interest in my odd little house by then, and so put aside these premium boards for me all summer. I piled those boards in a warm, dry place and let them season.

When it was dark and snowy and Tracy and I were alone, when nobody could see my mistakes, I built the cabinets. Their carcasses (the frames) are of plywood, but the doors and faces are fir, the Finlays' fir. I made each door myself by gluing and pegging together 4-inch strips of board, planing and sanding them, rounding the edges. The cabinets, finished, are clearly of the old school: solid, simple, and unique. We like them.

By mid-November the cabinets had risen sufficiently to support a kitchen sink. This was another important milestone, and in celebration we washed dishes, even some that didn't need it. Then we put away the plastic dishes that had been our table service for a month and a half. With the sink in place I pushed toward another key goal so that we might celebrate Thanksgiving with drawers. On the eve of the holiday it snowed hard. I spent that day in Bruce's workshop dadoing and gluing together drawers for the cabinets so we could unpack a box of silverware in time for Thanksgiving dinner. Bruce joined in. We wound up working together all day as a storm built steam outside. I took the finished drawers home, then continued working well into the night adjusting drawer slides and mounting fir fronts, but I made it. One more breakthrough.

The Moores—Michael, Wendy, and Kate—came over to share the holiday. We cooked a huge venison roast. Tracy and I had more or less lost track of our friends during the summer, buried as we were in our building. But by Thanksgiving the Moores were more frequent visitors to the land. Next door, their house was rising, a stout timber frame. Bruce and Mike were building it. I had no time to help, nor did Michael and Wendy. Both have full-time jobs, and so they hired the work done. Their building experience was very different from ours because of this. They were in a separate world. Through all this distance—our house from their house, them from their house—we lost track of them for a bit, but we caught up.

Most of Thanksgiving we spent in house talk, sources of tile, fixtures, wood. Michael and I took a few hours to tramp through the wind and snow looking for deer. We saw only one, although only a week before we had seen dozens of mule deer each day bounding up the ridges and draws. They had hunkered down in the dense woods, a sign of winter's deepening. We saw a set of fresh bear tracks working up the base of a draw, likely the trail of the bear's final stroll before hibernation.

At dinner we opened a batch of beer I had made and stashed just before we broke ground on the house. It was late summer then, and I had labeled the batch "Thanksgiving beer." We tasted it slowly, assessing any character it may have gained from the intervening months.

Then winter and work went on. In a few weeks our foothold on the house began to seem less tenuous. We closed some more holes. Winter appeared less menacing. Solstice was but a week or so away. It seemed we'd turned the corner, but then the sadness took Tracy for a while.

I hadn't expected this loss, although in hindsight it was understandable enough. We had spent months buried in the work, dust, noise, and clutter, all the time building a home but having no home. Outside it was dark, wet, and cold. Still, the worst of the building was over, and until then Tracy's spirits had held up remarkably well.

That's not to say there wasn't tension or even anger in the building. It was a tough undertaking, especially for newlyweds. Throughout, though, the anger that arose didn't last. Many couples have told us since that the process of building nearly destroyed or in some cases did destroy their marriages. Ours grew, and we developed a relationship of trust that was the key to a sort of division of labor. Each trusted the other to make decisions alone. Our values and tastes are similar, so each could readily extend this trust without fear of betrayal. In doing so, each tried to look out for the other's needs. Our decisions were quick and easy; our arguments were few, even during the most fatiguing of the building days. By early winter we were more or less through those rough days, which is why I was surprised to see that sadness hit her so hard.

In the years I had known Tracy I had never seen her melancholy. Yet on a day in December, some sort of bottom fell out, and she became deeply sad.

At first I wanted to fix it. That is my role in life. That's why I built a house. But this time, no. Maybe that's the line I crossed; maybe I finally had learned that one doesn't fix a life like a house. One doesn't even fix a house like a house. This sadness wasn't mine, it was hers. I took the episode to be a symptom of her health.

Here, above the 46th parallel, the swing of the seasons is severe. This swing is seen by others as the coming of the winter cold, but I mark it by the leaving of the light. In fall the sun sets further south each day along the rim of the valley. Each day the sun sets earlier, until finally it no longer really sets. Instead, about two-thirty in the afternoon the sky goes gray, then shade by shade mutes to a hushed black enforced by the sound-smothering snow. The world, day and night, shifts to monochromatic: gray, black, and white. Days become so short I begin to doubt their existence. I forget there is any green in the pine trees that are shrouded in hoar frost and snow.

The therapy faddists have a name for the mood swing that comes with this time: seasonal affective disorder. It makes a clever acronym, because the sufferer becomes truly and irretrievably sad. It is, plain and simple, a sadness borne of chemicals, a physical change in the brain produced by a decline in the light, literally the quantity of light passing through the eyes. Because this sadness is physical and therefore "artificial," the therapists label it a "disorder." They treat it by subjecting patients to arrays of artificial light.

I've lived in the north all my life and now refuse to call it a disorder. This sadness is the measure of a life ordered by the wax and wane of seasons, of cycles of time. I imagine it is how a bear must feel when this same light tells it to lie down for a winter's sleep, a sort of little death. In a sense, winter is a real death and a death deserves a grieving.

Each year that I spend listening more closely to the flow of nature all around me is a year of evaporating illusions. The cycles flow, and now I see them, especially as I weave my life to them. The trees grow up, fall down, rot, and die. My days warm and cool with the sun. The deer grow fat till fall. I eat one. The compost steams and molders. The frost of fall takes the tomato vines. All around the cycles whirl, fighting against and fueled by death. To me the cycles say always that my turn will come.

A friend once told me that she and a whole group of city people took an excursion that left them living for a long time on a Mexican beach, rocked by the waves and sleeping under the trees. She said all the women began menstruating together. She is the sort of woman who finds it difficult to talk about such things, but still she was thrilled. If permitted, our bodies will ebb and flow with nature.

Tracy has lived all her life with city people, among the climate-controlled and artificially lighted. Now she lives among the trees, and the price of that is a sadness inexorable and fine.

We don't have Christmas trees or really observe the holiday, preferring instead to examine its roots. Much of the tradition of Christmas is

plagarized from pagan rites of tree worship or celebration of the returning solstice sun. I like that. One day near Christmas I looked up from
my work to see Tracy out front of the house hanging ornaments on a
ponderosa pine. She had made them of blocks of scrap styrofoam left
from the house's insulation. She had cut the foam into small cubes,
smeared the cubes all over with peanut butter, then stuck bird seed in
the peanut butter. If the weather warmed a bit the nuthatches and
mountain chickadees would venture from the cover of the thick forest to
eat the precious fat and carbohydrates. Thus she called the birds to
chase her sadness.

A couple of days later we set the alarm clock for an hour before
sunrise, arose quietly, and pulled on long johns, sweaters, and boots.
Josh was staying at the house, and I whistled him out of bed. We cut
along the toe of the ridge heading east, then straight up the face of the
ridge through the trees, up where the deer live at the top of the hill.
There stands a rock pedestal jutting from the grass, juniper, and sage.
Together the three of us perched on it and scanned the southeast for
morning's first glow, the returning solstice sun. The tradition of climbing the highest nearby hill on solstice has practical roots, affording the
earliest view of the returning sun. The custom began in Iceland more
than a thousand years ago. How cold and dark the winter must have
seemed to them. How welcome the coming of the light.

Sometimes I want to repeal the twentieth century. Sometimes the
house affords the illusion I may succeed. One day I had spent the
morning cutting wood with my hand-powered saw, then splitting
rounds with a maul, hauling them inside, and basking in the instant
gratification of a wood-fire glow, the deep, resinous, antique smells. I
remembered then that potatoes still were buried under the snow and
mulch in the garden. They'd still be good, so I bundled up like a
peasant and pushed my wheelbarrow there to dig supper, hand to
mouth. Near the garden, Bruce was working on Michael and Wendy's
house, the timber frame now rising to full profile. He stood on a beam
just under its gable, handmade chisels and mallet at ready to cut
centuries-old joints. The illusion that I had defeated time seemed real
until Bruce saw me and shouted: "Hey, I got my fax modem working
last night. Try to send me something."

Michael Moore stopped to visit Tracy one afternoon. He asked her whether I would be able to stand the depression of finishing the house. I had not realized how well Michael knew me.

Out in the meadow a stranger hawk perched at the top of an infant ponderosa pine, six feet above the grass. Rough-legged hawks are comfortable on short perches. Normally they hunt the Arctic tundra, where there are no trees, and come south only in the winter, especially when Arctic lemming populations plunge. The hawks bring us messages. They are the envoys of earth's deepest cold.

I kept getting misaddressed mail. When we moved, I never got around to reprinting my business cards, and so when I needed one I would simply pencil in changes on an outdated card. "Sleeman Gulch," it said. And I'm sure my handwriting isn't that bad. The printing is perfectly obvious to me, and yet when I got mail derived from one of these hand-lettered cards, the sender often got it wrong. The mistake was always the same, an "F" for the "S."

I went to see the Finlays at the sawmill for a last load of lumber, rough-sawed pine siding. Enough siding for the whole house, top-quality pine that cost me three hundred dollars. The brothers asked me how the house was coming along and I said it was wrapping up, that I'd have to go back to making a writer's living. Mark said, "Yeah, I suppose with all the real work done, you'll have time now to dangle your participles."

The months of building wound down and I faced a return to my real craft. The touch of carpentry, however, prompted a crisis of faith, and so this dangling of my participles was no joking matter. A dilemma was emerging. I had been doing the job of writing for most of my adult years. It was my foundation. This house was a building, but on an existing foundation, a simple matter of walking through the construction of a house then locking myself away in a room and getting it all down on paper. Send it in and wait for the check. The room was built, and I needed the check, but I couldn't seem to face locking myself away.

The problem emerged early enough in this book, not visible to you, but obvious and overpowering to me here where I sit behind the curtain. I should have been back at the discipline and exquisite torture much earlier, but I couldn't face writing. At first I laid this to a sort of childish game of hooky, and so it was a development I greeted with some glee. There are not enough childish things in my life. In the early part of this writing I was like a kid with a bunch of new toys I called tools. I could live among a large pile of blocks that were all mine to stack as I pleased. I could play house. There were those long summer days of sheer independence, doing exactly as the house and I pleased. Pure sun and air. Bulldozers to drive. Climbing to the top of a stud-framed wall as if it were monkey bars, balancing on a ridge, and crowing like a chicken.

Yes, it was play, and I did not want to leave. I wanted to stay even more when I realized the play was valuable work, not the paperwork I had been doing all of my adult life. When I drove a spike in a stud it stuck, forming a wall and a roof, something good and real. My hands were no longer metaphors buried in words like "manipulation." My hands were just hands. Hands holding a firm grip on the world.

I had worked real work before and still always found myself back writing, as if compelled, but now I was being compelled away from writing and I couldn't understand why. Then I began to crack the case with an odd realization.

I had never brought the writing so close to home before, literally. I had never lived in my metaphor; sort of like a computer game programmer who suddenly finds himself transported into the guts of his computer and into the game, blasting away with a ray gun at the quarks, zots, and cyborgs of his imagination.

Many writers say they do this, let their writing invade their lives. I've said it, but what I have meant is that I let my writing invade my head. It's like a game. One creates a series of abstractions or thoughts so strong that they begin to form a sort of independent life form in the brain. Then the writer takes his place in this mental ecosystem. This, traditionally, is how we make our stories.

Yet in making up our stories we can let them be anything we want them to be. Mine, on the other hand, in the end had to be a house. It is at first a creature of the head but is nothing unless it becomes real. I was a writer whose story became real, and then I had to live in it, no respite. My story was and had to be my pipes, my toilet, my woodpile, my marriage, and the miter joints on the trim around my closet door.

Toward the end, just a couple of days ago as some of the notions of this last chapter pinned me to a wall and pummeled me, I said, "Trace, I've got an idea. Let's get away for a month so I can finish this book."

That was a cop-out, and I didn't do it out of fidelity to the idea of a house. What good is a house if it cannot hold one's life—all of one's life?

I was building a cabinet door one day, a particular day when the spotlight of the writing seemed intensely focused. It occurred to me I could not give an honest answer to a simple question: Was I building the door this way because it would make a good door, or because it would make a good paragraph?

Understand that for a journalist this is a horrifying question. The suggestion was that the needs of my writing were somehow influencing the subject. Journalists are taught that observer ought to be separate from observed. This is objectivity. It is an offshoot of Plato's idealism and the bedrock of all Western thought. It is where we derive our penchant for abstraction, that the ideal is separate from reality, that thought is an exercise removed from life. I had crossed the line and was now living a real life among my abstractions. This is a horrifying thought for a journalist because it smacks of staging the outcome of the story. Of contrivance, of artifice.

Yet instead of recoiling from this idea, I found myself wanting to push on through it. It and that cabinet door suddenly appeared as a barrier that had been fencing all of my life, indeed all of us. When thought is removed from the living of the thoughts, then thought and lives are removed from nature. This is what ails us.

I came back to the notion of writing as craft. What I once meant by that was a sort of putdown of writing, a forced humility, a reaction to the pretentious people of my trade. It was my own blue-collar reverse snobbery. I was raised with the old joke that says a journalist is a reporter with two suits, and so I always called myself a reporter. Those who called themselves journalists or professionals aspired to suits and country clubs. I wasn't altogether sure what I was, but I knew damned straight what they were. I wanted no part of that action. Yet defining our lives as a negative reaction to others' lives is a dangerous business, generally an admission that we fail to understand our lives. In my case, I failed to understand craft.

The cabinet-door question arose late in the house. It was a new tool really, a way for me to focus what I had learned from the carpenters and the rest.

Of course, shaping a cabinet door to make a good story would be contrivance, but so is shaping a cabinet door to make a good door. Craft, on its fundamental level, is contrivance. It is the act of making something useful. If I recoil from acts designed to make my writing useful, then I can have no respect for my writing. But if I stop with that, then I can have no respect for the notion of craft.

Craft is work. I learned it from woodwork, which is not an act of control. Rather it is a sort of covenant, a relationship, if you will; a marriage, a dance. It is an act of understanding at once what the wood is and what I am and denying the essence of neither. It is the act of finding, not making, the mask in the tree.

Once, in a second-hand store, I bought an old ash door. Solid ash, but of the antique office style that suggests ceiling fans and transoms. It has a message slot and a big glass panel reinforced by chicken wire. If one could find such a door new it would cost as much as a pickup truck, but I found it used and bought it for sixty five dollars. Just after I finished laying that fir floor in my study, I hung the door. It was to close me in, but for a while it closed me out.

I know the door once led to an office because it still says so. At its top, in gold letters, is a four-digit address: "2075." Below that: "Ruybal Custom Cabinets & Woodworks."

The door had hung for months, and Trace and I never got around to stripping off the lettering. It faces the living room, so visitors would often comment on it. One day a friend stopped by and exclaimed almost immediately, "Hey, you've got Louie's door."

It turned out Louie had practiced carpentry in Missoula before a divorce sent him back to Colorado. He was a softball player of considerable skill.

But even knowing the story didn't make it much easier to enter the study. Writing lurked in there. Then one day, as a joke, I used a felt marker to cross out the second "o" on "Woodworks" and change it to an "r." I wish this amendment would stick, but I fear there's still a ways to go.

It hasn't become any easier to write this, maybe even harder after the lesson of the cabinet door. Now my craft scares me even more. I understand now that I do not make this story what it is. Nor do my words. They are tools. Wonderful, fascinating, and useful tools, but tools nonetheless. I love to horde them, brandish them, and lay them all in rows in a box, but if I left them at that they would be ultimately as useless as a countinghouse full of gold. The life of this story is neither the words nor the writer. The analogous relationship to carpenter and wood is writer to reader. I have no control. If I controlled this story, it would be useless. Readers make this story. They give it life. This is what scares me witless about this craft, especially now that the stakes are so very high. By writing, I entrust the life of a story that matters so much to me to the hands of strangers.

In December I had a bad day—gray, close, and cold. I had been sawing firewood in the yard and seemed to be making no headway, as if the inexorable cold would eat my puny pile no matter how hard I worked. The fight went out of me. The rough-legged hawk had been circling around for days, and I got a good close look at it, at the eyes that burn with information of the deep Arctic cold, a place we can never know.

I hung up the saw and walked up the hill to a rock outcrop that invites sitting. There I perched like a raptor, looking down on my house and the frozen meadow below. My back was against the hills and trees, so I was sheltered by the wild. From this vantage I faced the little piece of ground I had tamed, a scar on the hillside, an incision to accommodate the artificial implant of a house. I tried, as Aldo Leopold suggested, to think like a mountain. I sat in the wild looking at the tame, and this led me to apologize for my life.

My house seemed such an imposition on the land. In a city such a house would go unnoticed, would even be an improvement on whatever had been there before. Yet here in the forest it is nothing but a blemish, and so perhaps I should have built it in the city. This is my dark little secret: that all of the good I have tried to build into this house is nothing more than a grand rationalization to hide my abhorrence of people. Not of individuals, but of the braying, collective mass. I can speak of energy consumption, fighting profligacy, even craft, but reduced to its simplest level, this house is about noise.

I no longer could stand the noise of the city, even a small city like Missoula—the rush and the crush and rude violations of space. A brain cannot work in this madness, and still we wonder why we are in such troubles, that our collective American brain seems broken. Cities, even small cities, are untenable, and so we face a dilemma, an old one that is the summation of our history. My house raises no new debate. By fleeing man, fleeing what we have become, I take man and our manipulations with me. I recreate what I flee, and so eventually I must flee again. True, I can be accused of this stupidity, yet even if this flight were the sole essence of the foundation of my house and I knew it, I would do it all again. What choice do I have? This is my basest line of self-defense. If I am reduced to protecting only my life, I will do it. I simply cannot stand the noise.

But I can roll the cycle of this paradox the other direction, to assert that my fleeing is a necessary step to fixing all of our lives.

This is not about flight. This is about landing.

The noise of the city stifles more than thought. It forces each person who suffers it to erect little walls, to numb the senses. We must insulate ourselves from our world; otherwise the pain would be unbearable.

Yet we need the information our senses bring. We need the pain because it is the teacher. There is no inherent virtue or moral high ground to my life that makes me want to live it by inflicting less damage. It is simply that I choose to live it in a quiet place where I can afford the luxury of reopening my senses. Here I can stand the noise. In the city Tracy and I often were awakened by the rude, late-night traffic of college-town hot rods. I felt assaulted, as if fascists had broken through my door. Now we sometimes are awakened in the early hours by coyotes singing near our bedroom window, and we are thrilled. I let myself hear them and come to care for the wild that they are.

Just over the ridge from our house there is a massive clear-cut, a felony against nature committed by a timber corporation. The logs were sawed and sent to build cities. Some of them built the houses of good people, and these people will never know what they have done. I am no better than these people, but my house is different, because I see these clear-cuts every day. I see them. I sense them. This is the advantage of a life lived close to its sources, a life landed.

I feel it necessary to apologize for my life, and I feel it necessary to apologize for my writing about it, because I know that in places I will be grossly misunderstood.

Among my friends the talk is of the Californication or Coloradical-ization of Montana. Montana is hot now. Movie stars are moving here. People are buying land and building houses because by urban standards it is ridiculously cheap. If you can stand the weather, it is paradise: pristine, wild, and free. There are elk and mountains and, placid, unsullied trout streams. Working ranches are being diced to 20-acre "ranchettes." The land I now occupy was spared this cute term, but that's what it is, the carcass of a ranch. Is this the death of Montana, a sentence carried out by people just like me?

Down the hill a neighbor built a suburban sprawler, then surrounded it with a sort of a 10-acre vegetative moat. He has landscaped the land with exotic species of plants and now keeps them alive in this near-desert by pumping the aquifer dry. Newcomers, for odd reasons, feel the West is to be won with irrigated lawns. He has built a brick garage twice the size of my house to shelter a fleet of recreational vehicles, snowmobiles, and motorcycles. He lights the spread, day and night, with a brace of mercury vapor lights.

A local paper reports that a city woman moved here to an elaborate log house. She promptly had it painted pink to match her Corvette.

Is this our future? Even if it is, the past was really no better. I refuse to mourn the demise of the ranchers. Their cattle were a blight. Bruce, a botanist before he was a carpenter, calls the land I'm on "cow-burned." Then he ticks off the native species of plants that should be thriving here but were grazed to extinction by our people's taste for cheap beef. Television mogul Ted Turner bought a ranch in Montana and announced, to the attendant hoots and hollers of the state's remaining ranchers, that he will return it to the buffalo. The good ol' boys of the local press have joined in the derision, pigeon-holing Turner as a misguided newcomer.

No one bothers to mention that the grassland ecosystems of Montana flourished for centuries under hordes of buffalo. That part of the state not forested was once a grand prairie with grass belly-high to a horse. Under the hooves of cattle it has been beaten into a desert. In biological terms, the cattle are the newcomers ignorant of tradition.

But if our replacements for the ranches are to be ski resorts, golf courses, Winnebagos, and rich people's ranchettes, then I will be among those longing for the good old days.

Now I realize that my role in all of this may be a part of this place's undoing. I write about it, and because I cannot control the relationship with readers I most certainly will be misunderstood. Some people will read this book as my description of the good life, and to me it is. If there is a future for our people and for thought, then part of it is rural. It is a future of simplicity and humility informed by a patient tuning to the needs of the land. We must learn to live among the trees. The future is not so much about the building of houses as it is about the building of lives.

Lately, we as a people have begun speaking about the collapse of the American dream. This was my bedrock concern in the building of a house, a topic so chosen because I believe the collapse is real. I now suspect the collapse has more to do with the fact that we do not so much build houses as buy them. Thus, a house becomes a product to be consumed like all others. That's why they're getting bigger. That's the problem with naked consumption. One gets what one wants, then finds it wasn't really what one wanted at all. It is a hollow experience, the chasing of our tails. We then believe that the hollowness was caused by an inadequacy of the house. Consumption begets consumption, and we trade up.

One cannot consume a house. A house is not product. A house is process. Yet there will be readers of this who will continue to think of Montana, houses, and lives as products they wish to consume. Some people will not hear me speak of the cold in this life, of the hard work. They will not hear that the joys and light derive from cycles of grief and death.

These people will come here with money and kill the land, trying to short-circuit nature and buy joy without work and grief. These people have bankrupted all of our nation. What will stop them from finding and bleeding the life from this place?

Our profligacy has imperiled our future. We are so removed from nature that we now are fully capable of destroying the planet's ability to sustain us, forgetting, as we have, that it does. Some of us won't even hear it whimper before the bang. It may already have sounded.

I wish I could say this clearly enough so that everyone will understand, but this is not possible. Each of us must see the mask in the tree. I cannot show it to you.

This poor house of mine, I am surprised it stands. Bruce and Mike and I framed it to bear its roof and walls, but I've laid all of this extra weight on the beams. I charged it with the healing of the troubles of the world, of carrying all my eccentric values like a coat of bright pink paint. I tried to make it fix all my relationships and live my life. More than live my life, to make me immortal. I'm middle-aged now, and just this past year admitted mortality. It is natural I would want something to take it away, but it is a terrible burden to place on a house. Yet it stands still in the woods where the trees fall and death comes to bring new life. Death comes, even mine. The forest gave me back that thought, and so gave me my life. It no longer seems like I need a house to live my life for me. It can go on being just a house. It is, after all, just a house. As Skinny Jim said, I wasn't building a fuckin' piano.

The light returned in January. Winter snapped like a twig. An early high-pressure system rolled in to melt the snow. I played some more with the house and found some gaps here and there, a vapor barrier I had forgotten, a few ashes blocking the draft of the wood stove. Those little details were causing the cold that had so worried me the month before. With them corrected I felt like I was beginning to, as Fred advised, sail the house. Suddenly, in late January, the whole design came together. The solar system, the insulation, the thermal mass, it all came together and worked. It held its heat, was always warm as it should have been, and dry. On midwinter days I see my neighbors' houses billowing sooty brown smoke, while my wood stove stands cold and clean. My house stands in the sun. The light bursts through it, and the light is beautiful. The rough-legged hawk stayed only a week, and then for reasons only its evolution understands it flew back, north of the Arctic circle. A red-tailed hawk returned to the now-vacant niche to scoop up the voles scurrying in the winter-matted grass. The summer hawk wheeled and dove in clear air.

It was a Sunday, two weeks into this unusual midwinter's balm, and some of us thought we should take a day off to go high. In Montana one can be a time traveler by legging up altitude, because when it's spring in the valleys it's still winter smothered in snow a few thousand feet up. I had not taken a day off from work in months, but this day was to play.

Bruce, Michael Gallacher, and I rattled up an old logging road as far as Bruce's four-wheel-drive pickup would slog the snow. Then we ditched it and unloaded our skis. There is a style of skiing here, resurrected in recent years, called telemark skiing. It is devilishly difficult and took me two years to learn, but I learned it. It is a bit of magic that opens to the skier oceans of unpopulated backcountry.

The equipment is basically the toehold floppy binding of cross-country skis, which are usually thought of as flat-country skis. The sport is executed (and that may be just the right word) on terrain precipitous enough to intimidate most downhill skiers. While careening straight down slope, usually a slope dotted with unyielding trees, the skier cushions his descent with the telemark turn. This is accomplished in a sort of half-kneeling position, with the knee of one leg placed down and directly beside the instep of the opposite foot.

A good day's skiing is generally one run, with half a day spent walking up the mountain and half spent skiing down. The up half is aided with devices called skins, long strips of plastic or mohair attached to the skis' bottoms to grip the snow. It looks like work, but we didn't think so that sunny January day, walking, talking, and sniffing spring in the air.

When we'd kick a bit of snow, it would roll downhill, growing as it went. In avalanche school they taught us that this phenomenon is a good sign. On days when this occurs, the snowpack is relatively stable and chances of a catastrophic slide decrease. Only decrease, though. There is always a danger of avalanche, so the only way to be safe is to avoid the backcountry until the snow is gone; to some of us, too dear a price for safety. The threat of avalanche was with us, and this focused the mind.

The backcountry always holds a sensation of walking on the edge.

This teaches. That's even how we learn to ski. A trick of rapid learning is to leave the open slopes and travel in trees, weaving a path among them. The prospect of careening into a tree at thirty miles an hour greatly enhances one's ability to turn. Necessity invents skills.

We walked up for hours, it seemed—patient, plodding, and sweating, talking now and again as men all nearly forty will do; how we survived the crazy years, bad jobs now and then, marriages of varying qualities.

We came to the summit. Talk stopped. The skins came off and we rolled them into our packs. Maybe 10 miles away from the peak we could see the outlines of the little mountain valley where Bruce lives, and he pointed out his house. We seemed so far above the houses, even far above the snow. Our jacket hoods went up, glove gauntlets were cinched to wrists, pole straps cinched to gloves. Then there were whoops, and we cut our way down slope, skiing free and fast for the second half of our day's journey. Sometimes we even cut long, graceful turns in the snow.

Sources

THE SOURCES used herein fall into two categories: those that supported the actual building of the house and those that informed the book. I will deal with the former first.

There are many how-to books to aid the amateur house builder, far too many to cover here. Accordingly, I will keep the list small, choosing sources largely on the basis of my own prejudices. This limitation yields a bit of advice for the owner-builder: Don't be afraid to do some research yourself. Much of the essence of a good house is specific to place, so it might take some reading to discover a technique suited to your purposes. Such a technique may be found in the very latest alternative building guide, or it may hide in a thirty-year-old carpentry manual in a second-hand bookstore. Shop around.

Particularly useful tools for designing a house come from a variety of areas. Foremost is something of a classic, now a difficult book to locate:

ALEXANDER, Christopher, et al. *A Pattern Language*. New York: Oxford University Press, 1977.

I also recommend a short essay that succinctly outlines the task before us, the notion of reintroducing nature into design:

ORR, David, "Education and the Ecological Design Arts," *Conservation Biology*, June 1992, pp. 162–64.

Design ideas might be found in:

METZ, Don, *New Compact House Designs*. Pownal, VT: Storey Communications Inc., 1991.
EASTON, Robert, and Peter Nabokov, *Native American Architecture*. New York: Oxford University Press, 1989.

A second category of useful design tools is the new generation of computer software specifically written for house design. Several programs are available for most models of personal computers. They can be worth the investment, because moving a line on a computer screen can be a good deal easier and less expensive than moving an actual wall.

Most of the work on my house was heavily guided by:

COLE, John N., and Charles Wing, *From the Ground Up*. Boston: Atlantic Monthly Press, 1976.

Specific help on timber framing—both theory and practice—came from:

BENSON, Ted, and James Gruber, *Building the Timber Frame House*. New York: Scribner's, 1980.
SOBON, Jack, and Roger Schroeder, *Timber Frame Construction*. Pownal, VT: Storey Communications, Inc., 1984.

To contact specialists in the field, try Timber Framers Guild, PO Box 1046, Keene, NH 03431.

For ideas on general construction techniques, check the library for the magazine *Fine Homebuilding*. It is a no-nonsense building magazine meant for contractors and will teach much. In particular I recommend the magazine's series of reprints organized as books on various construction topics abridged from the *Fine Homebuilding* Builder's Library. These are available at bookstores or from The Taunton Press, Box 5506, Newton, CT 06470.

Other building guides I used included:

CARLSON. G. E., and R. E. Putnam, *Architectural and Building Trades Dictionary*. Chicago: American Technical Society, 1974.

HAYNIE, Paul, *Cabinetmaking*. Englewood Cliffs, NJ: Prentice-Hall, 1976.

NATIONAL FIRE PROTECTION ASSOCIATION, *National Electrical Code*. Quincy, MA: Batterymarch Park, 1990.

WAGNER, Willis H., *Modern Carpentry*. South Holland, IL: Goodheart-Willcox Co., Inc., 1976.

There is a broad range of books dealing with solar energy, most dating from the 1973 energy crisis. Find one that contains specific insolation tables for your area. I used:

KREIDER, Jan F., and Frank Kreith. *Solar Heating and Cooling*. New York: McGraw-Hill, 1982.

A good source for information on energy conservation is Amory Lovins' institute, which publishes a long list of booklets on a variety of topics. Lovins is the nation's leading authority on energy conservation. The catalog of publications is available from the Rocky Mountain Institute, 1739 Old Snowmass Creek Road, Old Snowmass, CO 81654.

The *Alternative Energy Sourcebook* is a particularly useful publication, offering information on everything from composting toilets to photovoltaics. A cross between a catalog and an encyclopedia of sustainable technology, the *Sourcebook* is available from the Real Goods Trading Corporation, 966 Mazzoni Street, Ukiah, CA 95482 (tel: 800-762-7325), a mail-order company dealing in such products. It is well worth the $10 (refunded with the first order).

Sunelco also offers an extensive list of alternative products. Besides, they are good folks. Their address is Sunelco, PO Box 1499, Hamilton, MT 59840-1499 (tel: 800-338-6844).

The *Guide to Resource Efficient Building Elements* offers sources of energy-efficient, recycled, and wood-efficient building materials. It is available from Steve Loken's project, the Center for Resourceful Building Technology, PO Box 3413, Missoula, MT 59806.

Finally, as a source for advice on building techniques, do not overlook local suppliers. Construction materials, aimed at capturing the do-it-yourself market, have become more user-friendly in recent years. Accordingly, salespeople have become accustomed to providing solid advice and answers to stupid questions. A word of caution, though: Don't expect the local hardware store to be current on or even care about the latest word in energy efficiency. Listen to their advice, but keep some skepticism at hand.

Sources for material cited in the book include:

BROWN, Dee, *Bury My Heart at Wounded Knee*. New York: Holt, Rinehart & Winston, 1970.

BROWN, Lester R., et al., *State of the World 1991*. New York: World Watch Institute, 1991.

COX, Thomas R., Robert S. Maxwell, Thomas, Drennon and Joseph J. Malone, *This Well-Wooded Land*. Lincoln, NE: University of Nebraska Press, 1985.

FORD, Pat, "The Snake's Imperiled Salmon," *High Country News*, August 1, 1991, p. 1.

FORD, Pat, et al., *High Country News*, May 22, 1991, pp. 1–16.

LAMBOURNE, Lionel, *Utopian Craftsmen*. New York: Van Nostrand Reinhold, 1980.

LUOMA, Jon R., "Even If Rich, Shouldn't You Switch?" *Audubon*, May 1991, pp. 80–84. This article details efficiencies of compact fluorescent light bulbs.)

NABHAN, Gary, *The Desert Smells Like Rain: A Naturalist in Papago Indian Country*. San Francisco: North Point Press, 1987.

RYBCZYNSKI, Witold, *Home: A Short History of an Idea*. New York: Viking, 1986.

VAN DER RYN, Sim, *The Toilet Papers*. Santa Barbara: Capra Press, 1978.

WARDELL, Charles, "Composition Panels," *Fine Homebuilding*, April/May, 1991, pp. 77–81.

WRIGHT, Lawrence, *Clean and Decent*. New York: Viking, 1960.

WYMAN, Walker D., *Witching for Water, Oil, Pipes and Precious Minerals*. Park Falls, WI: University of Wisconsin River Falls Press, 1977.

FOR THE BEST IN PAPERBACKS, LOOK FOR THE

In every corner of the world, on every subject under the sun, Penguin represents quality and variety—the very best in publishing today.

For complete information about books available from Penguin—including Pelicans, Puffins, Peregrines, and Penguin Classics—and how to order them, write to us at the appropriate address below. Please note that for copyright reasons the selection of books varies from country to country.

In the United Kingdom: For a complete list of books available from Penguin in the U.K., please write to *Dept E.P., Penguin Books Ltd, Harmondsworth, Middlesex, UB7 0DA.*

In the United States: For a complete list of books available from Penguin in the U.S., please write to *Consumer Sales, Penguin USA, P.O. Box 999—Dept. 17109, Bergenfield, New Jersey 07621-0120.* VISA and MasterCard holders call 1-800-253-6476 to order all Penguin titles.

In Canada: For a complete list of books available from Penguin in Canada, please write to *Penguin Books Canada Ltd, 10 Alcorn Avenue, Suite 300, Toronto, Ontario, Canada M4V 3B2.*

In Australia: For a complete list of books available from Penguin in Australia, please write to the *Marketing Department, Penguin Books Ltd, P.O. Box 257, Ringwood, Victoria 3134.*

In New Zealand: For a complete list of books available from Penguin in New Zealand, please write to the *Marketing Department, Penguin Books (NZ) Ltd, Private Bag, Takapuna, Auckland 9.*

In India: For a complete list of books available from Penguin, please write to *Penguin Overseas Ltd, 706 Eros Apartments, 56 Nehru Place, New Delhi, 110019.*

In Holland: For a complete list of books available from Penguin in Holland, please write to *Penguin Books Nederland B.V., Postbus 195, NL-1380AD Weesp, Netherlands.*

In Germany: For a complete list of books available from Penguin, please write to *Penguin Books Ltd, Friedrichstrasse 10-12, D-6000 Frankfurt Main I, Federal Republic of Germany.*

In Spain: For a complete list of books available from Penguin in Spain, please write to *Longman, Penguin España, Calle San Nicolas 15, E-28013 Madrid, Spain.*

In Japan: For a complete list of books available from Penguin in Japan, please write to *Longman Penguin Japan Co Ltd, Yamaguchi Building, 2-12-9 Kanda Jimbocho, Chiyoda-Ku, Tokyo 101, Japan.*